UNITED STATES ARMY MILITARY POLICE SCHOOL
Fort Gordon, Georgia

SPECIAL TEXT

RIOT CONTROL

Fredonia Books
Amsterdam, The Netherlands

Riot Control

by
United States Military Police School

ISBN: 1-58963-460-8

Reprinted from the 1964 edition

Fredonia Books
Amsterdam, the Netherlands
http://www.fredoniabooks.com

RIOT CONTROL

TABLE OF CONTENTS

FOREWORD

The objective of this text is to provide law enforcement personnel with concepts, procedures, methods, and techniques which can be used in planning for peaceful assemblies, prevention of civil disorders, and restoration of order.

Theories, principles, and practices suggested for consideration of law enforcement agencies in their plans for prevention or control of civil disorders take into consideration due regard for the law, public safety, and the preservation of human dignity. It is anticipated that the material contained in this publication will increase the reader's ability to serve his country and its people.

The prevention or control of civil disorders is not an exact science New and better concepts are continually being developed. Those presented in this text are considered worthy of mention. Common sense and sound judgment are necessary in the application of any concept. Because of political, psychological, sociological, and judicial differences throughout the world, the reader must adapt and modify the contents of this text to the condition of the particular country in which he serves.

CHAPTER 1

CAUSATION FACTORS OF CIVIL DISORDER

1. INTRODUCTION.

     a. In the summer of 1961 in Osaka, Japan, club-swinging policemen charged through the slums at dawn, breaking up the third consecutive all-night riot. After the fighting was over, police listed 551 persons injured, including 389 policemen and eight Japanese newspaper reporters and cameramen. The next day, 6,000 more police were alerted for riot control duty. Officials estimate that at one point during the rioting, 5,000 police fought 3,000 rioters. The police arrested 97 persons. The surface causation of this riot is alleged to have been the manner in which police handled an auto accident that caused the death of an aged male pedestrian.

     b. From this brief account of the Osaka riot only superficial causal factors are identifiable. One must go much deeper in order to understand how civil disorders occur and how such outbreaks can be prevented or controlled. Confucius, the great Chinese philosopher, once observed that "to understand men is science."

2. OBJECTIVE.

     An essential function of the police at all levels of government is to maintain law and order. However, the police cannot perform this vital role without the wholehearted support of a community. The word "community" as used throughout this portion of the text highlights the need for combined efforts to prevent or control civil disorders. For example, a combined preventive or control effort may include the police, certain government officials, various civic leaders, and the press. It follows, then, that the prevention and control of civil disorders is not the exclusive function of the police. Actually, police agencies can most effectively and efficiently discharge their functions where there is community understanding of the various causes of civil disorders. Such understanding provides the broad basis for concerted action needed to successfully maintain law and order. The support and participation of the community are essential because many causes of social turbulence are not subject to elimination or control by direct police action. Where such causes are encountered, the police should provide appropriate officials with timely intelligence data on which to base remedial action. Human needs, rising human expectations, and pressure or influence by an opposing ideology are discussed in this chapter.

3. HUMAN NEEDS.

Individual or human needs may be separated into two different categories: physiological needs and social needs.

a. _Physiological needs_. Basic physiological needs of the human race include requirements for food, clothing, and shelter. Without these necessities human life perishes. History reveals that civil disorders have occurred when deprivation of these necessities became intolerable.

b. _Social needs_. Scholars do not agree on the exact classification of man's social needs. It is debatable as to whether or not these psychological factors could better be classified as social wants. Since want can be defined as a state of need, it is appropriate that these causative factors be discussed in this section under the heading of social needs. Appreciation of the fact that men do have psychological needs is necessary for a thorough study of civil disorder prevention and control. For the purposes of this text, the following are accepted as social needs of men: (1) security, (2) social approval, (3) recognition, and (4) group association.

(1) _Security_. The individual needs security both from the elements of nature and from fear. While real causes frequently exist, fears often develop from imaginary causes and may influence the actions of individuals as well as entire communities. In December 1944, during the battle of the bulge, the extent of the German penetration into France was still not clear. Historically, the logical "Axis of Approach" from Germany into the plains of France was through Sedan and the area which includes the towns of Mouzon and Stenay. German forces conducted extensive patrolling throughout the penetrated area and subjected the populace to extensive propaganda and psychological warfare activity. German agents moved in the area spreading rumors. These were supported and expanded by a powerful and cleverly operated German radio transmitter which purported to be the British Broadcasting System. While traveling north through Mouzon to Sedan, a U. S. military police patrol observed that the town was being evacuated. This was reported to U. S. military police headquarters in Sedan who initially assumed that German patrols had reached Mouzon. However, an immediate check with military police patrols which covered the entire area disclosed no evidence of German patrols or penetration into the Mouzon area. The military police battalion commander contacted the French Sous Prefect of Arondismont, Department of the Ardennes, whose area of authority included Mouzon and asked whether he knew why Mouzon was being evacuated. Upon contact by means of the French Gendarmerie communications network, the mayor of Mouzon advised the Sous Prefect that information had been received over the British Broadcasting System that the Germans were about to enter Mouzon. Upon being assured

by the Gendarmerie and other reliable sources that there were no Germans in the area, the mayor halted the evacuation and the people returned to their homes. Continued evacuation of Mouzon would have resulted in the evacuation of other towns and movement of large numbers of people into Sedan which was already overcrowded and susceptible to rumors or disorder created by agitators. In this case, it should be noted that removal of an imaginary fear and prompt action by responsible authorities prompted the people of Mouzon to return to their homes and prevented the evacuation of other towns.

(a) The need for security may manifest itself in the individual in different ways depending upon the environment to which he is accustomed. Any society in the world exerts pressure on its members and thereby affects their environment in either one of two ways: favorably or unfavorably. A change in the environment of an individual can result in a change of behavior. Collectively, a number of individuals with changed behavior can represent a group with changed behavior. The individual members of modern societies look to their governments for security. Where such governments do not or cannot provide for this need individual frustration may result. The feeling of frustration can lead to an individual's participation in a civil disorder.

(b) Another example of the individual's need for security is the frightened child who seeks the security of his mother's arms.

(c) A peoples' sense of security may be jeopardized when they are forced to accept the presence of an "outside" group. Such an "outside" group would be identified as such if it differed from the people in any of the following ways: racial composition, political ideology, religious beliefs, and social standards.

(2) Social approval. The desire for social approval is one of the strongest urges of man. Children are taught to cooperate with and respect other members of their society. They are taught the customs and traditions to which their society adheres. Normally, individuals who violate the customs and traditions of their society face the imposition of physical harm, material harm, or social ostracism.

(3) Recognition. Regardless of customs or traditions, individuals and societies the world over compete for recognition. Recognition is a psychological factor indicative of successful living which lends prestige to existence. The recognition sought varies as to degree It may be as simple as the need for respect and admiration of loved ones or as complex as the desire for recognition by a nation. Most men and nations will work long and hard to achieve recognition. If it is not obtained at least to some degree, men and nations may become frustrated.

(4) <u>Group association</u>. A man will seldom follow a course of action that will incur the disfavor of the group. He associates himself with a group and its objectives. Should a man be expelled from his group as an undesirable, he will in time seek association with another group. An individual who fails to attain a satisfactory degree of identification with one group is more vulnerable to the influence of other groups.

4. RISING HUMAN EXPECTATIONS.

The rising tide of human expectations is a real and tangible force that police officials must take into account. Many countries in today's world are experiencing a massive and revolutionary upheaval which can be interpreted as basically amounting to a sharp cleavage of the present from the past. As a result, the objective being sought is a better life here and now as compared to the previous aim of seeking only a better life for succeeding generations. Through the progress of modern technology, the time-distance problem that once hampered the intercourse of people has been reduced. Modern news and communication media flash reports throughout most of the world in minutes. People are increasingly familiar with their neighbors and their inherent similarities and differences. Awareness to these surroundings has made the world seem a smaller place. With this awareness has come the desire for a better way of life. This reaction to awareness is natural and can be expected to continue. Wars have been fought and nations have been conquered due to the aspirations of individuals or a society. The rising tide of human expectations is attributed to individual and collective aspirations for: (a) independence, (b) justice, (c) wealth, (d) recognition, and (e) self-esteem. (See Figure 1.)

a. <u>Independence</u>. Through awareness, people have developed the aspiration for independence from subordination. They are no longer satisfied to endure unnecessary restraints upon individual sovereignty. They aspire to choose their own objectives. The aspiration for equality of opportunity and right of personal selection may be expressed by individuals or societies in various ways. They may attempt peaceful approaches to accomplish their goals; however, once motivated and organized, they will move by any means to attain their objectives.

Figure 1. Desire for improvement.

b. _Justice_. Men aspire for equal administration of justice. They do not desire to be subjected to police brutality, unregulated search or seizure, or arrest without charges. Instead, they aspire to the right of equality before law for all members of society. Justice for the individual plays an important part in the rising tide of human expectations.

c. _Wealth_. The word "wealth" varies from society to society in its meaning and implications. An individual may be considered wealthy if he owns vast pieces of land; if he claims many friends; if he has health, vigor, and vitality; if he has a substantial sum of money; if he holds a prominent place in society; or if he possesses a large store of produce. Societies throughout the world use wealth as a measure of both individual and social progress. Men sense that wealth tends to add to their security regardless of their particular environment. With increased awareness of needs they are becoming dissatisfied with the presumption that wealth can never be acquired. The aspiration for wealth is closely correlated with the individual's desire to obtain personal, economic, and social privileges.

d. _Recognition_. Men throughout the world are seeking to communicate their needs, problems, and desires to their governments. Men are seeking the right to reason--to express themselves to other members of society. They are becoming dissatisfied with the role of subordinates who cannot assert themselves. In many instances, people are seeking to participate in their own government. They desire the right to arbitrate difference with their peers and their society. Some people have become aware that members of other societies in the world have attained this right; consequently, they are aspiring to attain the same goal.

e. _Self-esteem_. The aspiration for self-esteem is applicable to both individuals and societies. It is closely correlated with men's desire for the right to independence, justice, wealth, and recognition. Individuals want to be respected and considered equal to others of their society in their rights and privileges. Similarly, many formerly subordinated societies throughout the world are beginning to seek the same achievement. A group which has developed self-esteem will assert itself as it moves toward a predetermined goal. Self-esteem is a portion of the whole concept referred to as the rising tide of human expectation which must be recognized.

5. INFLUENCE OR PRESSURE FROM AN OPPOSING IDEOLOGY.

The remaining area for close attention in the underlying causation factors of civil disorders is the pressure or influence that may be caused by opposing ideologies, foreign or domestic. Since the earliest beginnings of civilized man, history has recorded one ideology pitted against another. Study of the Hannibalic War (2d Punic War) would provide the interested reader with an excellent example. However, competition between ideologies does not always result in armed conflict. The police official must understand that an opposing ideology can use subtle and outwardly peaceful means to influence the behavior of his society. Civil disorders become important tools by which governments are weakened, international relations jeopardized, and thousands of people injured or killed. There is every likelihood that these motivated civil disorders will continue to occur throughout the world just as they are occurring at the present time. This section will deal with some of the techniques used and purposes sought by an opposing ideology in recent civil disorders.

a. Exploitation. Pressure or influence by an imported opposing ideology is possible through exploitation of a relatively small but well-trained group of revolutionaries. The following is an example of such an exploitation.

(1) Setting. Twenty-one American Republics planned to assemble representatives at Bogota, Colombia, in the latter part of March, 1948. The purpose of this assembly of nations was to adopt a charter reaffirming the solidarity of the American states, pledging the member nations to mutual defense and resistance to international communism. This was to be the Ninth Inter-American Conference (Pan-American Conference). Almost immediately upon the announcement of the proposed conference, international communism moved with its available forces in an effort to destroy the conference.

(2) Communist actions. The time table of actions adhered to by the communists followed a carefully prepared plan with a sequence of events as outlined below.

2 January 1948 ---- The Communist party of Columbia began planning for "anti-imperialist" demonstrations to be conducted shortly before the Inter-American Conference.

23 January 1948 ---- Policy for the Inter-American Conference conflicts drafted by the Communist party.

29 January 1948 ---- Supplies and material necessary for use in the planned demonstrations were stored in Bogota.

2 February 1948 ---- The working plan for the communist inspired demonstrations was designed to include the following actions:

(a) Organization of public mass meetings.

(b) Organization of sixty cell meetings in outlying districts.

(c) Organization of fifteen syndicates in unions.

(d) Distribution of 50,000 handbills.

(e) Distribution of 3,000 posters.

16 March 1948 ---- Communist-appointed committee was positioned to observe the preparations of the participants for the forthcoming conference.

30 March 1948 ---- Reports indicated that molestations and agitation of arriving conference delegates had occurred.

9 April 1948 ---- Sequence of events, Bogota, Colombia:

-- 1:05 PM - A young lawyer and national idol of Colombia was assassinated. The assassin was mauled and subsequently executed by a "suddenly" formed mob. (This action was initiated during the noon period when all stores and shops were closed. Many people were on the streets. As a result of the mob action, transportation facilities in downtown Bogota were stopped.)

-- 1:20 PM - Radio stations were taken over by communist inspired groups composed mainly of students. The radio facilities were used to incite the people to revolt against the government. The people were instructed to destroy government property.

-- 2:30 PM - A mob succeeded in entering the capitol building and began to destroy office equipment.

-- 2:30 PM - Communist-held radio stations issued instructions to "assault and kill." The people were given a specific list of "target" individuals who were to be assassinated. The population was incited to form a people's militia.

-- 4:00 PM - Mobs began to plunder places of business within the city.

-- 5:00 PM - Downtown Bogota had been reduced to shambles through mob action. Fires raged. The Inter-American Conference was cancelled.

(3) Results. The rioting that occurred in Bogota was so successful that five days passed before the conference could be reconvened in a school building in suburban Bogota.

b. Strategy. Carefully planned civil disorders are an effective strategy used by International Communism in exerting pressure against an invaded society.

(1) <u>Planning</u>. Planning for inciting civil disorder is usually accomplished well in advance as was illustrated in the preceding incident. Planning is normally centered around one central incident or circumstance which will be used as the basis for the disorder. Contingencies that might arise are carefully considered. Proposed locations, weather conditions, police strength, and the morale of the population are carefully studied. Leader and agitator groups are appointed, prepared, and rehearsed.

(2) <u>Techniques</u>. Careful study of a society to be pressured or influenced will normally reveal definite problems facing that society. For example, a deficiency which exists in the human needs of the people could be used by a pressure group as a basis for inciting riots. If no well-defined problems face the whole society, the conflicting aspirations of various segments of the population can often provide the basic causes for inciting riots. Selected segments are influenced to become angry mob factions pitted against each other, e.g., workers against management, students against teachers, race against race, social class against social class. History indicates that many societies experiencing this type of pressure were not prepared to cope with the situation that developed.

6. POLICE RESPONSIBILITY.

As was pointed out in the first part of this chapter, the police cannot maintain law and order without the wholehearted support of a community and other governmental agencies. Because of their close and continual contact with the population, the police are usually in a better position than other agencies to analyze grievances which need immediate attention. Through close liaison with other local governmental agencies and free exchange of information with them, the police can insure that the peaceful pursuit of individual liberties will be maintained.

CHAPTER 2

CIVIC ACTION PROGRAMS

7. INTRODUCTION.

In Chapter 1, the underlying causation factors of civil disorders were discussed. It was stated that the police have a vital function to assist in the prevention of civil disorders. Since all societies in the world are vulnerable to civil disorders the police official must use knowledge of the emotions and drives of men to help eliminate or neutralize the susceptibility of society to civil disorders. This step can be accomplished through police participation in a well-conceived and efficient community civic action program. Webster's Student Dictionary says of the word "police" - "1. The control and regulation of the internal affairs of a state exercised by its government, especially in matters concerning public health, comfort, morals, and safety; hence, control and regulation of affairs affecting the general order and health of any community .... Also the organization or system for maintaining such control and regulation." Since the police are charged with interest in public health, comfort, morals and safety, and the control and regulation of such affairs as they affect the general order of society, it is the responsibility of police to be engaged in civic activities on a daily basis. The success of a police force can be measured, in part, by the degree of support and cooperation that it receives from the people served The police organization which has gained the confidence, respect, and approval of its society is far more able to prevent or control civil disorders than one which has not.

8. OBJECTIVE.

A strong civic action program can materially assist in the prevention of civil disorders. This chapter will present those aspects and theories considered important to the formulation of a sound, efficient, and beneficial civic action program and to the possible application that a civic action program can have in the prevention of civil disorders. Police participation in a civic action program will be discussed.

9. FORMULATION OF THE CIVIC ACTION PROGRAM.

a. General. Governments are becoming increasingly aware that a population which is allowed to express its desire for a better environment and way of life will be less sensitive to dissatisfaction. Most individuals experience frustration if they attempt single-handedly to attack the environmental factors to which they are opposed. Organization of a community civic action program is a method by which people are able to give expression to their desires while working towards beneficial goals in cooperation with their fellow men. It recognizes that the desire to work and associate with other men is a well-marked human trait. The community civic action program encompasses two major points: first, it encourages cooperative effort and second, such effort can be oriented toward community betterment. Basic to proper operation of the program are the following principles:

(1) Recognizing the social needs or aspirations of the community.

(2) Utilizing available human and material resources effectively and efficiently in satisfying needs and aspirations of the community.

(3) Providing the population with incentives, guidance, and support.

b. Community attitudes. The attitudes of a community are expressed in various ways. Significant indications of public dissatisfaction are apathy and noncompliance with laws. Indications of disaffection toward governmental policies may be observed through radio, television, and press media. Police activity is a vital community service; therefore, an informed public is essential in fostering proper understanding of police objectives and operations. Civil disorders can have a devastating effect on any community. The better educated the public becomes on the effects of civil disorder, the higher their state of awareness to the ramifications and consequences of social trends likely to produce civil disorders. An informed community increases the likelihood of gaining cooperative support from the people in the effective prevention of civil disorders.

10. POLICE PARTICIPATION IN THE CIVIC ACTION PROGRAM.

a. General. Police participation in a community civic action program has significant psychological objectives. It is undertaken to provide the public with tangible evidence of the police interest in the welfare and betterment of the community. The ultimate goal is to gain the confidence, respect, and active cooperation of the population. The formulation and implementation of an effective police civic action program should take place within the framework of and be in consonance with a well-conceived community program.

b. Police organization for civic action. Police participation in a civic action program requires extensive planning and complete utilization of all available resources.

(1) Basic policies. It is important for police officials to recognize that certain policies should be followed in maintaining the effectiveness of the civic action program.

(a) Interested agencies should present a united front in the regulation and enforcement of laws in consonance with the needs of the community.

(b) Public support and cooperation must be maintained by the governing body of the society.

(c) Inter-agency coordination leads to respect and mutual understanding of the problems encountered by different agencies of government.

(d) Information required for the operation of an efficient coordinated effort must be properly distributed.

(e) The police should deliberately seek to arouse, promote, and maintain an active concern for the public welfare within community organizations.

(f) The police should assist community organizations in an advisory capacity.

(g) The police should promote frequent conferences with community organizations to discuss laws, policies, and procedures of mutual interest.

(h) The police should solicit and evaluate advice, especially on matters pertaining to complex community problems.

(i) Membership in community organizations by individual policemen should be encouraged. These members can assist in the association and identification of police with the local population. They also provide the police agency with excellent sources of information valuable to police and community planning.

c. Police interaction with governmental and private agencies. Many elements of a society have interests in the preservation of order and the enforcement of laws. These agencies, depending upon the nature of the society, may include: legislative bodies, public administrators, judicial agencies, and other public welfare departments. Private citizens may belong to various civic groups. Each of these represents the needs and interest of the community.

d. Community civic organizations. Community civic organizations are usually headed by individuals who exercise influence over

diversified segments of the population. Police officials should therefore give careful consideration to the vital role that can be played by
these leaders in the prevention or control of civil disorder. Civic
organizations are normally composed of parents, residents of the community, businessmen, and professional men--people who have an inherent
interest in the character, welfare and prosperity of the community. The
study of community activities reveals that they are often basically organized in accordance with racial, economic, occupational, religious, or
social similarities and beliefs. Each community organization serves as
a clearing house for information relevant to its activities and field of
interest. Effective coordination by police agencies with civic organizations can materially assist the police education program if relationships are properly established.

        (1) <u>Understanding of the police position</u>. During a civil
disorder many individuals will forget that the police exist and function
to preserve law and order. Due to the possibility of resentment develop-
ing against the police during a civil disorder, it may be difficult for
police to convince factions of police impartiality. Police officials
through the sound relations achieved in the civic action program can en-
list the support of civic organizations. By favorably influencing their
members, maintaining open support of police impartiality, and demanding
peaceful settlement, these organizations can assist in the suppression
of mob action.

        (2) <u>Special police control measures</u>. Most control meas-
ures that might be necessary during a civil disorder could be considered
infringements of the law against the individual. Control measures should
be kept to the minimum necessary for the successful suppression of the
civil disorder and should be relaxed or removed as soon as the situation
permits. When control measures are employed, civic organizations can
give invaluable assistance in easing public resentment through educational
and persuasive measures. Misinformation and rumor will often complicate
the police task of maintaining law and order during a period of public
unrest. The united front that can be formed from the existing community
organizations will strongly affect public opinion and thereby either
simplify or complicate the police mission.

       e. <u>Arbitration of differences through conferences</u>. At the
outset of a civil disorder, police officials should immediately encourage
the conduct of conferences in which responsible community leaders are
participants. The objectives of these conferences are to analyze the
situation, plan actions designed to resolve differences, and discuss
the likely actions of the participants. Initial arbitration conferences
should be conducted before human passions are highly aroused and while
the police agency still enjoys a favorable public opinion. During the
opening period of the conference, police officials should emphasize the
necessity for the maintenance of law and order, and the means that will

be used to accomplish this end. Police officials do not take sides in any discussions. They simply stand on the firm ground of promoting the restoration of order.

(1) Arbitration committees. If the number of participants in the arbitration conferences become too large, adequate solutions may not be achieved. Police officials might well promote the formation of a special arbitration committee that will seek the settlement of the problem that created the disorder. The arbitration committee, since it repre sents both viewpoints of the disturbance, can be effectively employed as a supervisory panel to oversee the restoration and maintenance of law and order. Arbitration committees may effectively assist in the following important areas:

(a) The coordinating of remedial efforts of participating public and semi-public agencies.

(b) The protecting of the community officials from the influences of selfish minority groups that might act contrary to the public's interest.

(c) The influencing of public officials to act in the interests of public welfare by supporting the adoption of desirable programs and the discontinuance of those considered to be undesirable.

(d) Seeking public support of programs designed in the public interest.

(e) Winning public cooperation in the form of compliance with regulations and active intolerance of their violations.

11. POLICE PUBLIC RELATIONS.

a. Establishment of police public relation policies. Well defined policies must be established by police officials in the field of public relations. In the establishment of these policies, consideration should be given to the following factors.

(1) Causations of public resentment. To properly execute the police mission while maintaining the support of the population, the police official must be aware of those factors which might cause public resentment. With the realization that societies vary throughout the world, the reader will appreciate the impracticability of considering all applicable factors; however, some which might apply to the majority of societies are outlined below.

(a) Needless embarrassment or inconvenience of individuals by police authority.

(b) The demonstration of overbearing and unreasonable attitude by police.

(c) The failure to employ impartiality in the enforce ment of laws.

(d) The conduct of personal affairs while "on duty."

(e) The use of unnecessary force in apprehensions and arrests.

(f) Acts or deeds not in consonance with the social expectation of the population to include dishonesty, improper use of alcoholic beverages, and police violation of laws.

(2) Relationship with press and radio organizations. It is common knowledge that the radio and press media of a community have a great capability in molding public opinion. One of the main functions of the press or radio is to maintain contact with the public on matters of public interest. Good relations with the press and radio can assist police agencies in the accomplishment of their mission while stimulating good relations with the population. Definite handling techniques should be established by police officials for the following activities:

(a) The release procedures for newsworthy items of public interest.

(b) Restriction procedures on items that could be considered sensitive in nature or which might jeopardize the investigation of a crime, the reputation of an individual, or the security of the community.

(c) The methods by which press and radio facilities can be used to exploit the psychological value of photographs and commentaries in the maintenance of favorable public opinions.

(3) The police community relations unit. In large, congested, and complex communities, it may be advisable for police officials to consider the formation and employment of a specially trained police community relations unit. The unit should consist of well-trained and experienced police officers who have displayed an ability to meet the public and have a favorable reputation. The police community relations unit serves to accomplish five main points of importance to the police civic action program.

(a) It acquaints community organizations with police policies, procedures, and operation. When necessary, it interprets specific police actions, explaining their necessity and how they operate. It serves then, to educate the public.

(b) It transmits information to the police staff concerning problems and activities within the community that might otherwise remain undetected.

(c) It reports to police planners those police activities appearing discriminatory to the members of the community. It reports police practices which incur unfavorable public opinion.

(d) It operates as an intelligence listening post well situated within the framework of the community to receive early warning of trends and activities likely to result in civil disorders. (See Chapter 3, Police Intelligence.)

(e) It can provide members for and work in close coordination with a similar community relations unit which could be organized as part of the community civil action program.

(4) _The individual policeman._ To a great extent, a police agency is judged by the actions of the individual policeman in his daily contacts with the public. The individual policeman becomes the mirror in which the police agency is reflected. The wise police official will insure that, to the maximum extent possible, the individual policeman creates a favorable image in the public eye. How, then, is this favorable impression obtained?

(a) _Appearance._ The uniformed policeman should present a neat and clean appearance when he greets the public. Appearance assists the police officer in gaining a favorable public reaction.

(b) _Bearing._ Bearing reflects the individual police officer's confidence, professionalism, and training. Improper bearing detracts from the favorable impression that could otherwise be created. Bearing and comportment are synonymous in this context.

(c) _Attitude._ A police officer must reflect a feeling and purpose of interest and assistance. A police officer who displays an attitude which denotes an overbearing demeanor will seriously damage a favorable police image.

(d) _Knowledge._ All police, to be effective and efficient, must be well informed about the responsibilities of their office and of their mission. The individual police officer must have thorough knowledge not only of police science but also of the society with which he deals. A police officer who is not professionally qualified in the basic skills of his field will not create a favorable public impression.

(5) Relationships with children. Public attitudes are in part formed by the way children are handled and treated by police. Children can do much to assist in the creation and maintenance of a favorable image. In many modern societies police officials might appropriately consider ways and means of gaining the respect and admiration of the children.

(a) The establishment of youth activities which foster greater parent interest and assist in the suppression of juvenile delinquency.

(b) The sponsorship of youth activities such as scout troops, youth camps, and athletic leagues.

(c) The sponsorship of speakers, clinics, and safety programs for school and other youth organizations.

b. Determination of success of the program. The success of the public relations program depends upon the wholehearted support of every member of the department. Whether the program is successful or not will be determined by the attitude of the public toward the department and law enforcement in general. The press is a good barometer of public opinion and wields a great influence on the public.

12. POLICE TRAINING.

To uphold and enforce the laws of a society and maintain favorable public opinion, a police agency must insure that its members are well trained. Individual police officers must receive thorough training in subjects such as those listed below.

a. Knowledge and understanding of the police mission.

b. Knowledge of laws and ordinances and their application to the population.

c. The legal procedures of the society.

d. The employment of special police equipment.

e. The controlled application of force in keeping with the police mission, legal standards, and safety of the population.

f. The emergency administration of first aid.

g. Maintenance of equipment.

h. The arts of self-defense.

i. Information concerning existing subversive activities and their methods of operation.

j. The principles and importance of police intelligence.

k. Basic crime detection and investigational procedures.

l. The fundamentals of police public relations.

13. ADMINISTRATION.

The enforcement of law and the maintenance of order must apply equally to all members of a society. Impartiality and fairness are mandatory ingredients of a police civic action program designed to win popular support. It should be remembered that a police agency plays an important role in providing for the individual's requirement for security. Police officials who expand and develop this role of the police within a community will engender the support of the population. In many emergency situations people first turn to the police for protection and guidance, i.e., for the maintenance of security. The police agency that has been successful in winning the respect and trust of the people through civic action is in an excellent position to receive strong support in their efforts to preserve or restore order. At all times, however, the police must remain impartial and not show favoritism.

CHAPTER 3

POLICE INTELLIGENCE

14. INTRODUCTION.

Few individuals would attempt the passage of a dangerous mountain trail or trek through unchartered miles of desert without the sensory ability to see and hear. The mental application of these sensory abilities allows an individual to perceive varying situations. Once perception has occurred, the ability to comprehend enables a person to take whatever action is necessary in consonance with the demands of the situation. Efficient police operation occurs in part when perception and comprehension, through an organized intelligence system, are applied to the accomplishment of the police mission. The early perception of public unrest and subsequent comprehension of the problem can lead to timely application of remedial measures resulting in avoidance of civil disorder The development of intelligence information is quite simple for the typical police agency since its members are in close contact with the population on a daily basis. Police intelligence may be defined as any particle of information, news, or advice, the knowledge and application of which will assist the police in accomplishing their mission.

15. OBJECTIVE.

This chapter will present concepts in the development and application of an intelligence program to further a police agency's ability to enforce law and maintain order. The presentation includes a discussion of the intelligence cycle, the principles and application of overt intelligence, and the principles and application of covert intelligence. Specific emphasis is given to the use of intelligence in the detection of public unrest.

16. THE INTELLIGENCE CYCLE.

The development of the wheel and its applied use has allowed man to accomplish numerous technological improvements for his society. The intelligence cycle can be likened to a four spoked wheel which assists the police agency in efficient operation. The wheel of intelligence turns in perpetual motion. The four spokes that comprise the wheel are the four steps of intelligence: (1) the collection of information, (2) the processing of collected information, (3) the dissemination of resulting intelligence, and (4) the planning of the collection effort. In the organized intelligence program, these four steps occur continuously and simultaneously.

a. The collection of information. Operational planning based on police intelligence data will be unfavorably influenced where such data have been poorly processed or original information is not factual. The collection of accurate information is the most difficult step in the successful operation of an efficient intelligence effort. If members of an opposing ideology desire to create civil disorders within a community, common sense would dictate that they implement certain security measures. Those security measures would probably include the concealment of strength and identity of members, dispositions, intentions, movements, and plans. To prevent possible detection, it can be assumed that the opposing ideology would disseminate false imformation. To obtain accurate information, the police official must give careful consideration to two aspects which support the collection effort: the sources of information and the means of collection.

(1) Sources of information. A source of information is considered to be the origin of the information. Generally, any police agency has access to numerous sources of information in the course of its daily activities. For example, valuable information can be developed through the sources listed below.

(a) Local civic organizations.

(b) Businessmen.

(c) Social clubs, fraternities, and similar organizations.

(d) Political rallies.

(e) Parades.

(f) Churches and religious groups.

(g) Athletic events and informal crowds.

(h) Radio and press services.

(i) Other community services.

(j) Informants.

(2) Means of collection. Intelligence information may be collected by either individuals or organizations. Police agencies throughout the world generally have several means of collection at their disposal. The most common types of collection resources are discussed below.

(a) <u>The individual police officer.</u> The best collection resource available to the police agency is the individual policeman. The police officer's close association with the civilian populace can be used to provide the police agency with important and accurate information if two requisites are met.

1. <u>Intelligence indoctrination and training.</u> The police officer must be taught what to collect, where to collect, when to collect, and why to collect. He must be thoroughly indoctrinated on the importance of police intelligence. The officer must be trained in the application of man's five basic senses of sight, taste, smell, touch, and hearing, to the collection of information. Training in the collection of information for police intelligence broadens the officer's understanding as to its importance in the detection and prevention of serious incidents. The typical police officer discards daily, items of information that do not directly affect his immediate area of interest. However, what may seem unimportant to him may be of vital importance to the police agency. What the police officer is to collect is largely dependent upon information requirements formulated by his superiors; however, in the course of his duties he must evaluate <u>all</u> information which may be important to the collection effort. Where the officer is in doubt, he should report the information.

2. <u>Reporting techniques.</u> Information of intelligence value that is obtained but not reported accurately is of little use. The individual police officer must be trained in the reporting of information. A good notebook and pencil are as important in intelligence collection as they are in other areas of law enforcement. The police officer normally must answer the questions of who, what, where, when, why, and how. Clearly defined reporting procedures should be established to incorporate considerations listed below.

a. <u>What to report.</u> All information dealing with civil unrest or criminal activity should be reported. The police officer must make an initial evaluation of the information's validity and an objective appraisal of the source. Information should be as nearly complete and accurate as possible.

b. <u>How to report.</u> Information that may be of immediate intelligence value should be reported by the most expeditious means available. Rapid means of communication might include either radio, telephone, teletype, or personal report if distance between the policeman and superior is not extensive. In all other instances, an oral or written report should be utilized.

c. <u>Reporting channels.</u> A policeman should always report through an established chain of authority. If deviation from this rule is allowed, the circumstances surrounding the deviation should be clearly defined.

(b) Other collection agencies. Depending on the size of the community served and the nature of the society, police officials may consider the utilization of additional collection agencies necessary to supplement the effort of the individual policeman.

1. Special police intelligence. The police official can organize a small group of selected police officers who are utilized in the conduct of special investigations and the collection of police intelligence. Operations conducted by this group would normally be considered in the category of covert intelligence which will be discussed at length later in this chapter.

2. Community relations unit. The formation of a special public relations unit as discussed in Chapter 2 can serve the police agency as an efficient intelligence collecting agency in addition to functioning as a part of the civic action program. Its position in the community affords excellent early warning on the possible development of civil disorders.

3. Associated governmental agencies. Formal or informally organized intelligence systems may be operated by other governmental agencies dependent upon their needs. The development of efficient coordination and liaison can lead to the exchange of mutually vital intelligence information.

b. The processing of collected information. Processing is a three-step operation which includes recording, evaluation, and interpretation. Information is normally processed in accordance with priorities of importance. It is then correlated with other associated information.

(1) Recording. Recording is defined as the reducing of information to some form of writing and the grouping together of related items. The recording process simplifies the subsequent step of interpretation, rendering it easier to accomplish and more accurate in end product.

(2) Evaluation. Evaluation is the critical appraisal of information wherein it is determined whether or not the information was obtained from a reliable source and is accurate and pertinent.

(3) Interpretation. The final step in processing is when the significance of the information is determined with respect to what is already known. Conclusions are drawn as to the probable meaning of the evaluated information. Interpretation can be summarized as the concluded results of critical judgment, analysis, and integration.

c. The dissemination of intelligence. Information that has been processed must reach users in time to be of assistance in the formulation of plans. The means and methods selected for dissemination depend entirely on the detail, pertinence, and urgency of the information and its intended use. Police officials should carefully consider which branches of government may require processed intelligence information in consonance with the nature of the information. Intelligence indicating early occurrence of a civil disorder will require immediate dissemination so as to permit rapid planning and implementing of coordinated preventive actions.

d. Planning the collection effort and orders. Planning and guidance by police officials are necessary in the conduct of intelligence activities so as to maintain direction and continuity. Intelligence needs must be forecast in advance to allow sufficient collection time. The subordinate collection agency, whether it be the individual police officer or separate unit, must know the precise nature of information desired by their superiors.

(1) Essential elements of information. Police officials who anticipate civil disorders can direct the collection of specific data which are termed the essential elements of information. The collection of this information on a continuing basis facilitates accurate and timely revision of plans through the police officials' ability to remain abreast of the current situation. The essential elements of information for civil disorders might well include those listed below.

(a) Probable location(s) of civil disorders.

(b) Probable causes of civil disorders.

(c) Classification of individuals or groups who might create or support civil disorders.

(d) Estimated number of participants.

1. Initial number.

2. Anticipated reinforcements (by source).

3. Types and quantities of weapons.

(e) Probable assembly areas for crowds.

1. Assembly areas where riots might occur.

2. Assembly areas removed from site of disturbance.

(f) Routes available for police movement to crowd assembly areas or potential locations of civil disorder.

(g) Known leaders of past civil disorders and present potentially troublesome social movements.

1. Forceful influential members.

2. Professional agitators.

(h) Plans, activities, methods of operation prepared or used by disturbance leaders in the following areas of interest:

1. Possible destruction of property.

2. Possible interference with community utilities and services.

3. Possible assaults on nonsympathizers.

4. Agitation.

5. Embarrassment to government.

(i) Disturbance activities.

1. Passive resistance to control.

2. Verbal displays.

3. Violent acts.

4. Physical resistance to control.

(j) Organization.

1. Milling rioters.

2. Organized mob front.

(k) Prominent organizations supporting actively or passively the cause of the disorder.

(l) Location and nature of material and equipment available for use by the members of the disturbance.

(m) Location of unguarded material or equipment that could be seized by rioters.

(n) Location of important buildings.

    <u>1</u>. Public.

    <u>2</u>. Government.

    <u>3</u>. Private.

(o) Location of communications systems, transportation systems, public utilities, and stores of materiel and supplies subject to damage during civil disorder.

(2) <u>Orders</u>. Based on information obtained through the collection effort, police officials can form a fragmentary picture. Additional particles of information may be required for correlation and substantiation. Through timely collection and maximum utilization of available sources, information can be obtained that will enable the police agency to act before the development of a civil disorder. Through timely orders, the police official provides the intelligence effort with needed guidance thereby maintaining control and efficiency.

17. OVERT POLICE INTELLIGENCE.

The word overt literally means "open." Thus overt police intelligence activities are those undertaken openly and without attempted concealment from public view. For example, the individual police officer routinely collects information in an overt manner while performing his normal everyday duties. In some areas of the world he is the only individual commonly found closely associated with the populace; in fact, he may be the only government official dwelling within a community. In his capacity, he may perform other duties such as census taker, tax collector, distributor of public information, and local magistrate. In effect, he represents the government to the people. The police officer also plays the most important role in the overt intelligence effort of a police agency. Earlier in this chapter, police intelligence training and general reporting techniques were discussed. However, for an efficient overt intelligence effort, the police officer must know the principles that will assist him in the collection of information.

a. <u>Knowledge of area and populace</u>. A police officer can never know too much about his area. This rule applies not only to his ability to collect information but also to the successful accomplishment of his primary mission--the enforcement of laws and the maintenance of order. He is, in effect, a walking storehouse of information. Specific information that the police officer should know might include all items listed below.

(1) The economics or means of livelihood for the area.

(2) Industrial interests of the people.

(3) Cultural composition of the population.

(4) Religious differences and beliefs.

(5) Social aspirations of the group.

(6) Fluctuations in the strength and character of minority groups.

(7) Political beliefs.

(8) Popular trends of the people.

(9) Attitude of population toward international movement.

(10) Individuals considered popular or influential with the people.

b. Public relations and overt intelligence. The collection of information through overt intelligence activities is best accomplished in conjunction with sound police public relations. The police officer who has the respect and trust of the population is normally very effective. After gaining a thorough knowledge of his area and its inhabitants, the police officer must establish rapport with the people. The police officer then follows the general rules outlined below.

(1) Observe. Through observation the police officer is able to note accurately the occurrence, person(s), place, or thing that is related to the performance of his duty. The application of the ability to observe is important in overt intelligence. Observation should include the following:

(a) Patterns within the neighborhood. Generally, most neighborhoods develop standard patterns of operation or habits. The police officer must be familiar with these habits and note those happenings which do not fit into the normal scheme. When reported to superiors, information often can be correlated with other information to form a clear picture of an item of intelligence value.

(b) Meetings and rallies. Assemblages of this type normally alert the police officer to the moods of the population. Often, leaders and organizers are readily identified and controversial subject areas clearly defined.

(c) Athletic events and parades. The policeman can determine through observation, trends in nationalism, moods of the population, and the repressed feelings or sentiments of minority and majority groups.

(d) <u>Neighborhood businesses</u>. Continuing observation will reveal changes in activities that could be the result of subversive pressure.

(e) <u>Strangers</u>. The movement of strangers through the neighborhood when observed and correlated by further checks can disclose information concerning activities, associations, and interests which may be of intelligence value.

(2) <u>Listen</u>. The police officer must be a good listener. In the successful collection of information he must listen to many things spoken by many people; things which would include personal problems, opinions, interests, gossip, and grievances. He should listen to the conversations of people, speakers at meetings and rallies, and public expressions at informal assemblages. These particles of information collected from various sources may form an important intelligence picture.

(3) <u>Read</u>. The police officer must read. His ability to comprehend thoughts and ideas conveyed by literature is an important part of his effectiveness as a collector of information. He should continually review for intelligence value the information expressed on items such as those listed below.

(a) Handbills.

(b) Newspapers.

(c) Advertising.

(d) Business signs.

(e) Propaganda literature.

18. COVERT POLICE INTELLIGENCE.

The word covert has the meanings of sheltered, covered, and concealed. Covert intelligence refers to information collected by methods concealed from public view. Covert intelligence collection activities are considered secret. Since the intelligence effort of any police agency will be only as good as the collection techniques utilized, it is important that the subject of covert intelligence be discussed. The collection of covert intelligence may provide vital information concerning causes of public unrest and subversive agitation within the community. This paragraph will discuss covert intelligence collection techniques and their effective application and employment in support of the intelligence effort.

a. Informants.

(1) General. Informants are persons who give information to the police. They are sometimes compensated for their services, but compensation does not necessarily imply payment by the police officer receiving the informant's cooperation. For example, an informant may provide information to the police for purely altruistic reasons. The confidence of informants must be scrupulously respected by the police.

(2) Utilization. Informants are valuable only when they are in a position to obtain information of value to the police; good will or a spirit of cooperation is not enough. The police officer interested in obtaining information about action groups which might pose threats to internal political stability of a community will need informants who are members of such groups. For example, informants in politically conscious labor unions, student groups, and political party executive committees will be most helpful. Persons who have or can obtain access to information wanted by the police may be recruited as informants. Police officers must be exceptionally careful when recruiting informants. Each potential informant must be approached carefully, with the officer furnishing the motivation best calculated to appeal to the individual. The officer may have to spend much time in careful cultivation of the prospective informant before making any direct approach. There is no universally effective recruiting technique; each officer must discreetly plan his approach after making a complete evaluation of the prospective informant and the type of information he may be able to furnish. The virtues of patience and perseverance are of paramount importance.

Placed informants, known as "sleepers," can also be of great value to the police. These are individuals recruited as informants who infiltrate the action groups to be penetrated. Great care must be given to the selection and use of placed informants who may be compelled to remain without contacts with the police for extended periods of time while earning the confidence of groups penetrated. There is always a danger that placed informants will discard their allegiance to the police agency under the constant influence of new associates, so police officers must exercise caution when dealing with placed informants. The term "placed informant" can also be used to describe individuals who are recruited as informants and then placed in positions where they will come into contact with members of the action groups whose activities are of interest to the police. Barbers, cooks, waiters, and maids are examples of this latter type of placed informant.

(3) Special considerations. Police officers should treat their informants with respect and should not imply by word or deed that informants are anything less than patriotic public servants providing valuable services for their countries. However, the officers should not confide in their informants nor discuss investigations with them. Often

well-intentioned informants tend to assume control of investigations; police officers must guard against this development, particularly with informants who have been used frequently.

Protection of the identity of informants is the responsibility of the police officer. When confidence is implied or promised, it must be observed. Only by scrupulously observing all agreements made with informants can police officers hope to engender the confidence and enthusiasm that mark the valuable confidential source of information.

   b. Undercover police officers.

      (1) General. An undercover police officer is one who abandons his official identity as a law enforcement official and assumes an identity which will enable him to obtain information he would not otherwise be able to obtain. The assumed identity may merely involve the wearing of civilian clothing (an indication that the individual in mufti is something other than a member of a police agency), or it may require very elaborate preparations. In either instance, the preparations should be sufficiently thorough to preclude compromise, to minimize any danger to the undercover police officer, and to insure the ultimate success of the undercover mission. Normally, undercover investigations should not be attempted if other means of obtaining the desired information can be utilized effectively.

      (2) Considerations. The police officials charged with obtaining intelligence data should consider the following factors before authorizing an undercover mission: the exact results required, the importance of the mission, the availability of planning data, the availability of qualified investigative personnel, the equipment and preparation necessary, the danger involved, the time available for completion of the mission, and the prospects for success.

      (a) Selection of personnel. When it is decided that an undercover mission is the best means of obtaining required intelligence information, the best qualified police officer should be the candidate first considered for the assignment. The undercover police officer should be well trained and experienced in investigative work; he should be calm, mature, and resourceful; he should be completely self-confident and feel certain that he can assume an undercover role successfully; he should be courageous and able to deal effectively with unexpected and emergency situations; he must be able to avoid intemperance in all its forms; and he should be ready and willing to accept the undercover assignment. For a specific mission, the selected police officer should be convincing in the particular role he will be required to assume; he will need a good memory if it is not possible to make notes; he must be proficient in any occupational area in which he may be required to allege competence; he should have the physical appearance and characteristics consistent with his role; and he should have the background, education, or training which will enable him to wear his role like a well-tailored garment. The undercover police officer should also be completely familiar with the background and ramifications of the total investigation so that he will be able to assess accurately what he observes while undercover.

In addition to the above factors, superior officers must consider the linguistic talents, the educational background, the hobbies, the athletic abilities, the religious background, and other aspects of the prospective undercover agent's total personality when selecting a man for a particular undercover mission.

(b) Briefing. Prior to assuming an undercover role, a police officer must be completely briefed on the nature of the task he will be expected to accomplish. He should know as much as possible about his geographical area of operations, his expected contacts, and his reporting facilities and procedures. Obtaining the background information needed for this briefing before beginning an undercover assignment is essential for a successful mission.

(c) Preparation of "cover." A background or cover story for the undercover police officer will be necessary whenever he is required to infiltrate any organization or group of individuals. Every practical effort should be made to fit the cover story to the actual background of the undercover police officer. If it is even remotely possible that the fictitious background data of the undercover officer will be checked by members of the group being infiltrated, arrangements must be made in advance for prompt corroboration of the fictitious elements of the cover story.

(d) Rehearsals. The undercover officer, before embarking on his assignment, must carefully rehearse his cover story so that the fictitious elements appear to be genuine. He must also be certain to have on his person and in his personal effects only those items of clothing and equipment which are consonant with his cover story; nothing which might connect him with the police agency should be taken on an undercover assignment.

(e) Reporting and communication. Like bread, intelligence information becomes stale with age. Arrangements must be made in advance to permit prompt reporting of gathered data by the undercover agent. Mail drops, couriers, safe houses, and the telephone are among the means available for safe and rapid communication.

c. Surveillance.

(1) General. Surveillance is the investigative activity which consists of keeping persons, places, or vehicles under observation.

While a surveillance may be conducted by informants acting in behalf of a law enforcement agency, use of the term is usually restricted to describing the clandestine observations conducted by investigative personnel.

(2) Purpose. The surveillance technique of gathering information can be used effectively to obtain evidence; to locate wanted individuals by observing known acquaintances and haunts; to develop information about the activities of individuals; to secure a basis for the issuance of a search warrant; to check on the behavior of informants; to identify individuals frequenting or visiting a certain location or premises; to determine the nature of suspicious activities; to develop time-tables or schedules of the movements of suspicious or suspected individuals, or to develop sources of information which may not be already known to the police agents.

(3) Types of surveillance. Surveillance may be maintained from fixed or mobile observation points. Observations may be restricted to visual observations; they may involve the use of a variety of eavesdropping techniques; or they may include a combination of visual and aural techniques. The use of still and motion picture cameras to supplement or supplant ordinary visual observations should be encouraged when possible.

(a) Fixed surveillance. In selecting a fixed observation point, police investigators should consider the possibilities for observation that various prospective locations provide. They should also consider the need for movement of technical equipment and the opportunities for its use, as well as the number of surveillants the job will require. A fixed surveillance post should be close enough to the target location or premises to enable the surveillants to identify persons entering and leaving; binoculars and telescopes can be used to increase visual range when necessary. A communications system should be installed so that the surveillants can maintain round-the-clock contact with police headquarters and with other surveillants in other locations. Naturally the type of neighborhood and the availability of good observation points will influence the selection of the surveillance post, as will the kind of intelligence information required. If concealment is impossible to achieve, it will be necessary to inaugurate a system of intermittent surveillance using a number of investigators who will walk or drive past the location or premises periodically to maintain the surveillance; it may be possible, too, in cases of this type, to conceal hidden cameras or eavesdropping devices to provide aural coverage when visual coverage cannot be maintained without detection.

(b) Mobile surveillance. In mobile surveillance, the police officers may find themselves on foot, in public conveyances, in automobiles, or using all three modes of transportation. When the purpose of the surveillance is to gather intelligence information covertly, the surveillants may use either a loose (discreet) continuous surveillance, or a form of progressive surveillance in which the subject is discreetly followed for a certain distance each day and picked up the following day where the surveillance was discontinued previously. The progressive surveillance can be used effectively when the moving subject follows the same route daily; this type of surveillance will in time reveal the location of all premises visited by the subject.

(4) Considerations. In selecting surveillants, police supervisors should consider the aptitude, poise, experience, resourcefulness, alertness, patience, perseverance, and physical characteristics of the candidates for selection. The consideration of the prospective surveillant's physical characteristics is particularly important when a moving surveillance is contemplated and when an ordinary-appearing police officer will be less noticeable than one of exceptional height and girth or with other uncommon physical features. Before beginning a moving surveillance, the police officers should be furnished with suitable transportation, sufficient funds to defray any incidental expenses, a system of signals to be used by the surveillance team, adequate communication facilities, and a complete briefing on the subjects and the investigation to date. The area in which the surveillance will occur should be the subject of a complete reconnaissance, and all available information about the topography, the street layout, and locations frequented by the subjects should be provided to the surveillants. In using a surveillance as an intelligence-gathering technique, advance planning and judicious choice of surveillant personnel are the keys to successful completion of the mission.

d. Use of cameras.

(1) General. Photographic techniques and equipment can be very valuable for the police officer charged with the responsibility for gathering accurate and complete intelligence information. The judgment of the officer, his opportunities, and the photographic equipment available to him will influence the amount of pictorial coverage collected in any particular investigation.

(2) Considerations. Police agencies with ample funds will have available press-type cameras, portrait cameras, miniature cameras, 35mm cameras, fingerprint cameras, Polaroid cameras, and movie cameras of various types. In addition, there will be a selection of lenses, film, and accessories available for use by the investigative personnel. However, the best selection of photo equipment does not automatically provide the best photos. Police officers must be well trained in photographic techniques and training policemen to use their photographic equipment effectively is one of the responsibilities of the supervisory and command personnel. The opportunities for effective use of photographic equipment are legion; all cameras from the simple box cameras

to the most sophisticated miniature or aerial cameras can be invaluable tools in the hands of well-trained and imaginative investigative personnel. The conditions existing in particular jurisdictions during particular investigations will determine how existing opportunities can be exploited most profitably from an intelligence viewpoint.

(3) Uses. Undercover policemen and informants with access to the files of subversive action groups will have opportunities for effective use of miniature cameras and 35mm cameras with lenses suitable for document-copying work. Surveillants will be able to gather valuable intelligence data using the press-type cameras, the 35mm cameras, and the movie cameras, particularly when supplemental telescopic lenses are available. Aerial photographs have a practical value during briefings of surveillance teams or raiding details. Use of infrared techniques and film can help insure photographic coverage during darkness. The leaders of subversive groups, their visitors, members of the groups, and meetings of these individuals should be photographed surreptitiously whenever possible. Photographs, backed by unretouched negatives, provide convincing evidence of activities, contacts, and acquaintanceships that would otherwise be difficult to identify or substantiate. Photographs of suspect personnel are invaluable during briefings of informants, undercover police officers, surveillants, and raiding parties; they can also be used to identify subjects for uniformed policemen who will be responsible for providing overt intelligence-gathering services.

e. Use of sound detection equipment. Police cannot afford to ignore the possibilities for more complete and accurate intelligence coverage that science has provided. Short wave radios, portable transmitters and receivers, and other transmitting apparatus are among the items of equipment which may be utilized to increase the effectiveness of even the best-placed informants or the most resourceful undercover agents.

(1) Wire tapping. Wire tapping involves interception of messages transmitted over the telephone. When authorized, telephone intercepts can frequently be very productive in intelligence-gathering investigations. Direct wire taps are simple to install and difficult to detect; the investigator needs only to attach the terminals of a handset or magnetic earphones to the wires of the telephone to be tapped. Technicians can install equipment to the circuit which will prevent users of the tapped telephone from detecting the intercept when the phone is used. The telephone line may be tapped at any point in the lines between the instrument and the telephone exchange facility, and the intercepted conversations can be recorded easily by using tape or wire recorders that are actuated only when the tapped telephone is being used. By using an induction coil, telephone conversations may be overheard without making any direct physical contact with the telephone wires. The induction coil, when placed near the telephone or the wires, operates in and picks

up the magnetic field set up by the electrical impulses traveling along the telephone wires and surrounding space. The quality of induction coil intercepts is not as high as that of direct taps, but conversations can be recorded accurately when high-quality amplification equipment is used in conjunction with the induction coil.

(2) _Microphones_. Concealed microphones can also be used for surreptitious eavesdropping. Selection of the type of use depends on the job to be done. Frequency response, directional characteristics, and sensitivity must be considered. Some microphones are sensitive to sound from only one direction (unidirectional). Bi-directional microphones are sensitive to sound from front and rear, and nondirectional microphones are sensitive to sound without regard to direction. The correct microphone, used with appropriate acoustical improvement devices, will provide police intelligence agents with superior wire or tape recordings; however, the finest recording devices are of little value with poorly chosen or poorly placed microphones. Police officers ordinarily use carbon, dynamic, or crystal microphones.

(a) _Carbon and dynamic microphones_. Carbon and dynamic microphones are nondirectional and are recommended for use when concealment is of primary importance. The quality of reception is inferior with carbon and dynamic microphones, but they are easily concealed, inexpensive, readily available, sensitive, and usable at a considerable distance with a fine, unshielded wire that can be painted to blend into almost any background. To use carbon and dynamic microphones, electricity must be directly supplied to the microphones as an actuating power source. Dynamic microphones are more expensive than carbon microphones; both are low impedance devices. Dynamic microphones are more sound-sensitive in the high and low decibel ranges than carbon microphones which are effective only in the middle decibel ranges.

(b) _Crystal microphones_. Crystal microphones contain pressure-sensitive Rochelle Salts. When sound waves exert pressure on the surface of these salts, the opposite surface develops a minute electrical charge which is transmitted by wire to an amplifier for recording. Crystal microphones are very sensitive and have an excellent range and good sound quality reproduction capacity. However, these microphones are relatively expensive because they require the use of shielded wire and complicated amplification equipment for effective monitoring of intercepted conversations.

(c) _Common characteristics_. All microphones have three enemies in common; they are distance, reverberation, and background noises. For most eavesdropping, microphones must be located within six feet of the center of conversation. Reverberation (echoing) occurs when sound is reflected (bounced) from walls, ceiling, and floors; unfurnished rooms produce so much reverberation as to distort all of the sounds being picked up by the police officer's microphones. Rooms furnished with rugs, draperies, and furniture produce little reverberation. Unlike the human ear which can discriminate between audible noises and select ("tune-in") certain sounds while rejecting others, microphones cannot discriminate between sounds. Nothing is excluded, so traffic noises, dripping water, the scraping of feet, footsteps, and other non-conversational noises are picked up with the same fidelity as voices. Background noises which would not interfere with hearing a person who is speaking in the same room with the listener, often completely blot out the sounds of human voices for the police officer who is listening with the aid of a concealed microphone.

(d) Utilization. Concealment of microphones in locations where they will serve the police officer's purposes is a matter of ingenuity and opportunity. Microphones can be surreptitiously placed in hotel rooms, offices, homes, meeting halls, conference rooms, and any other locations by informants, undercover police agents, or overt police officers with opportunities to make the installations. The microphones can be installed in electrical receptacles, lamp bases, behind curtains, under furniture, in heating ducts, or in any other locations that will enable the concealed microphones to be effectively oriented for distance and direction. The main consideration is to conceal microphones and their wiring where they remain undetected and still operate satisfactorily.

(3) Recorders. Conscientious police officers usually record intercepted conversations. Disc, film, and magnetic recorders are used; magnetic recorders provide the best-quality sound reproduction, but are more expensive than disc or film recorders. All recorders work on the same principle; natural sound energy is coverted into electrical energy in the microphone, radio transmitter, or telephone, and then reconverted to sound energy in the amplifier, radio receiver, or second telephone. When the recorder is used, the reconverted sound energy is not expended; it is retained by the recording process for future use.

(a) Uses. Recording intercepted conversations enables police officers to devote all of their time to listening; they do not need to be stenographic experts to obtain verbatim records of conversations being monitored. Others, not present at the time, can also listen to the recorded conversations. Vocal identification of individuals can be made by using recordings; translations of foreign language dialogue can be made when convenient; verbal codes can be broken by cryptographers with access to recordings; and evidence of conspiracies and other crimes can be preserved on recordings for future courtroom utilization. Portable, concealable recorders are available for police intelligence use. These small wire and tape recorders can be used to record conversations that take place in the presence of the informant or undercover police agent carrying the recorders; when these miniature recorders are carried on the person, sensitive crystal-type "wristwatch" or "lapel button" micro-phones can be used profitably. When these recorders are planted or hidden in suspected premises or automobiles, crystal microphones or telephone induction coils can be used in conjunction with the recorders. Earphones permit monitoring conversations as they are recorded. These small recorders are battery-operated when used as portable equipment; they may also be operated on 110-120 volt current with a transformer rectifier.

(b) Characteristics. Tape recorders need not be watched constantly; large tape spools can be installed to provide long-time coverage with recorders that are actuated by sounds (used with planted microphones) or by electric impulses (used with installed telephone taps). Use of these types of recorders permits extensive eavesdropping coverage with a minimum number of police officers and also permits eavesdropping in locations where police officers can not be concealed.

(4) Short-wave radio transmitters. The necessity to in-stall wiring is a disadvantage when planting microphones or installing telephone taps. The use of short-wave radio transmitters eliminates the need for wire or cable installations. In recent years transmitters have been reduced in size without loss of efficiency; now some transmitters, using printed circuits and small batteries, are no larger than cigarette packages.

(a) Portable transmitters. Small short-wave trans-mitters may be concealed in automobiles of subjects, on the person of informants and police officers, or concealed indoors or outdoors. It is necessary to have short-wave receivers relatively near the transmitters, although the newest transmitter-receiver combinations are effective at ranges up to three miles under favorable conditions. The late model transmitters and receivers (and the "transceivers," the combination transmitter-receivers) are powered by nickel-cadmium long-life recharge-able batteries. Use of these batteries makes the old-style battery packs unnecessary. The new batteries provide eight hours of usable operating time, with about two hours of actual transmitting or receiving time, be-fore recharging is required. The batteries may be recharged by plugging their recharge cord into any 110-120 volt outlet overnight. For semi-permanent installations, these new transmitters are not as satisfactory as the older models with their larger, long-lasting, attached battery packs.

(b) Non-portable transmitters. Non-portable trans-mitters can be used to obtain valuable data; these transmitters operate on 110-120 volt electrical systems and can be spliced into existing wir-ing in the premises where coverage is desired. These transmitters have a tube life ranging from six months to one year, and once installed (be-hind radiators; in heating ducts; behind grilles, moulding, or plaster walls; in unused stoves or fireplaces; behind pictures; or elsewhere in a building) they may be left unattended to provide continuous operation almost indefinitely.

(c) <u>Telephone line transmitters</u>. Telephone line short-wave radio transmitters are designed to provide hard-to-detect telephone monitoring coverage. The transmitters are spliced into existing telephone lines with no additional wires needed. The receiver may be located up to three city blocks away and still pick up all transmitter signals. Ordinary telephone taps may be discovered when their installation affects the service or when the wires from the tap to the recorder are discovered; neither of these hazards exists when the telephone line transmitter is installed in a well-concealed location anywhere along the line between the phone and the telephone exchange facility.

(d) <u>Picture frame transmitters</u>. Picture frame short-wave transmitters are sometimes useful when long-time coverage is desired in a specific room. The transmitter and battery pack are concealed between the picture which faces the room and the cardboard covering the back. To outward appearances, all that is apparent is an attractive, but innocuous, picture mounted in a wooden frame hanging on the wall. The batteries provide about 200 hours of transmission time.

(e) <u>General requirements for antennae</u>. Concealable antennae are integral parts of each of the transmitters mentioned above; when transmitters are secreted in the automobiles of subjects, they may be connected to any existing radio antenna or used with their own antennae

(5) <u>Vehicle application</u>. Special inverters permitting operation of standard AC 110-120 volt equipment from direct current voltage are available, thus making it possible to operate recorders and other equipment in automobiles. The inverters and other special equipment discussed in this chapter are available commercially from business firms which specialize in supplying law enforcement agencies.

CHAPTER 4

LAWS AND ORDINANCES

19. INTRODUCTION.

It is appropriate in the discussion of the prevention, suppression, and control of civil disorders to give consideration to the preventive application of the laws enacted by society. The measures taken by the government of a society to maintain public order and safety must be balanced against the needs of the population. Laws and ordinances designed to control the population are enacted under the general authority of the police power of government. The English philosopher, Jeremy Bentham, stated that, "Police is in general a system of precaution, either for the prevention of crime or calamities." Such laws bear a direct relation to the health, morals, safety, and general welfare of the society. Any extensions of government police power must have some basis in necessity. A law necessary in one community may not be needed in another. Similarly, a law not justified at the present time might well become justified in the future. The laws of a people must be developed in accordance with the changes that continually occur within the society. The Supreme Court of the State of Illinois, in the review of a case concerning the legality of an ordinance stated,

".....the consistently increasing density of our urban populations, the multiplying forms of industry, and the growing complexity of our civilization, make it necessary for the state, either directly or through some public agency by its sanction, to limit individual activities to a greater extent than formerly. With the growth and development of the state the police power necessarily develops, within reasonable bounds, to meet the changing situations....."

20. OBJECTIVE.

This chapter will deal with the application of certain public laws which, if enacted, will assist police in the prevention of civil disorders. Laws and ordinances mentioned in this text will identify enforceable penal sanctions which enable law enforcement agencies to counter threats of impending civil disorders.

21. TYPE LAWS AND ORDINANCES.

a. Noncongregation. The use of laws or ordinances which regulate or restrict public or private gatherings of individuals is appropriate when such assemblies tend to promote a public disturbance.

(1) Laws or ordinances to prevent gathering. Under conditions of extreme public tensions it may be advisable to prevent people from assembling. In such circumstances, the extremes of this requirement might range from prohibiting congregation at any place and time within a city or a given area to restrictions applicable only in certain places especially subject to unruly gatherings of people such as the city hall, courthouse, governor or mayor's residence, and other government buildings. This type of law or ordinance might be limited to the prohibition of gatherings at designated places during certain specific times. It might also designate the number of people in one group that may lawfully gather, such as ".....and it shall be a violation of this law for more than three persons to gather....." in a particular area at a specific time. Noncongregation established by law or ordinance could well serve to eliminate at an early stage any danger of disorder and riot by large groups of people.

(2) Permits to gather. When tension has eased it may be possible to allow public or private gatherings if permission has been granted by proper authority. The representative of a group could be required to apply for a permit to meet at a certain place and time for a specific reason. This requirement will allow police officials sufficient time to prepare for possible outbreaks of disorder and alert them to potential "trouble areas." Permits to assemble would be appropriate for certain events involving large numbers of people such as festivals, parades, rallies, athletic events, political meetings, labor meetings, and similar gatherings. Government officials should make every effort to advise the leaders of organized groups as to local laws and ordinances which are applicable to the contemplated group activity.

b. Restriction on movement. The movement of individuals within a city or other area, especially during the hours of darkness, can be effectively controlled by a strictly enforced curfew. Certain individuals may be granted passes so that essential businesses and public utilities can operate after curfew. As tension eases restrictions on movement can be eliminated gradually. It may prove necessary to restrict all modes of travel until the cessation of trouble. Again, as tension subsides, limited travel by permission granted from competent authority can be instituted as a less restrictive form of control. Such laws and ordinances can be put into effect by the local police by establishing road blocks and check points for control over all incoming and departing persons.

c. Registration. A law or ordinance requiring registration of all persons in a city is a valuable aid in maintaining surveillance of known troublemakers and in providing an excellent locator service. Minimum information, consisting of name, date, place of birth, occupation, and current home address should be obtained. The law or ordinance might further require registration of all new arrivals, those intending to depart, and visitors into the area.

d. <u>Communications</u>. All communications equipment having a capability of transmitting or interfering with official messages could be required to be registered. Also, the authority for public officials to requisition, seize, or confiscate such equipment should be defined. The law or ordinance should include all electronic or wire communications equipment whether it be of professional or homemade origin. Sound trucks and electronic megaphones could also come under the restrictions of laws of this type. Such laws and ordinances would serve a dual purpose; they would eliminate the possibility of any interference with official messages intended to reach the public and would also place an effective limitation on the ability of agitators and mob leaders to reach large numbers of people.

e. <u>Newspapers and other printed matter</u>. These media of communications provide another means through which moral suasion can be used to minimize or prevent threatened civil disorder. Cooperation of these media should be sought in avoiding unnecessary emphasis on obviously inflammatory or derogatory news articles and stories which, if not handled discreetly, pose a discernible danger to the public interest and safety.

f. <u>Conspiracy as associated with civil disorders</u>. It could be made an unlawful act for two or more persons to meet for the purpose of planning an act which is designed to create violence, rioting or other forms of civil disturbances. Laws and ordinances might also prohibit inciting or participating in any rioting or public disorder. Acts which would violate laws of this nature might include making hostile or derogatory speeches or threats regarding public officials or which are aimed at the overthrow of the lawful government. Any group action which would have the result of fomenting civil disorder could be incorporated into conspiracy type laws and ordinances.

g. <u>Noninterference with government functions</u>. Since the unimpeded operation of the government is essential it may be desirable to enact laws and ordinances making criminal offenses of certain acts of interference with governmental functions. Public transportation, public communications, and public utilities must be allowed to continue throughout periods of unrest and tension since disruption of such services increases unrest and the possibility of group violence. In addition, police should be able to perform their duties unhampered by intentional interference.

h. <u>Prohibition or restriction against possession of weapons</u>. It may be necessary to enact laws or ordinances prohibiting possession of or requiring the registration of firearms, ammunition, and explosives in order that they may be controlled. Such laws should pertain to automatic weapons, grenades, sporting rifles and shotguns, pistols, revolvers, firing devices, and certain chemical agents. In some instances it may be necessary to requisition, seize, or confiscate privately owned weapons during periods of public unrest. Receipts should be given to assist in eventual return of the property where appropriate. In addition, law enforcement officials might be given authority to confiscate any other items that could be used as weapons. Searches of automobiles and individuals entering a tension-filled area should be accomplished and objects such as clubs, bottles and chains, should be taken so they cannot be used as weapons.

CHAPTER 5

CROWD AND MOB BEHAVIOR

Section I

PSYCHOLOGICAL ASPECTS OF MOB BEHAVIOR

22. INTRODUCTION.

An unruly, wanton mob bent on destruction, assassination, or other overt illegal ventures can be awesome even to the law enforcement officer who must disperse the mob. Typical law abiding citizens allow themselves to lose control and obey the "Law of the Pack," a law which identifies man as an animal lacking morals, ethics, or inhibitions. Personal conduct that ordinarily would be regarded as contemptible is readily acceptable to the standards of the "Pack." A civil disorder need not be planned or even deliberate. It can result from a disaster which so disrupts the community that the populace behaves in a frenzied and distraught manner. The more knowledge a police officer has regarding the characteristics of crowd and mob behavior, the better are his chances of effectively dealing with civil disorders. This section will enumerate characteristics of mob action and will identify some techniques that rioters probably will use to annoy or obstruct police during the restoration of order.

23. MOB CHARACTERISTICS.

Mobs are characteristically emotional and frequently irrational The members of a mob normally share the same emotions. Mobs, according to their intent, can generally be classified by type. The following list ing describes various types of mob classifications.

a. Aggressive mob. The aggressive mob riots and terrorizes. It is classically illustrated by race riots, assassination mobs, polit- ical riots, and prison riots.

b. Escape mob. An escape mob is one whose frightened members are attempting to reach safety. Panic motivates the escape mob. Members of an escape mob, because of panic, normally lose their power to reason. Escape mobs which tend to overrun anything in their paths can create great damage and loss of life.

c. Acquisitive mob. An acquisitive mob is motivated by a de- sire of its members to acquire something. A classic example of an acquis itive mob is one which riots because of a shortage of food.

d. _Expressive mob._ The expressive mob is one whose members express fervor or revelry such as following a sporting event or holiday celebration.

24. PSYCHOLOGICAL INFLUENCES THAT WORK IN FAVOR OF AGITATORS.

Often the following questions are asked. Why do peaceful people participate in mob violence? What is there about a large crowd or mob that causes an individual to react differently from the way he does in his normal daily living? What are the psychological forces that cause a temporary breakdown in an individual's ability to control his emotions? The answers to these questions can be found in the psychological influences that contribute to the seemingly abnormal behavior which dominates most mobs.

a. _Novelty._ When an individual is confronted with new and strange circumstances, the habits that he has formed may not fully continue to dominate his drives. The specific stimuli which usually govern his actions may be absent. Lessons learned from previous experience may not be applied to the new situation. The individual subconsciously tends to welcome the break in his normal routine and thereby reacts enthusiastically to the new circumstances.

b. _Anonymity._ When an individual is within a mob, he may tend to lose his self-identity. As a result of the temporary loss of identity, he may sense a freedom from restraint and feel that he will not be blamed for his actions.

c. _Release from repressed emotions._ Prejudiced and unsatisfied desires of the individual which are normally held in restraint may be readily released after joining a mob. This temporary release of repressed emotions is a powerful incentive for the individual to participate in mob action since it provides him with opportunities to deviate from normal patterns of socially acceptable behavior.

d. _Force of numbers._

(1) The size of a mob provides an individual with a sense of power which most people like and desire to use. The feeling of power that may prevail among members of a mob is often augmented by a feeling of irresponsibility, resulting in a combination of dangerous factors.

(2) The force of numbers in a large mob action may create a feeling of righteousness within individual members and convince them that their actions are justifiable.

e. Suggestion. People normally will accept the ideas of a dominant personality. Ideas spread throughout a mob without a restraining thought, question, or objection being raised in the minds of its members.

f. Contagion.

(1) People are naturally curious. They are attracted by a large noisy gathering or mob.

(2) People become emotionally stimulated by the actions of others even though they may not have shared the experience from which the emotion originated. Usually this contagion is started by a feeling of sympathy which often develops into anger. The individual tends to imagine himself in the same position as those members of the mob who may advance a similar cause or belief; by associating himself with their cause, he also becomes angry.

g. Imitation. The urge to do what others do is strong in man. Only individuals with strong convictions normally resist the urge to conform and join. Pressure for conformity becomes strong in an emotional crowd or mob which may turn its anger against a dissenter.

25. PANIC IN CROWDS AND MOBS DURING DISTURBANCES AND DISASTERS.

a. General. Panic is terror created by overpowering fright which inspires highly emotional behavior or unreasoning and frantic efforts to reach safety. Panic mobs are violent and extremely difficult to control. People comprising a panic mob become so irrational that their actions become increasingly dangerous to themselves and others. There are four main characteristics of panic producing situations.

(1) Perceived threat. A perceived threat may be physical, psychological, or both. It is usually regarded as being so imminent that nothing can be done to solve the situation short of frantic efforts to escape and survive.

(2) Partial entrapment. There is normally only one, or at best, a limited number of escape routes from a situation dominated by a perceived threat.

(3) Partial breakdown of the escape route. The escape route becomes blocked or congested thereby precluding effective passage.

(4) Front-to-rear communications failure. When the escape route precludes an effective escape and people continue to assume falsely that the route is open, the panic producing situation is

completed. The physical pressure of the people advancing towards the escape route causes those in the front to be smothered, crushed, or trampled, thus producing widespread panic.

b. <u>Panic during civil disorders</u>. Panics are generally short-lived and usually affect only a relatively few individuals. In those cases where police forces are committed to a civil disorder, individuals who formerly were not members of the disorder may become frightened by the show of force or use of riot control agents and resort to frantic efforts to escape.

c. <u>Panics following disasters</u>. Panic in the wake of a disaster is an ever-present possibility. The success of public preparation for a disaster will greatly reduce the possibility of mass panic. Panic can result where thousands of injured, confused, or stunned survivors are seeking escape from such things as fire or flood. The major potential problem stems from the likelihood that large numbers of people will converge upon limited escape routes.

26. MOB ACTIONS.

a. <u>General</u>. The formation of mobs results from certain stimuli within individuals as discussed in paragraph 24. Outside promotion by means of propaganda, rumors, or individuals of an opposing ideology further stimulates the formation. The mob leader is of great importance in inciting a crowd to mob action. Mob action depends to a great extent on the ability of the mob leader to bring the emotions of individuals to a peak of intensity and subsequent release. Mobs naturally tend to follow the leader's suggested courses of action; however, justification for a course of action may be necessary before a mob can be incited to violence. Mobs under the influence of an opposing ideology may be so well organized that leadership is not apparent. In these instances, the mob is not the result of spontaneous, natural human reactions. The nature and purpose of the deliberately planned mob actions are carefully concealed. Although appearing to be separate and distinct actions resulting from supposedly local problems, disturbances led by opposing ideologies are in reality attempts to weaken or destroy the influence of constituted authority. Death, injuries, extensive damage, and looting must be expected when riots occur. The state of emotion and the violence of the rioters will depend upon a number of factors to include the composition of the mob, the number of people involved, the cause of the disturbance, and the location of the disturbance. Weapons in the hands of rioters and malicious rumors spread by mob leaders cause police officials deep concern. (See Figure 2.)

b. <u>Verbal abuse</u>. Police should anticipate verbal abuse in the form of obscene remarks, taunts, and jeers when encountering a mob. Confidence in their leaders and a sense of responsibility and discipline are vitally important to police officers in carrying out their orders in the face of verbal abuse. (See Figure 3.)

Figure 2.   Rioters with clubs and weapons pose a
threat to police officials.

UPI

Figure 3.   Policeman ignoring taunts of mob member.

c. Attacks on policemen and police vehicles. Groups of
rioters can be expected to give vent to their emotions upon individuals
or small groups of police officers. Vehicles may be overturned, set on
fire, have their tires slashed, or otherwise damaged. Police officers
performing duty during a civil disorder may be beaten, injured, or killed.
To guard against such attacks, police patrols must be sufficiently equipped
and capable of self defense. (See Figures 4 and 5.)

Figure 4. Police vehicle burned by mob.

d. Thrown objects. The members of a mob can be expected to
throw filth, trash, and missiles of varying types at uniformed police.
Mob action of this nature constitutes an attack upon the police who must
be free to use the degree of force necessary to handle the immediate situation. Officers performing duty near multistoried buildings or other
elevated structures must be alert for objects dropped by rioters. Normally these objects will include anything available within or near a
building which may produce casualties.

e. Vehicles and objects used against police. When police are
located at a lower level of an incline or slope, rioters may be expected
to direct vehicles, trolley cars, carts, barrels, rocks, liquids, and

Figure 5. Damaged police vehicles.

other objects against the force constituting authority. On level ground,
wheeled vehicles can be employed effectively by rioters against law enforcement elements. Where possible, animals may be stampeded toward
police.

       f. Demolitions. Rioters may employ natural gas, dynamite, or
other explosives to create damage, demolish buildings, or block movement
routes. An explosion can be timed to occur as police elements are in their
most vulnerable position. Police must anticipate the employment of demolitions in numerous places. Good police intelligence, careful planning,
and constant vigilance are required to prevent or cope successfully with
these situations.

       g. Weapons fire against police. Weapons fire against police
may take the form of selective sniping or massed fire. Mob leaders can
employ weapons fire against police elements to inspire more daring and
violent action by rioters or cause police to employ more severe measures
against the mob. The latter would tend to foster antagonism toward the
police force.

h. Use of women, children and elderly people. Mob leaders may place women, children, and elderly people in the front of the mob. This is done to gain police sympathy and to discourage police countermeasures. Where countermeasures are undertaken by the police, mob leaders may have photographs taken to create further public animosity and police embarrassment.

Section II

PSYCHOLOGICAL ASPECTS OF CROWD CONTROL

27. INTRODUCTION.

Under normal conditions when a crowd is orderly, violating no laws, and causing no danger to life or property, it is of little concern to police agencies except for possible circulation control. However, experienced police realize that problems often arise when groups are formed and an incident may occur which may excite or inflame human emotions. A crowd, although innocent in its origin, nature, or purpose, can become a mob; a mob in turn can generate rioting. Police history is replete with examples which indicate that the application of training skills and knowledge of crowd psychology could have prevented serious incidents or the loss of lives. The purpose of this section is to provide background knowledge concerning crowd behavior.

28. TYPES AND CHARACTERISTICS OF CROWDS.

a. General. A crowd may be defined as a large number of persons temporarily congregated. Contrary to our definition of a mob, the crowd does not have leadership, the members of the crowd generally think and act as individuals, or it might be said simply that the crowd is not organized. It is significant to note that where the mob is ruled by emotion, the crowd reacts with reason. Actions by the crowd are strongly influenced or controlled by law, custom, convention, or habit, to name a few.

b. Physical crowd. The crowd in its simplest form is called a "physical" crowd, or a temporary collection of persons. An example of a "physical" crowd would be people in a shopping area.

c. Psychological crowd. The "psychological" crowd is a group of people with a common interest. There are two categories or types of "psychological" crowds:

(1) Casual. The common interest may be any event which receives the crowd's attention for only a few minutes. Examples of the

casual crowd are those which congregate at the scene of a traffic accident, a fire, or a street fight.

(2) _Intentional._ The common interest is any event which receives the crowd's attention for several hours. Examples of the intentional psychological crowd are groups of people at sporting events, funerals, labor meetings, and political rallies. The intentional psychological crowd is the most prone to riot and should be of special interest to police agencies.

29. PSYCHOLOGICAL ASPECTS OF CROWD CONTROL.

Psychology has a definite place in police work dealing with crowds and crowd control.

a. The police officer who has a knowledge of human behavior simplifies his task when performing duty which requires contact with crowds. He should understand the general characteristics of the individuals who constitute the crowd. Further, he should have a detailed knowledge of the area in which the crowd is assembled or intending to assemble. Finally, he should know the purpose of the assemblage.

b. Readily available manpower is important when dealing with a crowd. The use of police officers with above-average height is a beneficial psychological control factor.

CHAPTER 6

TECHNIQUES OF CROWD CONTROL

30.   INTRODUCTION.

Experience has shown that the possible eruption of mob violence cannot be confined to any particular type of crowd. A crowd that assembles to witness a national sport, strengthen a picket line, or view a political rally contains the ingredients of force and violence. In the preceding chapter, the general behavior of crowds and mobs was discussed. This chapter will be concerned with techniques that can be employed by police for the efficient control of various types of crowds formed in pursuit of peaceful activities. The understanding of crowd and mob behavior; the use of sound public relations, efficient police intelligence, basic psychology, good judgment, common sense, and the principles contained in this discussion will facilitate the effective prevention of a civil disorder.

31.   TYPES OF SPECIAL EVENTS.

Special events that attract crowds may be categorized into the following types:

    a.   Political rallies.

    b.   Athletic contests.

    c.   Religious meetings.

    d.   Recreational activities.

    e.   Unusual occurrences.

    f.   Strikes or demonstrations.

    g.   Parades.

32.   CHARACTERISTICS OF TYPE CROWDS.

Crowds attending various types of special events have certain characteristics or peculiarities which, if thoroughly understood, can be of material assistance in crowd control planning.

    a.   Political rally. Crowds at political rallies are definitely partisan. Often the opposing party may "pack" meetings or send agitators to disrupt proceedings. Early identification of these individuals and subsequent assignment of police in close proximity to them will greatly curtail their activities. Party leaders who have the support of the crowd should be called upon to give assistance to any police efforts or make any announcements of a police nature. Through this action, possible resentment may be avoided.

b. **Athletic events.** Crowds attending athletic contests are generally divided by team loyalties. Feelings often run quite high and arguments are frequent. Usually these arguments are of a "safety-valve" nature of little or no concern to police. Fights based solely upon the progress of the game or activity are usually settled quickly without material harm or damage. Caution must be taken, however, to assure that this type of event is not used as a means for fomenting riots.

c. **Religious meetings.** Particular care must be exercised by police and other authorities in their official actions where religious meetings are used as a front for efforts to incite civil disorders. This presents a very delicate situation to the police and each such situation must be handled in its own way by authorities concerned. However, the creation of religious martyrs must be avoided if possible. Time and the delicacy of the situation may be of the essence, hence it is imperative that the covert police intelligence apparatus effectively keep authorities informed with accurate intelligence upon which proper and discreet counter measures can be based. History records that the most fanatic violence has erupted from circumstances held to constitute religious persecution.

d. **Miscellaneous recreational activities.** Crowds at public beaches, amusement centers, parks, large picnics, and other kinds of miscellaneous recreational activities may occasionally become threats to public order. For example, serious accidents, unexpectedly severe weather, excessive altercations are illustrations of special circumstances which might lead to inflamed emotions and subsequent violence.

e. **Unusual occurrence.** Crowds gathering due to curiosity at unusual occurrences such as fires or accidents usually have no other purpose or preconceived ideas connected with such events. Make-up of these crowds changes constantly due to individuals losing interest. Failure of such crowds to undergo this change should warn the police that some influence, possibly one which could lead to trouble, is retaining the crowd's interest.

f. **Strikes or demonstrations.** Conflicting interests are usually present during strikes and demonstrations. As a result such situations are violence prone due to the strong emotions involved. Because of these emotional pressures it is often difficult for the police to preserve a public image of impartiality. History indicates that police are not always successful in their prevention and control efforts and sometimes must be reinforced by military forces. Police planners should recognize that such situations can have very grave consequences.

g. Parades. Where parades are used as a form of demonstration by political, religious, economic, student, and other groups having intense emotional feelings, a basis of potential civil disorder exists. Parades in connection with holiday celebrations or festivities are less likely to produce violence unless the preceding period of time has been marked by intense agitation or other signs of public unrest.

33. PROBLEMS OF CROWD CONTROL.

a. Overcrowding. This problem is best controlled by the establishment of shut-off lines. These lines should be laid out and manpower and facilities assigned in advance so that upon a signal the shut-off can be established. Three principles are applicable in the establishment of a shut-off line:

(1) It should be established at a point where the people who are unable to gain access to the area can be turned back without creating a congestion problem.

(2) It should be established at a point where the physical features tend to channel the flow of pedestrians to its narrowest width.

(3) It should be established at a point far enough beyond the crowd to prevent the shut-off point being overrun by the normal crowd. Room for police to maneuver must be provided between the edge of the crowd and the shut-off point. Communications should be established between police at the shut-off point and at the crowd. Portable radios are excellent for this purpose. Consideration should be given to the establishment of an overflow area for accommodating those who wish to remain in the vicinity even though they may not be able to go to the main assembly area. (See Figure 6.)

b. Clashes between opposing groups. Political meetings or those concerned with labor disputes are good examples of controversial meetings in which there is a strong possibility of clashes between opposing groups. Probably the best solution to this problem is to separate the groups and prevent any physical contact between them. This involves assigning each group to a specific area. Often each group will assist in diverting its adherents to the correct area. Equally desirable locations and equal opportunity for publicity should be provided. If possible, a different departure time should be given each group. If this is impossible, the groups should be dispersed in different locations, exit routes policed, shut-off lines established and transit facilities policed. Obviously it is not always possible to completely segregate opposing groups. In many cases the varied opinions represented may not be formally organized. In such instances assignment of detectives or plain-clothes men should be made in the crowd to identify leaders or potential troublemakers, determine plans of the group and enable prompt action in the event of disorder. Police should be on their posts and police lines should be established before a crowd arrives.

Figure 6. Police Lines Form to Control Crowd
Around Washington Monument, Washington, D. C.

c. Panic. Panic is the fear of the unknown. In crowds panic can be highly contagious. Floods, fires, serious accidents, fights, or other critical emergencies may occur with such shocking suddenness that man's reasoning processes are suspended and panic results. There is only one truly successful way to control panic--prevent it. Nothing should be left undone. Plans for panic prevention should include:

(1) Separation of crowds into smaller groups by establishment of aisles, barricades, shut-off lines, and other restrictive measures.

(2) Provision of sufficient exits so that the area can be quickly cleared.

(3) Strategic placement of uniformed police throughout the area so that prompt preventive or control action may be taken.

(4) Inspection of the area before the crowd gathers to assure that no explosives, fire hazards, or other panic-producing conditions are present.

(5) Adequate protection of light control switches to include provision for auxiliary lighting.

(6) Provision for keeping exits clear. Width of exits should increase as the distance from the center increases.

(7) Assurance that control personnel are thoroughly familiar with the evacuation plan.

(8) Assurance that doors open outward and that revolving doors are not used.

(9) Provision of a public address system.

d. Criminal activities. A crowd presents an ideal environment for pickpockets, sex offenders and similar criminals. All police personnel should be fully instructed in the "modus operandi" of these types of criminals. Plain-clothes personnel should be assigned who are experienced in detecting pickpockets, dope peddlers, and degenerates. Assignment of policewomen in civilian clothes is very effective in detecting sex offenders.

e. Sickness and injury. First aid stations should be strategically located in coordination with health and other responsible agencies. The emotional tension normally associated with a crowd situation and the necessity for standing or walking in a congested area creates an atmosphere in which some people become ill. It is good practice to pre-position an ambulance or patrol car equipped with emergency medical supplies and equipment to care for the sick and injured.

f. Lost children. Provision should be made for the security of children who become separated from their parents. A shelter should be provided which should be under the supervision of a policewoman. Toilet facilities and facilities for the children's amusement should be provided. Communications should be established so that information regarding lost children may be quickly disseminated.

g. Traffic congestion. A simple plan involving a minimum degree of control should be established to facilitate flow of traffic. Traffic must be diverted in order that vehicles will not flow through the crowd area. Detours should be established a considerable distance from the area involved. Communications should be maintained between these outlying detour points and traffic headquarters so that a complete detour may be instituted. In the interest of public relations detour routes should be adequately policed. Traffic stoppages should be prevented by tracing traffic density for a considerable distance from the area occupied by the crowd. Consideration should be given to temporarily changing traffic patterns at the conclusion of an event in order to accommodate the mass exodus of vehicles. Widespread publicity should be given to all traffic plans and detours. Where applicable, full advantage should be taken of automobile radios and radio stations to broadcast traffic news.

34. CROWD CONTROL PLANNING PROCEDURES.

a. Obtain information. The first step in planning for control of a crowd is to obtain all available facts and rumors. Information of planning value may be categorized as factual or hearsay.

(1) Factual information.

(a) Some communities require a permit for parades, rallies, or similar events. Such a permit provides an excellent initial element of control because desired rules and regulations may be instituted as a prerequisite for issuance. A requirement for conspicuous display of the national flag is an example of an appropriate requirement.

(b) Time and location of event.

(c) Purpose and sponsor of event.

(d) Physical features of the area. Information pertaining to entrances, exits, transportation facilities, and other physical features which may affect operations is best secured by an on-site inspection under conditions similar to those which will exist at the time of the event. Maps, sketches, and photographs should be obtained.

(2) Hearsay information.

(a) Expected attendance.

(b) Climate or atmosphere of the event.

(c) Anticipated presence of opposing groups.

(d) Psychological background of expected crowd.

(e) Expected trouble or disorder.

b. Coordinate activities. There are numerous agencies and individuals with whom coordination may be effected to gain valuable assistance. Municipal agencies may institute special regulatory requirements such as establishment of a curfew or a curb on the sale of liquor. Transit companies may establish special loading and unloading points. Public utility companies may assure that emergency crews are available if required. Detailed coordination should be effected with the sponsor to accomplish such things as a clear delineation of his responsibilities; a thorough understanding of any legal restrictions or requirements; and a determination of identification procedures to be established. Other agencies with whom coordination may be effected are the fire department, weather bureau, health or sanitation department and street department. Coordination with adjacent communities, including military installations, may be appropriate.

c. Identify problem areas. A reconnaissance of the area should be made and maps or sketches prepared indicating potential problem areas such as transportation terminals, hotels, parking areas, and buildings housing offices of various groups identified with the crowd situation.

d. Prepare traffic plan. Traffic circulation plans should be prepared indicating entrance and exit routes, bypasses, detours, parking areas, and routes for emergency vehicles.

e. Determine personnel requirements. The number of police personnel required should be based on an analysis of intelligence reports, reconnaissance, previous similar events, number or magnitude of potential problem areas, and information provided by sponsors of the event. Whenever possible, police officers with previous experience regarding a particular post or patrol should be utilized. A lapel pin or other means should be used to identify police officers wearing civilian clothing. Emphasis should be placed on the establishment of a mobile reserve force with good communications.

f. Determine equipment needed. The equipment required will depend on the type of event and the information obtained from sponsors, reconnaissance, and experience with previous similar events.

(1) Weapons. As a minimum, a hand gun or riot stick, or both, will probably be required. In this connection it is well to consider psychological factors. For example, unruly members of a crowd may have more fear of a riot stick than a gun where usage limitations are placed upon the latter.

(2) Communications. Some means of communication will be required for all members of the police force. It may be in the form of simple visual or whistle signals or electronic communications may be

required. A communications center should be established through which information regarding all aspects of the crowd situation can be channeled. A communications code should be adopted and appropriately safeguarded. Repairs and replacement posts should be maintained at the crowd scene. A truck appropriately stocked and equipped for repair purposes provides an excellent solution to this problem.

(3) Vehicles. An adequate number of vehicles should be available to provide rapid movement of police officers to any point of a crowd commotion. Vehicles should be equipped with radios to permit sudden changes in assignments. Patrol or medical vehicles should be located in a central location which facilitates rapid dispatch.

(4) Barriers. Police type barriers are helpful in crowd control. A typical barrier is made of wood and may consist of a long horizontal plank supported by wooden legs. Usually the top of the plank is about 40" off the ground when the barrier is in position. Rope lines can also be employed as a barricade device. The advantages of using these barriers in controlling an orderly crowd include provision for maintaining police lines with a minimum of manpower, channeling movements of the crowd, and delineating the police line. For less orderly crowds, they provide a barrier which can be used to divide the crowd into smaller and more easily controlled groups. However, they are of little value in controlling a violent, disorderly crowd since they may be seized and used as weapons.

(5) Signs. A crowd provided with directions usually tends to be more orderly than one which is not. Temporary signs properly located are an excellent information medium. Directional signs not only reduce police manpower requirements but also tend to eliminate congestion caused by people who stop to ask questions of police personnel.

g. Inform police personnel. Advance orders given to police officers should be timely, complete, and in writing. Orders should be accompanied by a map, sketch, or overlay of the individual's assigned area of responsibility. The chain of command and the communications net must be thoroughly understood by police officers. The location of facilities such as the communications center, first-aid station, and lost children shelter should be included. Orientations should also include a review of the essentials of crowd control training such as the following:

(1) Observe spectators rather than event.

(2) "Baiting" by spectators should outwardly be ignored; however, such spectators should be kept under surveillance as potential leaders of disorders.

(3) Prohibit use of heavy sticks or boards to carry signs which can be used as weapons.

(4) Do not bluff.

(5) Avoid unnecessary conversation.

(6) Remain impartial.

(7) Avoid bodily contact.

(8) Keep outside of crowd.

(9) Identify and watch crowd leaders or potential leaders.

(10) Employ crowd psychological factors to advantage.

35. PROTECTION OF DIGNITARIES.

a. History of assassinations. In almost every society there have been actual or attempted assassinations. Many assassinations have been accomplished in spite of large numbers of protective personnel. In the United States practically no protection was afforded the Chief Executive from 1801 to 1901, with the result that Presidents Lincoln, Garfield, and McKinley were assassinated, and an attempt was made on the life of President Jackson. From President McKinley's assassination in 1901 to the present time, presidents of the United States have been protected by the United States Secret Service. Until the assassination of President John F. Kennedy on 22 November 1963, no president had been killed since McKinley. No elaborate or fanciful weapons have been used in most assassinations. In some instances, clever bluffs and treachery have played important roles, but most of the weapons were small arms.

b. Basic causes of assassinations. The majority of assassinations or attempted assassinations are basically caused by revolutionary, economic, ideological, psychological, personal, or mercenary factors. In some instances several of these factors may simultaneously be involved.

(1) Revolutionary causes. Individuals or groups who aspire to overthrow a government may seek this goal through selective assassinations. The revolutionary aspiration itself may be the product of economic, ideological, psychological, and personal factors, or some combination of these considerations.

(2) Economic causes. An assassin is motivated by a belief that his victim is responsible for currently unfavorable economic conditions or will create such conditions adversely affecting his country, a certain group, his own family, or himself.

(3) Ideological causes. Assassinations may be adopted as a means to remove individuals having political or other views considered intolerable by fanatical opponents.

(4) Psychological causes. Along with other causal factors most assassins are suffering from some degree of mental derangement, fanaticism, or emotional instability.

(5) Personal causes. Assassins may be primarily motivated by intense personal feelings, such as rage, hate, jealousy, or a desire for revenge.

(6) Mercenary causes. The assassination is attempted for monetary reward; however, the assassin's sponsor may himself be motivated by one or more of the other causal factors previously discussed.

c. Nature of the assassin. Assassination plots usually begin in the mind of a discontented individual who has reached the conviction that the only solution is to kill the person he considers responsible for his difficulties. This type of individual may have no legal basis or means of taking action against, for example, a highly placed political or military figure. The assassin will attempt to gain advantage by the use of surprise. He will endeavor to select the best opportunity by seeking information about his intended victim. For example, through reconnaissance, shadowing, inquiries of servants and neighbors, magazine or newspaper stories, and radio announcements, the assassin may gain a detailed knowledge of the habits and movements of the individual marked for death. The assassin may not be discouraged or deterred by observance of strong security measures. If the assassin attacks and is foiled but not captured he is likely to try again. Difficulties for a security force are increased by the fact that an assassin may not have distinctive features, that he may not fear capture or death, and that he may even desire to become a martyr. Moreover, the assassin may have one or more accomplices. Many potential assassins are suffering from severe mental disorders. They may experience hallucinations, delusions, and obsessions. Demented cranks who are suffering from delusions of persecution are particularly dangerous.

d. Planning. Police planning must strive for simplicity yet be thorough enough to consider every probable contingency.

(1) Factors to be considered in planning include: composition of the party protected, the itinerary (routes, modes of travel, time factors, division of security responsibilities, engagements, eating and sleeping stops and refueling points), defense areas, security personnel and equipment requirements, coordination matters (including methods for cross-identification of various security agency personnel), communications, secrecy requirements, public relations, security post designations,

advance screening and reconnaissance needs, emergency procedures, alternate plans, and miscellaneous administrative matters such as eating and sleeping arrangements for security personnel.

(2) The complete security plan should be prepared in the minimum essential number of copies and given a carefully limited distribution. Each copy should be assigned a number for positive control purposes. Security agencies or other vitally important officials receiving copies should be required to adhere to a receipt system established by the agency preparing the plan. The preparing agency should habitually destroy all notes, drafts, used carbon paper, and copies containing errors or not required for use. Only completely trustworthy typists should be used. Coordination of the entire plan should be limited to those indi viduals or agencies considered absolutely essential. Individual knowledge of the plan should routinely be restricted to what he has to know to carry out his particular duties.

(3) Absolute and complete protection of a dignitary against assassination or other types of attack is seldom possible. The goal is to minimize the chances of success of any contemplated attack. The privacy of the dignitary must be considered, and care should be taken to avoid his embarrassment.

(4) Every phase of security must be carefully planned in advance. Additional pertinent factors considered in this planning include importance of the protected person, political attitude of the local population, distances involved, and duration of the security mission. Consideration must be given to the prevention of accidents and the possibility of attempts to kidnap the protected person.

(5) Physical protection consists of a series of protective rings or cordons, each complete in itself. These defensive rings may be composed of security personnel, physical barriers, or both. An example of this type of security is the protection established around a house designated as a residence for a dignitary. A number of walking patrols around the grounds would comprise the first protective cordon. A series of fixed posts covering entrances would form the second ring. Security personnel stationed within the house would form the third echelon of protection. The depth of the protective forces and the degree of security established will be governed by the factors considered in the planning stage.

(6) Security arrangements and plans must be flexible enough to respond to sudden changes in the protected party's itinerary or in emergencies. For example, weather conditions and mechanical failures (including failure of lighting systems) are two ever-present potential hazards. The unexpected arrival of large numbers of visitors is another situation frequently encountered. Last-minute changes in the schedule of events occasionally occur. The security must be sufficiently flexible to cover these and many more eventualities.

(7) Central direction and unity of effort are of special importance because of the nature of this assignment. The officer in charge should be designated with full responsibility for all phases of the security mission. Responsibility for each component phase of the security plan must be clearly defined. All available information channels should be utilized for information of potential danger areas. Most of this coordination can best be accomplished by an advance party after receiving the official itinerary.

(8) The security of the protected party may be placed in serious jeopardy by undue publicity. Where considered necessary, police officials should seek the cooperation of the press and other public relations media in minimizing this danger. The consequences of making public the details of an itinerary other than those deemed absolutely essential may gravely endanger the effectiveness of police security plans. Those aspects of an itinerary made public should receive particular scrutiny in police planning. In some cases absolute secrecy may be essential to the success of the police mission.

e. Protective techniques.

(1) Protection requires teamwork. Success depends upon the cooperation and assistance of others. The failure of one individual may nullify the efforts of an entire organization. It is impossible to devise protective techniques which are totally foolproof. All personnel should be trained for the ideal system and attempt to approach that system insofar as circumstances permit. Protective personnel must be rehearsed to assure that in an emergency, despite the excitement and emotion, they will instinctively act correctly.

(2) All areas to be occupied or visited by the protected person should be surveyed in advance. The procedure that is used for building inspections must be complete. In many instances, the dignitary is a house guest of an individual. At times, he may stay in a hotel occupied by numerous other guests. The officer in charge and his advance party must use common sense and sound judgment in establishing the best security possible under existing circumstances. In some instances, the advance party can improve security plans by arranging for a separate house, separate floor, or wing of a hotel as a billet for the official party. Normally, billeting arrangements are included in the itinerary prior to the start of the protective mission. Proper building inspection entails a thorough examination from roof to basement. Detailed plans, such as engineering drawings or blueprints of the building, should be obtained. Rooms and hallways are measured visually and compared with the dimensions indicated on the building plan to locate any hidden passageways or alcoves. Each room is examined systematically. Walls, ceilings, and floors are mentally divided into three-foot squares and each

square minutely examined for cracks, evidence of recent repairs, or any unusual features. Suspicious areas should be explained satisfactorily by reliable operating or maintenance personnel. All doors are opened; all furniture is carefully examined; and drawers are removed as a check for concealed compartments. All wires leading into or leaving the various rooms are traced and all devices connected with them identified. Heating radiators, plumbing, pipes, and similar equipment are carefully examined for dummy installations. All locks and locking mechanisms are inspected. After the inspection is completed, the room or building is secured until used.

(3) One protective ring should be established within the residence when it is occupied by a dignitary. At least two additional areas should be established on the outer perimeter. There must be a pass system for the staff members and frequent visitors. Food suppliers should be checked and food selection and handling should be controlled. Mail and packages should be fluoroscoped or inspected. Periodic inspection should be made of premises for safety hazards, lethal devices, and sufficiency of security equipment. Adequate communications should be maintained. All possible emergency situations should be considered.

(4) Protection while the dignitary is riding in a vehicle requires special attention. Cars to be utilized should be procured from a reputable source and be in excellent mechanical condition. They should possess ample power and be able to travel considerable distances at widely varying speeds without difficulty. Drivers should be well trained, and reliable, and thoroughly familiar with the route they are to follow. Alternate routes should be established. Sharp turns or other features requiring slowdown should be avoided. Overpasses and other areas overlooking the route must be policed and cleared during passage of the motorcade. Routes should be divided into sections so that detours may be expeditiously placed into operation with minimum effect on normal traffic flow. An escort vehicle should precede the protected vehicle and should be followed as closely as possible consistent with driving safety. Observers in an advance vehicle should precede the motorcade by approximately one-half mile to report hazards and unusual conditions. Whenever possible at least one member of the protective detail should be in the protected person's vehicle. Additional protection with limited manpower may be effected by notifying the routine patrol force to converge on the route in their respective areas at the time the motorcade begins.

36. CRITIQUE AND AFTER ACTION REPORT.

a. The critique. This is the final stage of the crowd control mission. It is conducted to provide all participants with a clear, concise, and objective idea of what was done correctly and what was done incorrectly. Intelligent, tactful, and constructive criticism is necessary to improve operations. The critique can be most effective if held as soon as practicable after the mission is completed. The critique is important. Its success depends upon the flexibility with which the officer in charge employs it. He should criticize individuals in private and praise them in public. Participants should leave the critique with a favorable attitude toward the security mission and a desire to improve the next one. Examples of personal initiative or ingenuity, types of errors, and proposals for corrective action should be specified. Personnel should be encouraged to participate in the controlled discussion and led to feel that the critique is a period for learning rather than a time set aside for criticism of their performance.

b. Critique planning. The critique cannot be planned as thoroughly as other phases of the mission because the points to be covered are influenced directly by the performance of personnel. Advance planning can include the time and place of the critique and the general outline to be followed. The officer in charge can insure complete coverage of essential elements by following a general procedure similar to the outline below.

(1) Restate objective of the mission. This will enable participants to start on a common ground. This is necessary because the participants who were concerned with a particular aspect of the subject may have forgotten the overall objective.

(2) Review procedures and techniques employed. In this step briefly summarize the methods used to attain the objective.

(3) Evaluate performance. This is the most important part of the critique. Using notes taken during the operation, the officer in charge discusses strong points, identifies weaker ones, and makes suggestions for improvement. He must be careful not to "talk down" to the group. All remarks are sufficiently specific and impersonal to permit all personnel to profit from the experience.

(4) Control the group in discussion. The person in charge should clarify the points he has mentioned and guide group discussion of other relevant topics which arise.

(5) Summarize. The critique is concluded with a brief, comprehensive summary. The person in charge can suggest study and practice to overcome deficiencies.

c. After action report. The after action report is a narrative of the highlights of the operation. It is written as soon after the completion of the mission as practicable. Notes taken during the operation serve as a basis for compiling this report. Emphasis is placed upon

difficulties which were encountered and the procedures necessary to elim
inate them. Recommendations for improvement concerning planning, coordi
nation, personnel, and equipment are written in detail. A file copy is
retained for use in improving future operations.

CHAPTER 7

APPLICATION OF FORCE

Section I

GENERAL

37. INTRODUCTION.

People who have deep-seated hatreds, fears, or desires may not respond to the preventive techniques employed by police to prevent a civil disorder. When a riot occurs the mission of the police is to restore and maintain order. Decisive control measures are absolutely necessary for the successful accomplishment of this mission. Sound judgment dictates that only the minimum force necessary be used against rioters; to do otherwise may unnecessarily jeopardize life and property. Members of a mob are quick to sense fear, indecision, and poor organization of a police agency performing riot control duty. Therefore, successful riot control is dependent upon efficiently executed tactics by a group of law enforcement officers dedicated to team work, mutual support, and the principles of law and order. The individual police officer performing riot control duty must possess thorough training in tactics and techniques, confidence in himself and his leaders, and faith in his unit. A feeling of unit esprit de corps is essential.

38. OBJECTIVE.

The successful execution of a riot control mission depends to a large extent on advance planning considerations, organization of the police force, adequate intelligence information, thorough training of the committed forces, knowledge of control tactics and techniques, a sound tactical plan of operation, coordinated action of individuals and units, and bold, aggressive leadership. The objective of this chapter is to discuss factors which are important in performing a successful riot control mission.

39. MEASURES OF FORCE.

A discussion of riot control techniques centers in the types or measures of force which may be applied by police to restore law and order.

a. Show of force. A show of force represents the intention of the duly constituted authority to maintain order through the employment of organized police forces. A show of force is intended to induce a psychological reaction within the mob causing it to disperse. Normally it is used prior to the application of more severe control measures.

b. <u>The employment of riot control formations</u>. Fear is often created within individual members of a mob who find themselves in the path of an advancing, armed, determined, and organized force of uniformed police. This is the psychological intent of the riot control formation. Through a series of preplanned maneuvers, it is possible to disperse a mob while avoiding physical contact between rioter and policeman.

c. <u>The employment of water</u>. Water applied under high pressure from fire hoses or water cannons is practical and effective against mobs. Its use is considered humane since few serious casualties are apt to result.

d. <u>The employment of riot control agents</u>. The use of irritant nontoxic gases against a mob is also humane in its application, although temporary casualties are produced. The application of riot control agents by police against members of their own society may readily disperse a mob; however, it may cause resentment toward the authorities.

e. <u>Fire by selected marksmen</u>. A determined mob that is well organized and guided by intelligent leaders may resist lesser measures of force. Members of the mob may attempt to inflict casualties within the police unit through the use of small arms fire, demolitions, grenades, and other lethal devices. Police must be prepared to counter this type of mob action with a more severe measure of force such as fire delivered by selected police marksmen.

f. <u>Use of unit fire</u>. The most severe measure of force that can be applied by police units against a mob is that of available unit fire power with the intent of producing extensive casualties. This extreme measure would be used as a last resort only after all other measures have failed or obviously would be impractical, and the consequences of failure to completely subdue the riot would be imminent overthrow of the government, continued mass casualties, or similar grievous conditions.

g. <u>Selecting a measure of force</u>. The measures of force discussed in this section differ in degree of severity. Police commanders should select and apply a particular measure based on a careful estimate of each riot situation. Only the measure of force needed to control a specific situation should be used.

Section II

RIOT CONTROL PLANNING

40. INTRODUCTION.

The police official charged with the responsibility of riot control must consider well in advance those planning factors which basically influence the accomplishment of his mission. Planning is a continuing process involving personnel, operations, and logistics. This section is concerned with general advance planning considerations which will enable police reaction time to be minimized.

41. PERSONNEL PLANNING.

The standards governing the process of selecting police officers for riot duty must be given careful consideration. Police officers assigned to riot control duty must be able to retain their composure while operating under physical, mental, and emotional strain. They must respect all individuals regardless of race, color, or creed and maintain an impartial, patient attitude. They cannot reveal signs of fear. They must be able to issue orders in a manner that rioters can easily understand and obey. They must be in good physical condition. Personnel plans must also consider sources of reinforcement. Requirements for special categories of personnel such as doctors, nurses, ambulance attendants, dog and horse trainers, aircraft pilots, armored vehicle drivers, and boat operators should be provided for.

42. OPERATIONAL PLANNING.

a. Training requirements. Individual police officers and police units must be maintained at a peak of readiness for riot control duty at all times. Training for riot duty includes comprehensive instruction in the subject areas outlined below but is not limited to these matters.

(1) Causes of civil disorders.

(2) Mob behavior.

(3) Riot control tactics.

(4) Use of force.

(5) Use of dogs and horses.

(6) Characteristics and employment of riot control agents.

(7) Security.

(8) Intelligence.

(9) Characteristics and employment of special equipment.

(10) Police plans of a semi-permanent nature such as alert plans, standing operating procedures, loading plans, and others as necessary.

(11) Use of the riot gas mask.

(12) Map reading.

(13) Communications.

(14) Road blocks and barricades.

(15) Physical conditioning.

(16) Legal aspects.

(17) Care and maintenance of riot control equipment.

(18) Civil disorder prevention and the police civic action program.

(19) Disaster control operations.

(20) Weapons.

b. Operational requirements.

(1) Unit alert plan. Each police organization which may be involved in riot control duty should maintain a detailed alert plan based upon anticipated missions. The alert plan is the step-by-step procedure that is used to bring the unit rapidly to a state of operational readiness. The alert plan should be designed for implementation in the event of fire, disaster, or civil disorder. The details of the plan are based upon local operating conditions and should be revised through the result of experience gained in rehearsals or mission changes. Each individual affected by the plan must know his personal responsibility and the responsibility of his unit. Prior to departure for the scene of disorder or before a practice alert terminates it is important that officers in charge make detailed yet rapid inspections of their elements.

On the spot corrections should be made. The alert plan should incorporate an inspection checklist. Other matters covered in the alert plan are contained in the following list.

(a) Authentication procedures for the alert order.

(b) Required actions by individuals.

(c) Required action by individual sections of the organization.

(d) Procedures for issuing special equipment, supplies, and material.

(e) Vehicle preparation.

(f) Security.

(g) Administrative details.

(h) Tentative briefing schedules.

(2) Standing operating procedures. Unit standing operating procedures (SOP) are designed to simplify, clarify, and standardize methods of operation that are considered permanent procedures within the organization. Standing operating procedures are normally divided into two categories.

(a) Administrative standing procedures include, but are not limited to, matters such as food and water, medical aid, casualty reporting, basic loads of ammunition, riot control agents, resupply procedures, vehicle distribution and usage, and certain communications instructions.

(b) Tactical standing procedures include, but are not limited to, matters pertaining to construction, defense and displacement of roadblocks, patrols, security, designation of and instructions for selected marksmen, plans for the employment of riot control agents and designation of personnel involved in such plans.

(3) Determination and selection of probable problem areas. Responsible police officials through the evaluation of their community and its environment can predict with reasonable accuracy those areas which might be prone to experience civil disorders. Evaluation of intelligence information will indicate trends within the population and causes of public unrest. Each area selected as a possible disorder site should be reconnoitered with attention to locations of key facilities, primary

and alternate routes of access, and tentative areas available for the use of police forces. Maps and aerial photographs should be secured for the areas of concern.

(4) Employment of aircraft. Consideration should be given to the possible employment of either fixed-wing or rotary-wing aircraft in support of riot control operations. Aircraft can extend the capability of the police commander to observe, communicate, and control. If available, coordination should be effected for the necessary police use of aircraft. The use of mechanical riot control agent dispersers mounted in helicopters can materially assist the police commander in large scale riot operations.

(5) Tentative planning. Tentative operations plans should be formulated for areas in which a civil disorder is anticipated. These plans should include possible assembly areas for police forces, routes of access, possible location of roadblocks and observation points, tactical concept of the possible operation, and temporary quartering of control forces.

(6) Preparation of proclamation. Where proclamations are used in conjunction with the show of force, it is feasible to prepare draft copies of the proclamation in advance. Normally, the senior police commander will issue a short oral proclamation during a show of force and prior to commencing actual dispersal operations at the scene of a disorder. If the situation permits, the reading of the entire proclamation directing the dispersal of the mob by constituted authority has a good psychological value.

(7) Communication planning. Organic police communications equipment and facilities should be maintained in first-class operating condition at all times. In addition, a primary objective of advance communications planning and coordination is to insure that supplementary media such as local radio stations, newspapers, sign-making firms, and printing firms will support the police as necessary during civil disorders. Local radio stations can provide assistance in fixed station, mobile unit, and aircraft broadcasting. Newspapers can also communicate police messages or announcements to large numbers of people. Sign-making firms can provide vital aid. Printing firms can publish leaflets and other material for public distribution. Advance police planning should provide for appropriate standing arrangements for support from these or other media. Materials which may be written, printed, or recorded in advance include scripts, leaflets, and recordings. These materials must be prepared in the appropriate language. The psychological value of efficient use of all available communications media by the police should never be discounted.

43. INTELLIGENCE PLANNING.

The value of an efficient police intelligence effort was discussed in Chapter 3. The application of the intelligence cycle becomes increasingly important in advance planning for riot control. Police planners must review and revise requirements for essential elements of information as public unrest gathers momentum. The continuing efficiency of the intelligence effort can assist in minimizing loss of life and damage to property. Timely collection of accurate, usable intelligence assists the police planner in evaluating accurately the scope and nature of an impending or actual riot. Based on this evaluation, the planner can better determine the composition and size of the police force required to contain the threat or to restore order. Further, he is able to prepare more effective concepts for police tactical and logistical operations.

44. LOGISTICAL PLANNING.

Logistical planning is accomplished to determine accurately the requirements for supplies, equipment, transportation, shelter, and other types of support needed by the police force engaged in riot control duty. Poor logistical planning can seriously interfere with the effective execution of a riot control mission.

a. Supply and equipment planning. This planning should provide for adequate stocks of heavy single strand or barbed wire, heavy stakes, nails and spikes, hammers, wirecutters, gloves, shovels, picks, axes, wood planks, and heavy rope. These materials are useful in the preparation of street blocks and barricades. Other equipment or supplies may be required such as armored vehicles, gas masks, riot control agents, mechanical riot control agent dispersers, flood lights, bullet proof vests, helmets, searchlights, movie cameras, public address systems, heavy construction equipment, aircraft, ambulances, supply vehicles, spare parts, first aid kits, fire hoses, fuel stocks, food, bedding, command post needs, maintenance tools, weapons, radios, and such other materiel as may be considered necessary in particular circumstances. For example, in situations where a number of horses or dogs are used, special care and feeding problems may exist. Landing pads or strips may be needed where the police use helicopters or light fixed-wing aircraft. Boats and certain marine supplies may be required.

b. Transportation. Logistical planning for civil disorders must include provisions for sufficient transport of personnel and equipment. Transportation requirements for reserves or reinforcements should be considered.

c. Basic loads. Preparation of basic loads of certain supplies and equipment for both individuals and units is important in efficiently planning for rapid police reaction in emergency situations. Among the items which can be grouped into basic loads are ammunition, food, water, gasoline, lubricants, spare parts, patrol kits, riot control agents, maps, and administrative supplies. Basic loads for individuals should be stored with the basic load of the police element to which they belong. The storage pattern should follow the vehicle layout and loading sequence used in the element's personnel and equipment loading plans for its assigned vehicles. It may be helpful to paint an outline of the vehicle on the storeroom floor. A running inventory must be kept and complete inspections should be made monthly. Based upon the characteristics of each item in the basic loads, a procedure for periodic exchange of certain items should be established. For example, riot control agents, ball ammunition, food stuffs, and gasoline deteriorate in prolonged storage. Retention of unserviceable materials can have grave consequences in the event of an emergency.

d. Medical aid stations. Plans should provide for the establishment of medical aid stations at the scene of civil disorders. This planning should include provisions for medical personnel, ambulance services, medical facilities, medical supplies, medical evacuation, casualty reporting, fatality registration procedures, and other appropriate considerations that may be considered necessary.

e. Personnel loading plan. Police units must be prepared for rapid deployment in a riotous situation. It is imperative that police elements adhere to the principle of unit integrity during the loading of personnel in the deployment phase. Advance loading plans that have been rehearsed and proven effective should become standing procedure within the police unit. Personnel loading plans must be adaptable to movement by organic vehicles, buses, trains, and aircraft.

f. Equipment loading plan. In consonance with the maintenance of unit integrity through personnel loading, attention must be given to the advance planning and standardization of equipment loading. Equipment loading plans must be adaptable to each of the transportation modes discussed above. Subordinate elements of the police organization travel with required equipment and a small reserve of ammunition, riot control agents, and basic supplies.

g. Motor movement. To facilitate command and control, advance planning for motor movement should consider several factors.

(1) Reconnaissance patrols. It is advisable for police commanders to establish advance reconnaissance patrols to the front of the main police body during movement to an area experiencing civil disorder. The reconnaissance patrol becomes the eyes and ears of the commander and provides him with timely data on the situation.

(2) _Bivouac and detrucking areas_. Tentative bivouac and detrucking areas should be selected in advance of the motor march of a police unit. During actual deployment into an area experiencing civil disorder, bivouac and detrucking sites should be secured in advance of the arrival of the main body.

h. _Rail movement_. Police may move into an affected area by rail. It is advisable to consider the following factors in this situation.

(1) Coordinating with railroad police.

(2) Special trains should be used for the movements. Use of cars in regularly scheduled trains can lead to serious complications. For example, special trains can preserve unit integrity. Also, they can be placed on sidings easily.

(3) The entraining point should be secured and unauthorized personnel excluded from entry into the immediate area.

(4) If the civil disorder is severe and violent, agitators may place explosive devices along the rail line. If this eventuality is anticipated, several flatcars should be pushed ahead by the engine.

(5) Rioters may create problems at the detraining point. Advance security parties can prevent such occurrences by securing the area. It is advisable for police commanders to refrain from contact with rioters until operational positions have been reached and secured.

i. _Deployment by aircraft_. Where deployment by aircraft is practical, advance planning should determine exact characteristics of available aircraft so as to properly plan loading. Plans should permit preserving the integrity of subordinate police elements enroute. Equipment and personnel weight must be calculated with a high degree of exactness. Special aircraft should be used so as to preclude the complications which could arise if police units attempted to move piecemeal aboard scheduled passenger flights.

j. _Assembly areas_. Logistics planning includes the advance selection of assembly areas. Assembly areas should be located out of sight from the mob but within reasonable marching distance to the disorder site.

Section III

TACTICS AND TECHNIQUES IN THE APPLICATION OF FORCE

45. INTRODUCTION.

Tactics and techniques in the application of force vary with the needs of the specific situation; however, the control of a riot is based on the precept, "contain, isolate, disperse." The intent of this section is to discuss certain fundamental tactical considerations which generally apply to police forces engaged in the restoration of law and order.

46. RIOT CONTROL PRINCIPLES.

Certain principles are basic considerations in the execution of riot control operations. Their proper application is essential to the exercise of command and the effective conduct of the tactical police mission. Each principle is a vital consideration in itself but is related to the other principles. Depending on specific circumstances, each tends to be either in conflict with or support others. Consequently, the degree of application of any specific principle will vary from situation to situation.

a. <u>Principle of the objective</u>. The basic objectives of riot control operations are the destruction of the mob's organization and the breaking of its will to resist. Police operations must move toward these objectives by the most rapid and direct means. The operations are planned in consideration of the resources available, the nature of the mob, and the physical terrain. The ultimate objective is the restoration of law and order.

b. <u>Principle of the offensive</u>. Offensive action is necessary to achieve decisive results and to maintain freedom of action. It permits the police commander to exercise initiative and impose his will upon the mob; to set the pace and determine the course of operation; to exploit the mob's weaknesses; to take advantage of rapidly changing situations; and to meet unexpected developments. The defensive may be forced on the police commander, but it should be adopted only as a temporary status for the purpose of economizing forces in an area in which a decisive action has not been concluded or used as a delaying tactic until the offensive can again be regained.

c. <u>Principle of mass</u>. Superior power can result from the most effective combining of police strength with carefully selected measures of force. Correct application of the principle of mass, in conjunction with the other principles of riot control, may permit numerically inferior police forces to achieve desired results.

d. Principle of economy of force. Skillful and prudent use of force will enable the police commander to accomplish the mission with minimum expenditure of resources. This principle tends to be in conflict with the principle of mass.

e. Principle of maneuver. Maneuver is an essential ingredient of force. It contributes materially in exploiting successes, in preserving freedom of action, and in reducing vulnerability. The object of maneuver is to dispose a police force in such a manner as to place the mob at a relative disadvantage and thus achieve results which would other wise be more costly in men and materiel. Successful maneuver requires organizational flexibility, administrative support, and command and control. It is the antithesis of permanence of location and implies avoidance of stereotyped patterns of operation.

f. Principle of unity of command. The decisive application of necessary force requires unity of command. Unity of command obtains unity of effort by the coordinated action of all police forces toward a common goal. While coordination may be attained by cooperation, it is best achieved by vesting a single commander with the requisite authority.

g. Principle of security. Security is essential to the preservation of force. Security is achieved by measures taken to prevent surprise, preserve freedom of action, and deny the mob information of the police force. Since risk is inherent in riots, application of the principle of security does not imply undue caution and the avoidance of calculated risk. Security frequently is enhanced by bold seizure and retention of the initiative which denies the mob the opportunity to interfere.

h. Principle of surprise. Surprise can decisively shift the balance of power. By surprise, success out of proportion to the effort expended may be obtained. Surprise is achieved by striking a mob at a time, place, and in a manner for which it is not prepared to react effectively. Factors contributing to gaining surprise include speed, deception, application of unexpected force, effective intelligence, and counterintelligence, to include communication and electronic security, and variations in tactics and methods of operation.

i. Principle of simplicity. Simplicity contributes to successful operations. Direct, simple plans and clear, concise orders minimize misunderstanding and confusion. The simplest workable plan is best.

47. CONTAINING AND ISOLATING THE CIVIL DISORDER.

As soon as police units are committed to an area experiencing civil disorder, police commanders should act to confine the disorder to the affected area. This isolating measure is critical in preventing further growth of the disorder and the possible development of tumultuous conditions beyond the control of the police. People not yet involved in the disorder must be prevented access to the affected area. Contagion emanating from the disorderly area can be a serious problem to the police commander.

a. Patrols. Patrolling of the boundaries and points of entry into the affected area accomplishes several important objectives.

(1) Patrolling reduces the opportunity for unauthorized persons to circulate between the secure area and the affected area. Patrols can normally cope with individuals and small groups composed of two or three persons.

(2) Patrols prevent the assembly of people by dispersal of individuals who begin to congregate.

(3) Patrols can provide the commander with timely information of possible problem areas, movement of the rioters, and conditions within the respective patrol areas.

(4) Several types of patrols can be employed effectively depending upon the exact nature and location of the civil disorder.

(a) Motor patrols. Motor patrols are valuable because of their ability to cover distance rapidly. Through radio communications, contact with the controlling headquarters can be maintained. Motor patrols can maintain contact with stationary posts that may lack dependable communications. Because of their speed and mobility, motor patrols are able to provide the commander with timely ground reconnaissance.

(b) Foot patrols. Foot patrols can be employed effectively in some areas for detailed reconnaissance and where population movement is heavy. Patrols of this type are limited in the effective range of operations. When foot patrols are used to seal a disturbed area, adequate communications, equipment, and personnel should be provided. Foot patrols can be coordinated through the use of motor patrols. Foot patrols must be capable of defending themselves and coping with limited numbers of disorderly individuals.

(c) Air patrols. Air patrols perform reconnaissance and surveillance missions of the disturbed area. They are an excellent means for providing timely information on the actions of rioters, damage, status of access routes, barriers, and other important points of information. They assist the commander in directing police movements within the affected area.

(d) _Water patrols_. Water patrols can be employed where the affected area has access by navigable water.

b. _Roadblocks and barricades_. In the initial stages of the restoration of order, police officials must consider the situation prior to implementing a tactical plan of operation using the measures of force The concept of the defense requires fewer personnel to accomplish than the concept of the offense. The execution of the defense through the use of roadblocks and barricades assists the commander in isolating the affected area and preventing further complication of the problem. Roadblocks and barricades help channelize movements of people, block routes, prevent assembly of hostile or agitated crowds, and isolate affected areas. Roadblocks and barricades should be manned by trained police observers and the positions must be defensible. Such positions must not be located so as to permit them to be easily surrounded or cut off. Roadblocks and barricades may be constructed from such available materials as trolley cars, buses, trucks, other vehicles, sandbags, earthworks, trees, timbers, wire, or various combinations of such materials. Materials tending to chip, shatter, or splinter can be covered with canvas, to minimize casualties caused by flying fragments.

(1) _Types of roadblocks_.

(a) _Roadblocks against personnel_. Concertina wire is considered the best material for the rapid construction of temporary roadblocks against personnel. These roadblocks should be prepared in advance of the main riot control effort. Signs should be clearly placed indicating that unauthorized persons are not allowed to approach the position. Police officers defending the position should be protected by sand bag emplacements if small arms fire is anticipated. Provisions for lighting approaches to the position during the hours of darkness should be made; however, care should be used to avoid silhouetting the position or officers manning it.

(b) _Roadblocks against vehicles_.

1. _Motor vehicles_. Barricades against motor vehicles can be fabricated out of large, heavy objects and earth. Barri cades should extend the complete width of the roadway to include sidewalks. Several parallel barricades placed at an interval of from 25 to 50 feet can provide depth which may be desirable to insure against the possible passage of large or high speed vehicles through the position.

2. _Trains_. The passage of trains may be prohibited by wrapping a heavy chain around one rail, with each wrap placed on top of the other. The chain should be padlocked at the ends. The chain barricade should be placed sufficiently away from the point of

blockade to prevent the train from crashing into the position when it becomes derailed. Signs and warning lights should be placed in advance of the chain barricade to provide the engineer time to comply with the no-passage order.

                    3. <u>Trolleys</u>. Techniques similar to those used to stop a train may be used to effectively block trolleys. In lieu of a chain, material such as sand, earth, or gravel in adequate quantity is sufficient to derail the vehicle.

            c. <u>Search and seizure</u>. Depending on the situation, it may be desirable for police to conduct early search and seizure operations to prevent or limit the use of weapons by rioters and to take known agitators into custody. Search and seizure operations may be expanded to include propaganda material, communications devices, flammable materials, explosives, and other casualty-producing materials to which the mob might have ready access. If intelligence information indicates the existence of lines of communication being used by a mob they should be located and cut. By tracing such lines to their sources it may be possible to capture key mob leaders and important documents or equipment.

            d. <u>Curfews</u>. The implementation of an ordinance or law imposing curfew upon the population assists police materially in isolating the affected area. Law-abiding citizens of the society not affected by the disorder will normally comply with curfew regulations. Violators of curfew restrictions can be prosecuted.

            e. <u>Pass systems</u>. To facilitate ready identification of individuals and to control their circulation in and out of an affected area a pass system can be of assistance to police officials. If restrictions are continued for an extended period of time, police officials can anticipate the use of counterfeit passes by unauthorized personnel. To counter this possibility, the color of passes can be changed frequently at irregular intervals.

            f. <u>Control of sensitive items</u>. It may be desirable to enact laws and ordinances to permit the control of sensitive items during the civil disorder. Sensitive items can be defined as those things that could add to the further agitation of the civil disorder. Examples of sensitive items might include intoxicating beverages and firearms.

            g. <u>Administrative techniques</u>. When committed to a civil disorder, police commanders should take necessary measures to record the chronological sequence of events. Recorded information will be of critical value for analysis and use both during and after an operation. Administrative recording should include entries in four separate areas.

(1) Operations journal. The record of all events affecting the operation.

(2) Intelligence journal. The record of collected intelligence information.

(3) Administrative journal. The record of those items of information not otherwise directly bearing on the operation.

(4) Situation map. The record of the situation by graphic means as it developed.

h. Police security measures. Police security measures continue throughout an operation. In some situations the number of rioters can be expected to outnumber police forces. Police commanders should know that an unexpected attack against the rear or flanks of a police unit can have serious effects and may render the unit ineffective. This consideration applies during any phase of riot control regardless of whether police forces are engaged in motor movement, foot marches, or tactical riot control formations. To give advance warning and prevent surprise, flank and rear security forces are recommended. Security forces should be equipped with adequate communications and be capable of self-defense.

i. Communications techniques. Communications play a vital role in the successful execution of riot control missions. In addition to advance planning considerations, as discussed earlier in this chapter, it is important that police commanders be familiar with certain techniques applicable to communication.

(1) Community communications facilities. The ability of police to communicate must not be solely dependent on community facilities. However, such facilities may be used to augment organic police equipment where practicable.

(2) Radio. Skillful use of police radio equipment provides for greater operational flexibility and can be vital to the successful execution of a riot control mission. Procedures used should be carefully prescribed. Routine instructions can be incorporated into regular standing operating procedures. However, to minimize the danger of compromise, police codes, authentication systems, procedures governing frequency changes, and other highly sensitive matters should be published in confidential communications operating instructions. These confidential instructions must be periodically changed to avoid compromise. During actual riot control operations such changes may be required on a daily basis. Confidential communications documents must be rigidly controlled. Distribution and location of each copy can be regulated by

means of control numbers and a receipt system. All police officers must be instructed to expeditiously report the loss or capture of a confidential document. Orders should be issued which place the police radio net on listening silence whenever the loss of such a document is made. An alternate set of instructions should be available for immediate distribution. Radio listening silence should not be terminated until each station in the police radio net has received a copy of the alternate confidential instructions. Police radio communications should be controlled through a central facility known as the Net Control Station. This station is located at or immediately adjacent to the main police command post. It opens and closes the police radio net, monitors transmission traffic, receives messages for the command post, and disseminates the police commander's orders to subordinate police elements. The Net Control Station is supervised by a police officer appointed for this purpose This officer must be highly skilled in radio communications techniques.

(3) Communications security. It must be anticipated that unauthorized persons may monitor police radio nets or attempt to send false messages over the nets. Continuous emphasis must be placed on requiring all police personnel to follow established security procedures. Messages must be authenticated. Simple codes should be used. Frequency changes should be provided for where characteristics of radio equipment permit. Where several law enforcement agencies are involved in the same riot control operations, joint operating agreements may be necessary to avoid communications security problems. Such agreements could establish uniform security procedures, provide for exchange of communications liaison personnel and equipment, and clarify other matters deemed appropriate

(4) Messages. To maintain control and response in radio communications, it is imperative that all messages be as concise as possi ble. The importance of brief and clearly interpreted messages cannot be overemphasized. Long, complicated messages tend to create confusion and misunderstandings which in turn may jeopardize the success of riot control operations.

(5) Messengers. Messages which are necessarily long and complicated should be delivered by messenger service wherever possible. Attention to messenger security is required to prohibit possible compromise.

(6) Communications during dispersal operations. A police commander employing his units against a mob must be able to continuously communicate instructions and orders to maneuvering elements. The riot control unit should be equipped with portable radios, sound-powered megaphones, or battery operated loudspeakers. Public address systems can be utilized from vehicles. Runners should be available. With these aids the police commander will possess necessary communications.

48. QUELLING THE RIOT.

a. Initial action. A mob will normally move from one location to another. Initial police action in quelling a riot will normally consist of blocking the mob at a point short of its objective. Blocking is accomplished through the rapid positioning of personnel barricades. Once the mob has been blocked, a police commander can use a show of force and issue a proclamation directing the dispersal of the mob. Instructions as to the routes of withdrawal should also be given.

b. Riot control formations. A complete discussion of riot control formations may be found in Chapter 9.

c. Employment of water. Water applied from fire hoses can be effective in defense of a narrow front such as a street, a narrow passageway or defile, or in defense of a fixed police station such as a roadblock Personnel applying the water should be protected by riflemen, and in some cases with shields. Concerning the use of water, the following factors apply:

(1) Water may be applied in a flat trajectory stream if sufficient pressure is available. Water is extremely effective when applied in a high trajectory stream during cold weather.

(2) Harmless dye can be used with water for future identification of mob members through stained clothing.

(3) If available, a truck-mounted water tank and compressor can be effectively employed to deliver water under high pressure against a mob. The water tank should have a capacity of 750 to 1,000 gallons. A reserve compressor should be available in case of mechanical failure. Hoses capable of withstanding high pressures must be used. Extra sections of hose should be available in the event distances involved require them or in case of hose ruptures and hardware malfunctions.

d. Movie cameras. Movie cameras are especially effective when photographing a mob. Movie cameras, to a greater extent than still cameras, tend to dispel feelings of anonymity that may exist within the mob. Movies also record the actions of a mob and aid in identifying members.

e. Special psychological activities. In addition to other police measures discussed in this text which have important psychological effects, police planners and commanders may encounter circumstances or conditions requiring formulation and use of special measures wholly psychological in nature and intent. For example, countering rumors with facts may become a vital necessity. Facts can be prepared for dissemination through skillful combinations of words and symbols, valuable tools in communicating ideas. Police agencies having staff psychologists or access to psychologists should solicit their aid in preparing such materials. Means of dissemination can include dropping leaflets from aircraft, posting signs, placards, and posters in public places or conveyances, radio or public address system announcements, and any other available method. Timing is of particular importance.

f. Routes of withdrawal. The police commander should never exert pressure against a mob unless it has available to it an open route of withdrawal. Such routes should be designated in advance and announced to the mob through public address systems or leaflets. Withdrawal routes should terminate in areas of little tactical value and should avoid industrial areas, public service facilities, and vital installations. Where possible, rioters should be dispersed in residential areas thereby permitting them to reach their homes.

g. Operations against large mobs. A large mob which is compactly massed may be difficult to disperse. Riot control agents applied to that portion of the mob to be moved first usually will initiate dispersal. Riot control agents can continue to be employed until complete dispersal has been accomplished.

h. Operations in built-up areas. Riots usually occur in business districts, industrial areas, and around key facilities. Special tactical factors to be considered prior to implementing the measures of force include those listed below.

(1) Roof tops. Police should secure control of roof tops before attempting to use force against a mob. Both sides of the street must be secured. Where roof tops vary in height, selected marksmen may cover with small arms fire adjoining lower roof tops to prevent casualty producing objects from being thrown onto the riot control force. Roof tops also provide excellent positions from which riot control agents can be delivered against the mob.

(2) Side streets. The route along which a mob is to be moved will normally contain several side street intersections which must be crossed by the mob prior to reaching the selected dispersal area. Police commanders must seal these side streets so as to canalize the movement of the mob along the desired route. Under certain circumstances, it is possible for the police commander to displace the sealing force from intersection to intersection, in leapfrog fashion, thereby adhering to the principle of economy of force.

(3) Buildings. Rioters will often attempt to secure control of buildings. Buildings that might contain rioters should be cleared systematically from the top floor toward ground level. This method permits use of a minimum number of police. When this method of clearing

is not possible, buildings should be cleared systematically one floor at a time. Additional police are normally required since individual rioters will require escort. When clearing from the bottom toward the top, escape routes for rioters are cut off; therefore, resistance to police efforts should be anticipated.

i. Operations against barricades. Barricades erected by rioters are designed to impede effective police action. If rioters defend a barricaded position, the use of riot control agents is normally an effective means of neutralizing the position. Barricades erected in buildings, narrow passages, defiles and elsewhere may have to be overcome and removed. Fire can effectively destroy barricades that are constructed of combustible material; however, caution should be exercised to prevent the spread of the fire to nearby areas. Police should assume that hostile barricades may be booby-trapped by explosives, mines or electricity.

j. Operations in residential areas. Techniques used in residential areas are essentially the same as those for built-up areas. A requirement may exist for more numerous sealing parties since the distance between houses is normally greater than it is between buildings anywhere else in the community.

k. Operations at vital installations. Vital installations such as banks, hospitals, utilities, and government buildings are normally protected by security forces and devices as discussed in Chapter 13. If all access points of an installation are beseiged by rioters and it appears that penetration will be effected, additional measures of force should be employed immediately. If a penetration has been effected, police forces must gain entry, secure sensitive areas, and thereafter initiate a progressive series of blocking, clearing, and sealing-off tactics to remove rioters.

l. Pursuit operations. When the mob line has been broken and rioters withdraw, police forces should enter the pursuit. Pursuit of a mob is normally begun by police marching rapidly on foot. When the mob breaks and runs, contact is maintained by special pursuit vehicles which pass through police riot control formations to continue the dispersal of the rioters. Police commanders who fail in the pursuit phase may encounter a rapidly reformed mob.

m. Defensive operations. Under some circumstances, police elements may be required to conduct defensive operations during the dispersal phase. Defensive action would normally include the designation of a predetermined line past which the mob is ordered not to move. Police defending this line should apply the minimum measures of force necessary to enforce the order. Some means of denying an area to rioters are indicated below.

(1) Flood the area with water.

(2) Contaminate the area with riot control agents.

(3) Barricade approaches to the area.

n. Post-dispersal operations. Once a mob is dispersed, police must prevent it from reforming.

(1) Large-scale search of built-up areas. It may be necessary for police to conduct search and seizure operations within a large portion of a community. To accomplish this, the area to be searched should first be divided into sections. As each section is searched, it must be sealed off. The adjoining section may then be searched. No unauthorized personnel are allowed to enter or depart a sealed area until the search has been terminated. Although difficult to accomplish, the use of motor patrols, aerial surveillance, and fixed observation points will minimize violations.

(2) Preventive patrols. The use of preventive patrols is important in dispersal operations. For example, where widespread public unrest exists, agitators may attempt to form additional mobs for the continuation of violent action. Police patrols should be well equipped and capable of dispersing small crowds as they occur throughout the entire community. Patrols also can provide timely intelligence information concerning the attitude of the population.

(3) Release from restrictions. A community which has experienced a civil disorder should not be released from restrictions imposed by police until public unrest has disappeared. The decision to release restrictions should be based on sound intelligence information obtained through both overt and covert collection techniques. Factors causing the disorder should be carefully analyzed and corrective action initiated.

Section IV

USE OF MAPS

49. INTRODUCTION.

Most individuals understand a picture more easily than a mass of words. There is merit in the saying, "One picture is worth a thousand words." The use of maps in riot control operations is so important and relevant to the application of force that it requires consideration in this separate section.

50. OPERATIONS MAPS.

    a. <u>General</u>. The use of an operations map enables the police commander to progressively monitor a civil disorder as it develops. Timely posting of information relating to the situation can point up details that could otherwise be overlooked. The map picture of the civil disorder simplifies the commander's ability to accurately estimate the situation, make timely decisions, and issue clear, concise orders.

    b. <u>Information recorded</u>. The information routinely recorded on an operations map includes the following data:

    (1) Locations of rioters.

    (2) Mob patterns of movement.

    (3) Possible mob objectives.

    (4) Locations of critical areas.

    (5) Mob dispersal areas.

    (6) Mob dispersal routes.

    (7) Police troop dispositions.

    (8) Possible positions for police barricades.

    (9) Police patrol routes.

    (10) Critical intersections.

    (11) Routes for traffic re-routing.

    (12) Areas which might prohibit the use of riot control agents.

    (13) Police routes of advance.

    (14) Police assembly areas.

    (15) Locations for police reserves.

    (16) Police control and communication points.

    (17) Possible positions for medical aid points.

c. Techniques. Operations maps should be kept at police command posts. Incoming information should be promptly posted by trained police personnel. Special situation maps attached to plywood backing and covered with acetate can be issued to patrols and other police elements as necessary. These maps and map boards should be routinely maintained in the basic load.

51. TYPES OF MAPS.

a. Planimetric. A map which shows only horizontal (flat) positions of features on the ground. This is the type of map normally used in riot control situations. Various scale maps are usually published. Scales are used to relate map distances to ground distances, e.g., one inch on the map is equal to one thousand inches on the ground. Planimetric maps are also referred to as street or road maps. (See Figure 7.)

b. Topographic. A two-dimensional map which shows relief (elevation) and planimetry in a measurable form. Topographic maps obtained from military sources may not be scaled suitably for riot control operations. (See Figure 8.)

c. Aerial photography. Aerial photography can be of value in riot control operations. Such photography can include pictures made from both oblique (angular) or vertical camera positions. Vertical photographs may easily be used as photo maps where the scale is determined and the appropriate grid is superimposed. (See Figure 9.)

52. MAP AIDS.

a. Symbols. A map symbol is defined as a diagram, a number, a letter, an abbreviation, a color, or combination thereof which is used to distinguish a specific feature, unit, activity, or installation on the ground. Symbols used for operations maps should be standardized and well known by police personnel. Symbols may be affixed to the map by grease pencil or small pieces of cut acetate and pins.

b. Overlays. Overlays correlated to specific maps are useful in recording information. Multiple overlays can be used where necessary. Information may be too voluminous to enter on a single overlay. It may be desirable to place one category of information on one overlay, a second category on another overlay or on additional overlays as required.

c. Area identification systems.

(1) Military coordinate scale system. (Universal Transverse Mercator.) This is a system of grids that are superimposed on a map and used to identify specific locations against a base of reference.

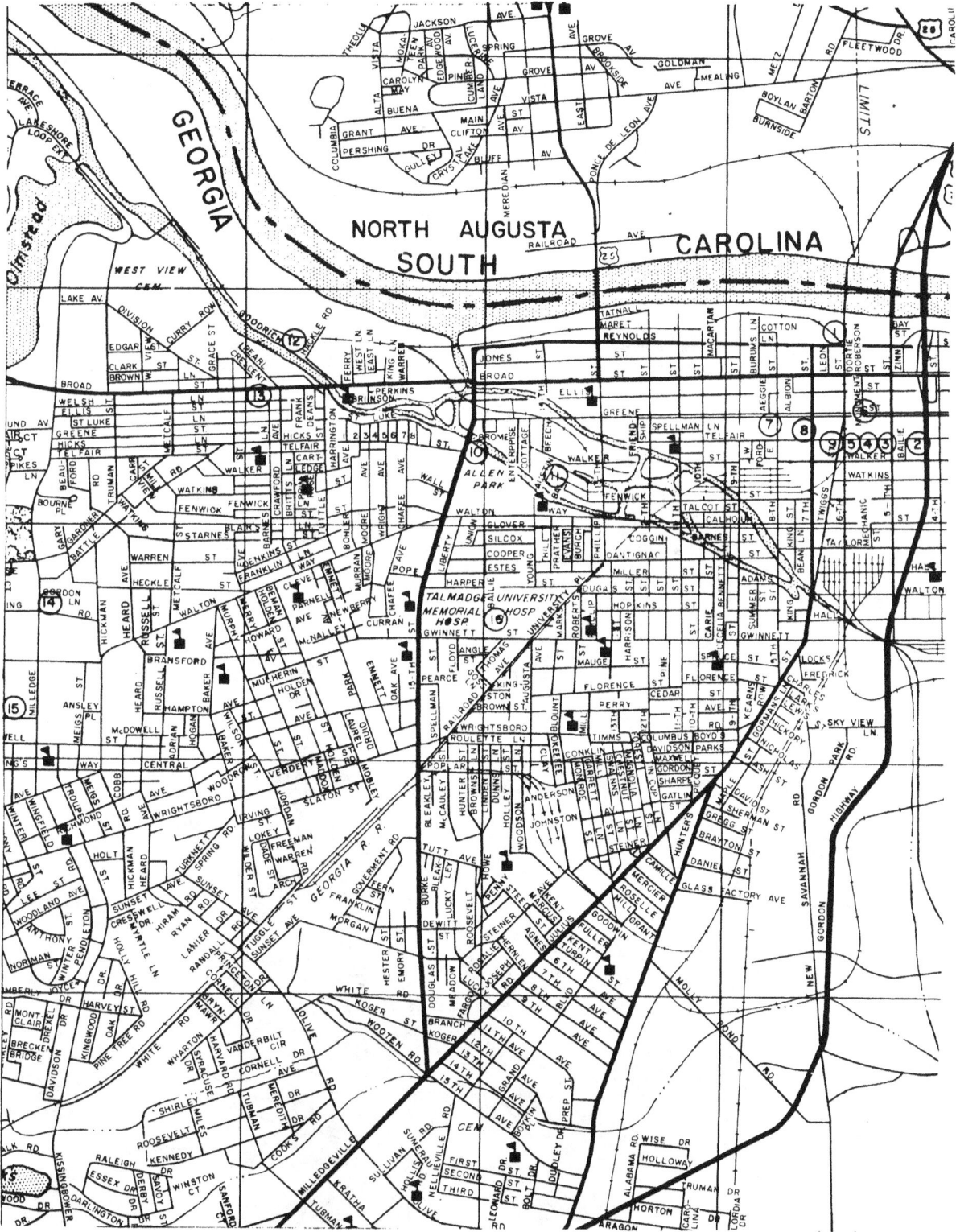

Figure 7. Planimetric or city map.

ST 19-180; 87

SERIES V845
SHEET 4550 I NE
EDITION 2-AMS

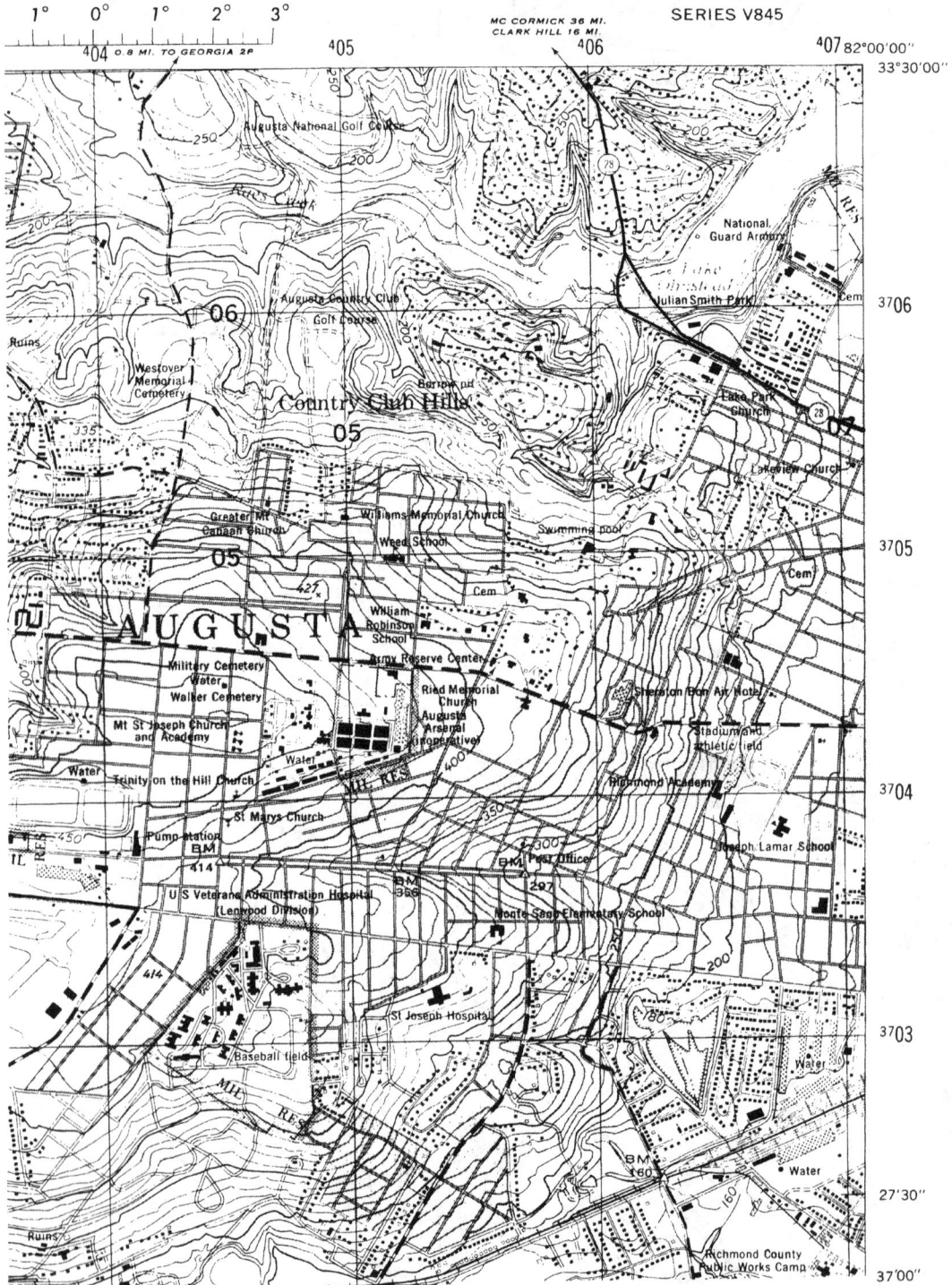

Figure 8. Topographic map.

ST 19-180; 88

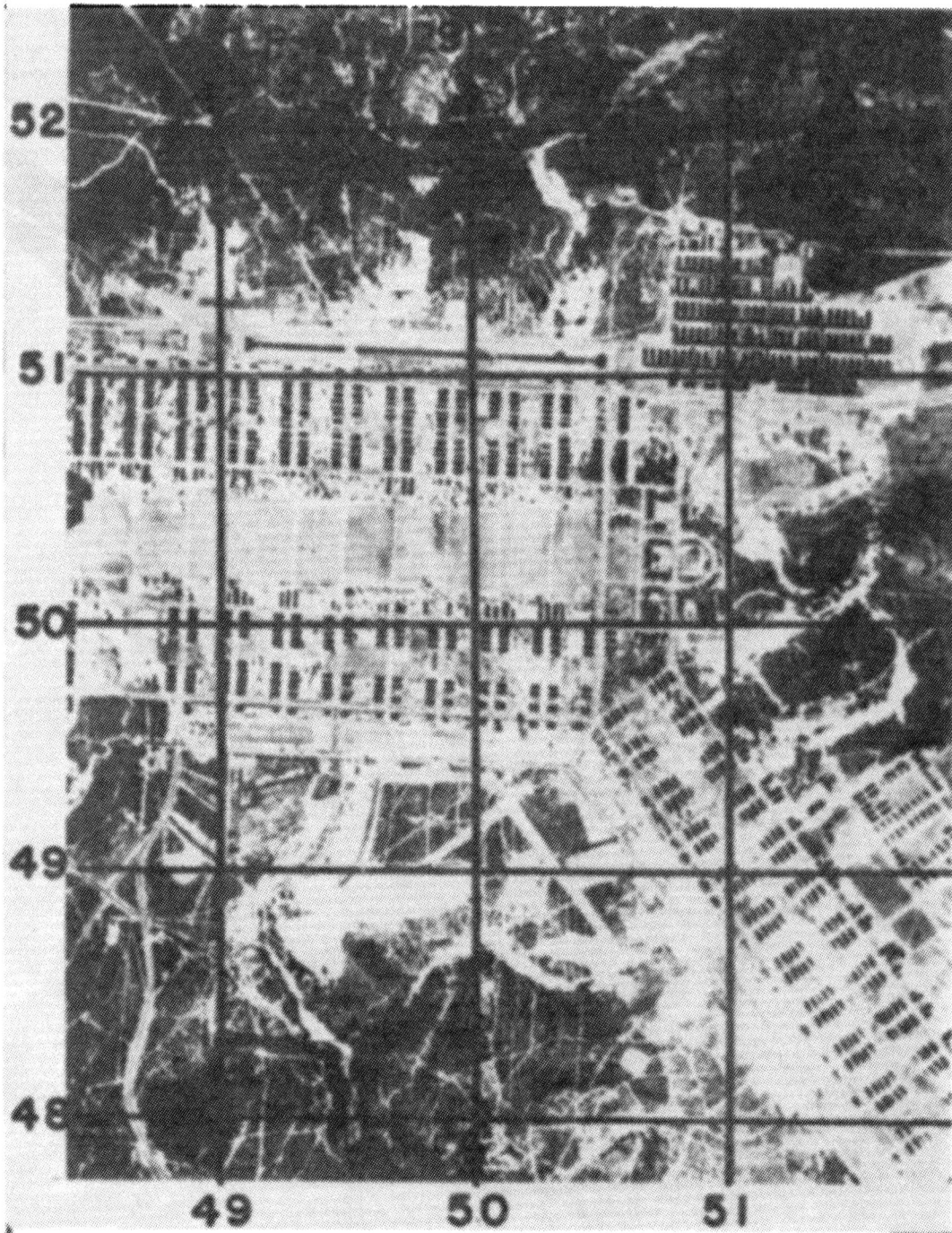

Figure 9. Aerial photo map.

ST 19-180; 89

(2) <u>Map reference code system</u>. (Figure 10a.) Use of a map reference code involves placing circles on a map or overlay to desig nate check points, barricades, posts, road junctions or other critical locations. Each circle is numbered. The numbers can be used to refer to a point or location without actually mentioning what is there. For example, this procedure is very helpful in radio communications because of the obvious security advantage. The numbers can be changed daily or as frequently as considered necessary. To demonstrate use superimpose Figure 10a, map reference code, over Figure 10b, a town map.

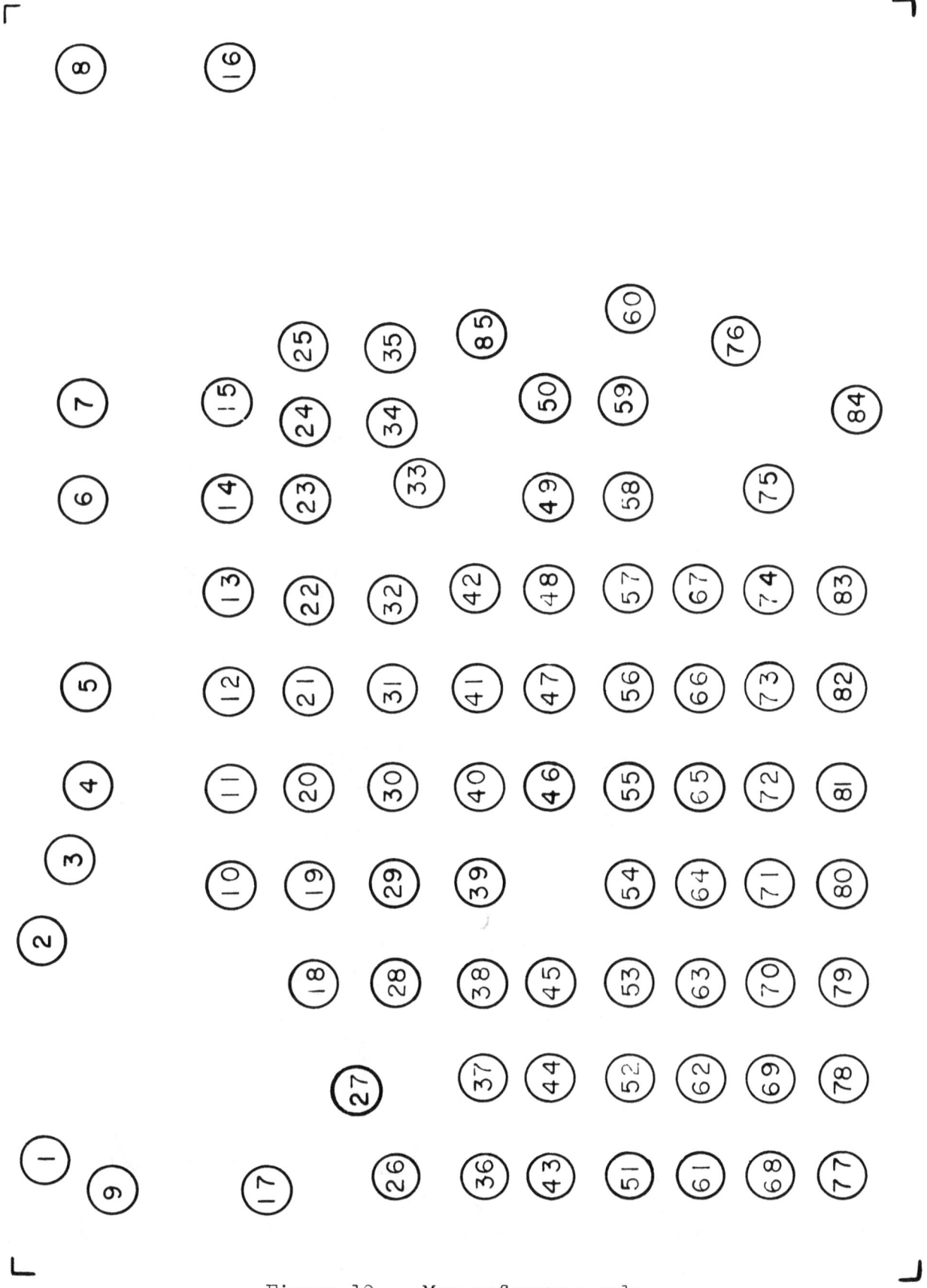

Figure 10a. Map reference code.

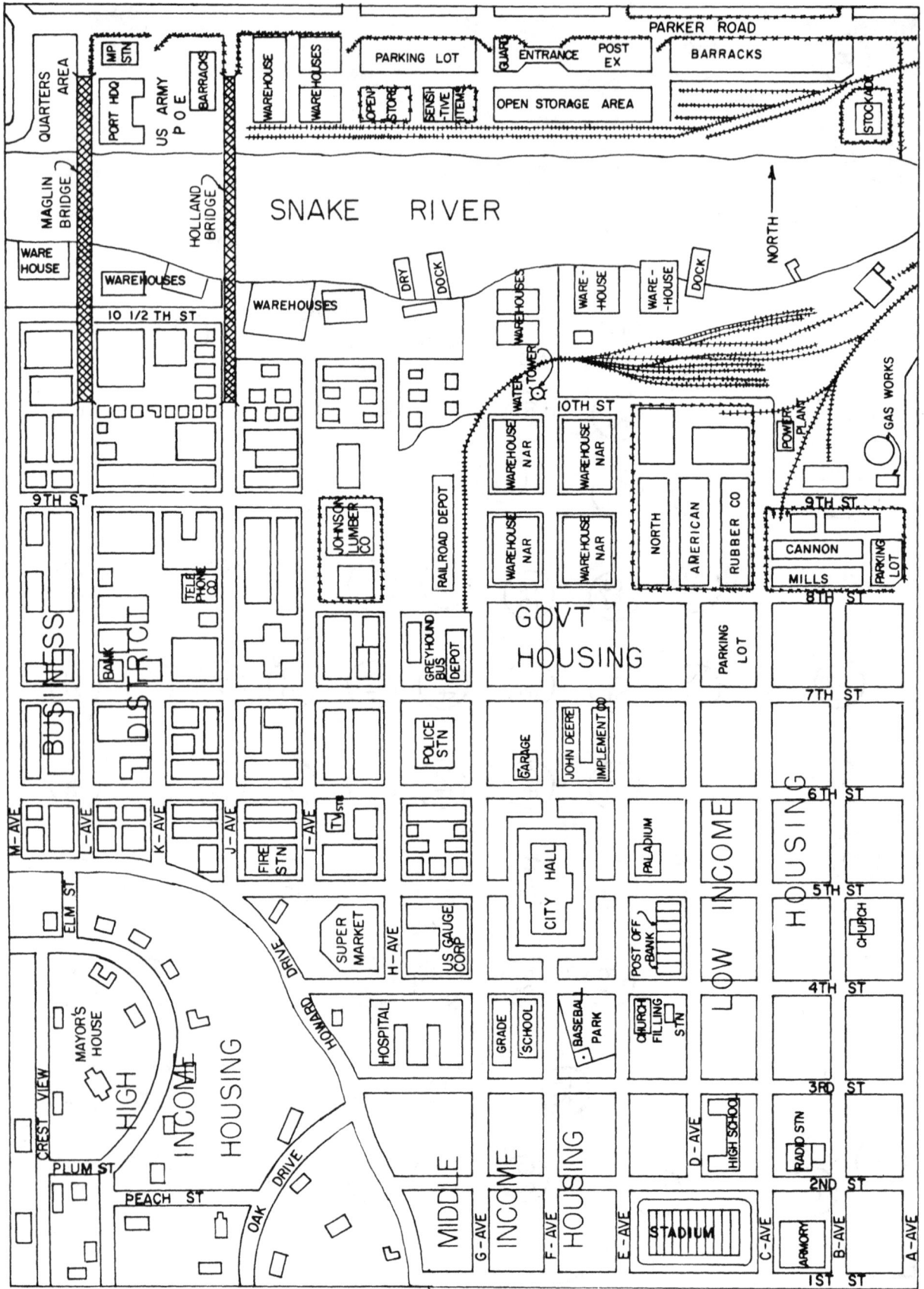

Figure 10b. Town plan.

ST 19-180; 92

CHAPTER 8

ORGANIZATION FOR RIOT CONTROL

53. GENERAL.

In most civil disorders members of a mob will outnumber the
police. Consistent with the principle of economy of force, police commanders must organize riot control units to permit efficient employment
and control. The tools available to a commander to execute a riot control mission are police personnel, their organizations, and their equipment. It is of utmost importance to the success of riot control operations that the organization of police forces be established along predetermined lines which carefully consider individual responsibilities
and relationships. For purposes of this discussion and to clearly indicate the principle of organization, a type police battalion will be used.

a. Police battalion. A police unit typically consisting of
a headquarters, at least three subordinate operating elements, and a
support element. The strength of a battalion will approximate 600 individuals.

b. Police company. A police unit typically consisting of a
headquarters and three subordinate operating elements. It may be subordinate to the command and control of a police battalion. The strength
of a police company will approximate 200 individuals.

c. Police platoon. A police unit typically consisting of a
headquarters and four subordinate operating elements. The strength of
a police platoon will approximate 50 individuals. It may be subordinate
to a police company.

NOTE: Figures 11, 12, and 13 depict a type police battalion and the
subordinate police companies and platoons of the battalion.

54. ORGANIZATION.

a. Battalion headquarters.

(1) Command and the commander. Command is the authority
which a commander lawfully exercises over subordinates by virtue of rank,
assignment, or responsibility. Command includes the authority and responsibility for using available resources effectively and for planning,
organizing, directing, coordinating, and controlling his unit in accomplishing assigned missions. The commander alone is responsible for all
that his unit does or fails to do.

A TYPE POLICE BATTALION

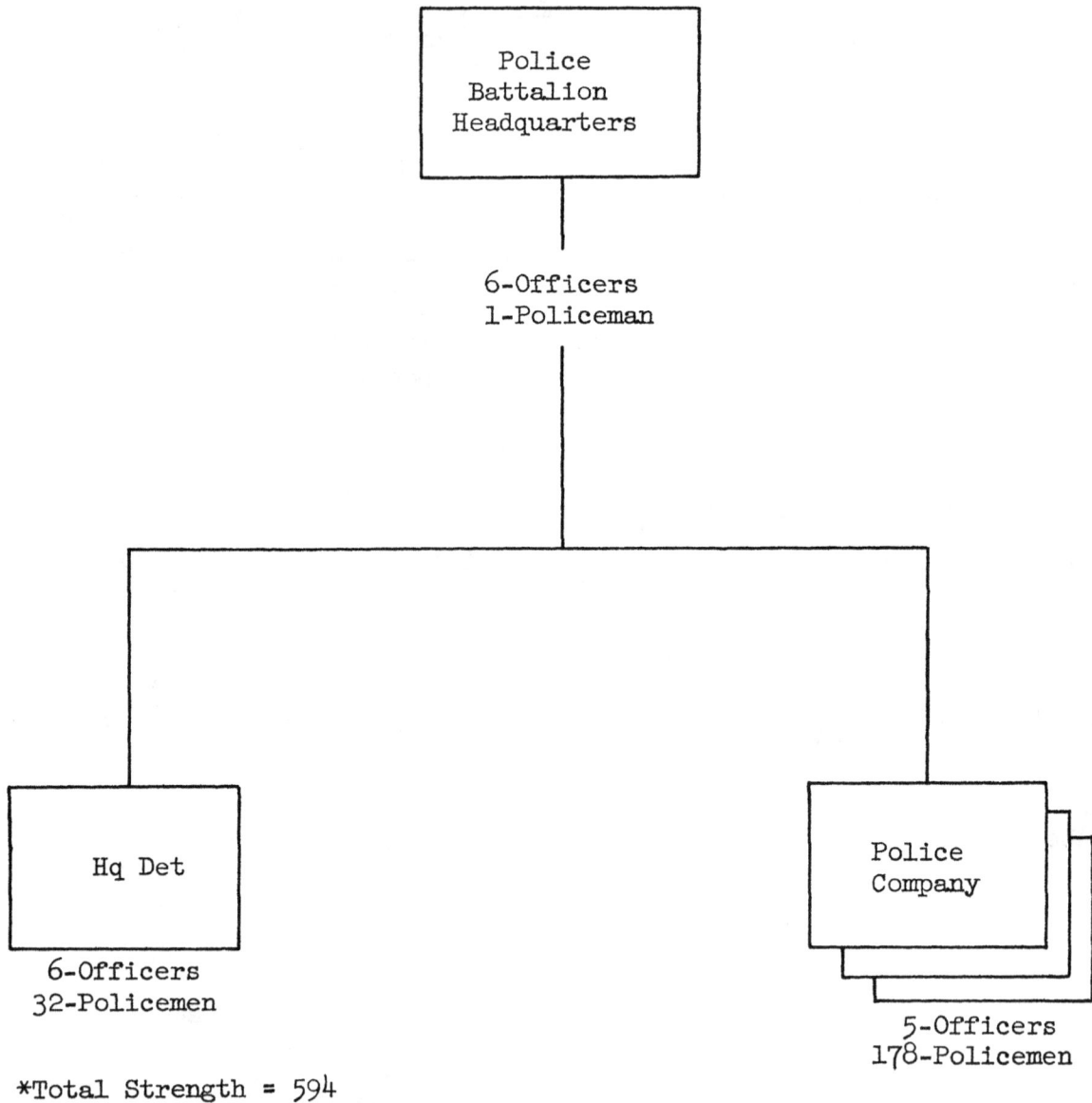

```
                    ┌─────────────────┐
                    │     Police      │
                    │    Battalion    │
                    │  Headquarters   │
                    └─────────────────┘
                             │
                             │
                        6-Officers
                        1-Policeman
                             │
          ┌──────────────────┴──────────────────┐
          │                                      │
          │                                      │
   ┌─────────────┐                        ┌─────────────┐
   │             │                        │   Police    │
   │   Hq Det    │                        │   Company   │
   │             │                        │             │
   └─────────────┘                        └─────────────┘
     6-Officers                             5-Officers
    32-Policemen                          178-Policemen

 *Total Strength = 594
```

Figure 11. A type police battalion.

ST 19-180; 94

A TYPE POLICE COMPANY

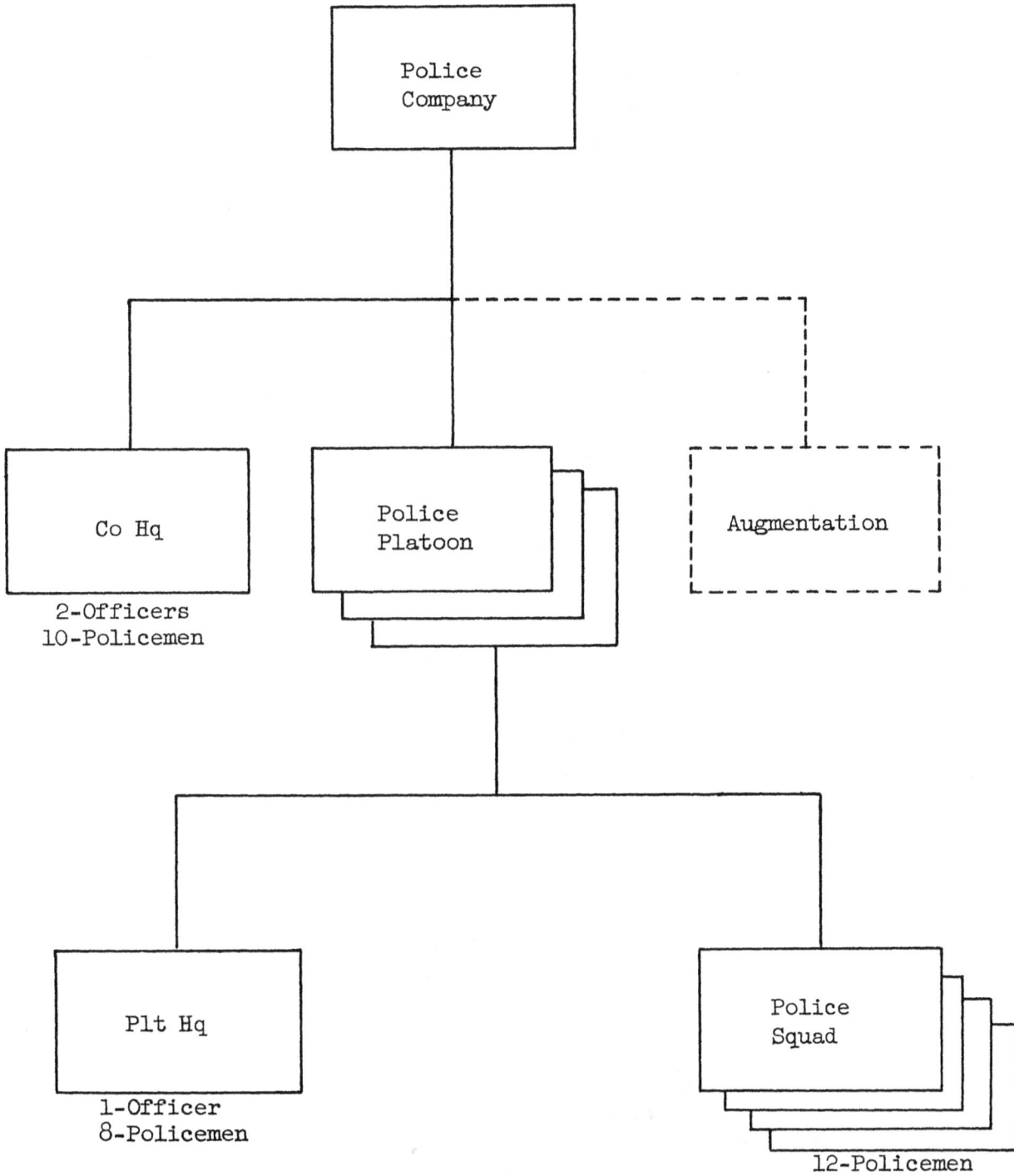

```
                    ┌─────────────┐
                    │   Police    │
                    │   Company   │
                    └──────┬──────┘
                           │
         ┌─────────────────┼─────────────────┐ (dashed)
         │                 │                 │
   ┌───────────┐     ┌───────────┐     ┌───────────┐
   │           │     │  Police   │     │           │ (dashed)
   │   Co Hq   │     │  Platoon  │     │Augmentation│
   │           │     │           │     │           │
   └───────────┘     └─────┬─────┘     └───────────┘
   2-Officers              │
   10-Policemen            │
                           │
              ┌────────────┴────────────┐
              │                         │
        ┌───────────┐             ┌───────────┐
        │           │             │  Police   │
        │  Plt Hq   │             │  Squad    │
        │           │             │           │
        └───────────┘             └───────────┘
        1-Officer                 12-Policemen
        8-Policemen
```

*Total Strength = 183

Figure 12. A type police company.

ST 19-180; 95

A TYPE POLICE BATTALION

Personnel

I. Battalion Headquarters

Battalion Commander	1
Executive Officer	1
Adjutant, S1	1
Operations and Intell, S2, S3	1
Supply and Maintenance, S4	1
Investigations Officer	1
Sergeant Major	1
	6 Officers
	1 Policeman

II. Headquarters Detachment
Detachment Headquarters

Detachment Commander	1
Detachment Sergeant	1
Supply Sergeant	1
Detachment Clerk	1
Light Truck Driver	1
	1 Officer
	4 Policemen

Battalion Administration Section

Personnel Officer	1
Operations Sergeant	1
Personnel Sergeant	1
Clerk, Typist	2
Clerk, General	1
Light Truck Driver	4
	1 Officer
	9 Policemen

Battalion Supply and Maintenance Section

Supply Sergeant	1
Motor Maintenance Sergeant	1
Sr Wheel Veh Mech	1
Wheel Veh Mech	2
Light Truck Driver	1
Mechanic Helper	2
Supply Clerk	1
	9 Policemen

Figure 13. A type police battalion.

A TYPE POLICE BATTALION (Cont)

Communications Section

Commo Sergeant	1
Chief Radio Operator	1
Radio Operator	3
Message Clerk	1
	6 Policemen

Investigations Section

Asst Investigations Officers	4
Investigators	3
Stenographer	1
	4 Officers
	4 Policemen

III. Company Headquarters

Company Commander	1
Executive Officer	1
First Sergeant	1
Supply Sergeant	1
Company Clerk	1
Chief Radio Operator	1
Radio Operator	1
Wireman	1
Light Truck Driver	2
Policeman	2
	2 Officers
	10 Policemen

IV. Police Platoon Headquarters (3)

Platoon Leader	1
Platoon Sergeant	1
Radio Operator	1
Senior Policeman	2
Clerk, General	1
Policeman	3
	1 Officer
	8 Policemen

Police Squad (12)

Squad Leader	1
Asst Squad Leader	1
Senior Policeman	5
Policeman	5
	12 Policemen

(2) <u>The commander's staff</u>. The commander and his staff operate with one purpose in mind: successful execution of the unit's mission. To this end the staff must be organized to provide the commander with the most effective assistance. The commander normally delegates authority to his staff to take final action on matters within command policy thereby freeing himself to focus attention on the essential aspects of command. In performing its functions, the staff secures information and furnishes estimates and advice as required by the commander; prepares the details of his plans; translates his decisions and plans into orders; and causes such orders to be transmitted to each command element. It assists, to the extent authorized by the commander, in the supervision of the execution of plans and orders and takes other action necessary to carry out the commander's intentions.

(a) <u>The Executive Officer</u>. The commander himself commands the staff, but the executive officer directs, supervises and coordinates the activities of all staff members. He also assumes command of the battalion in the absence of the battalion commander and under this circumstance actually exercises command.

(b) <u>The Adjutant</u>. This officer is the principal staff assistant in administrative and personnel matters pertaining to the battalion. His major areas of responsibility include: correspondence, records, reports, files, operating the battalion message center, publishing orders and directives, personnel management, supervising the battalion mail service, and other headquarters management activities.

(c) <u>Operations and Intelligence Officer</u>. This officer is the principal staff assistant in matters pertaining to organization, training, operations, and intelligence. His major areas of responsibility include:

1. <u>Organization</u>. Recommendations on the organization and equipping of the subordinate police companies.

2. <u>Training</u>. Preparation and execution of battalion training programs to include the organization of battalion schools and compilation of training records and reports.

3. <u>Operations</u>. Preparation and publication of operational plans and orders, and supervision and coordination of the execution of battalion operations.

4. <u>Intelligence</u>. Preparation of plans and orders for the collection of information.

(d) <u>Supply and Maintenance Officer</u>. This officer is the principal staff assistant on matters pertaining to materiel and services. His major areas of responsibility include:

                    1. <u>Supply</u>. Determines supply requirements. Requisitions, procures, stores and distributes supplies.

                    2. <u>Transportation</u>. Operation of battalion motor pool.

                    3. <u>Services</u>. Provides utilities for facilities as needed.

                 (e) <u>Investigation Officer</u>. This officer is the principal staff assistant on matters pertaining to investigations. (He may be subordinate to the operations and intelligence officer.) His major responsibilities include investigating serious incidents and preparing physical security surveys.

                 (f) <u>Sergeant Major</u>. This man is the senior police sergeant in the battalion who acts as an administrative assistant to the adjutant.

        b. <u>The support element</u>. This element consists of the administration, supply and maintenance, communications, and investigations sections. Personnel in these sections work for and support the activities of the principal staff officers to whom they are assigned. These sections are staffed by the Battalion Headquarters Detachment to which they are organic. (See Figure 13.)

        c. <u>Police companies</u>. There are three companies which are organized alike. They consist of a company headquarters and three platoons. Each platoon consists of a platoon headquarters and four squads. A police company has the capability of being augmented by other units such as smoke generator units or medical units.

    55. EQUIPMENT.

        Regardless of the competency of its commander and police officers, or its strength and status of training, the police battalion cannot perform its mission without adequate equipment. Figure 14 indicates those items of equipment that are considered essential to the police battalion in its mission of restoring order in an area experiencing civil disorder. Other equipment may be necessary depending on local conditions.

ESSENTIAL EQUIPMENT OF A TYPE POLICE BATTALION

Item	Squad	Platoon Hqs	Company Hqs	Battalion Hqs
Rifle w/grenade launcher	12	6	9	27
Rifle, sniper		1		
Pistol		2	2	18
Machine gun		1	1	1
Bayonet	12	6	9	27
Riot control agent disperser		1		
Smoke disperser		1		
Water disperser		1		
Reconnaissance vehicle	3	3	3	9
Truck, cargo-personnel*		2	3	4
Trailer, recon. veh.	3	3	3	9
Trailer, truck, cargo-personnel		2	3	4
Radio set, medium range	3	3	3	9
Radio set, short range	1	2	2	
Antenna		1	1	1
Public address system			1	
Gas mask	12	9	12	45
Helmet	12	9	12	45
Gloves, heavy duty	12	9	12	45
Protective vest	12	9	12	45
First aid kit	12	9	12	45
Canteen	12	9	12	45
Photographic set			1	
Medical chest		1	1	1
Concertina wire, roll**	1	2	4	4
Fire extinguisher, portable		1	1	

*One vehicle in each platoon headquarters and in the company and battalion headquarters are equipped with a winch.

**50 feet of wire per roll.

Figure 14. Essential equipment of a type police battalion.

ST 19-180; 100

CHAPTER 9

RIOT CONTROL FORMATIONS

Section I

CHARACTERISTICS AND CONSIDERATIONS

56. RIOT CONTROL FORMATIONS AND THEIR USE.

      a. <u>Line</u>. The line may be employed as either an offensive or defensive formation. It is a continuous formation without gaps along the front. The flanks of a line must be anchored by obstacles or protected by reserve units.

          (1) <u>Offensive</u>. The line is used to push or drive mobs in a rearward direction along a confined frontage such as might be found on a city street.

          (2) <u>Defensive</u>. The line may be used to hold or deny the mob access to sensitive areas or to control its movement.

      b. <u>The echelon, left or right</u>. The echelon is an offensive formation used to turn a mob away from an obstacle such as a wall or a building or to direct its movement in a certain direction.

      c. <u>The wedge</u>. The wedge is an offensive formation employed to split a mob into smaller segments. Unless the flanks of the wedge are firmly anchored, it should not be driven into a mob. This action could result in encirclement of the police unit.

      d. <u>Modified formations</u>. Under unusual circumstances, the formations above can be readily altered into modified formations as the situation dictates. Such formations might include a square, circle, or diamond.

57. NORMAL EMPLOYMENT PROCEDURES.

      Riot control formations are effective in a show of force. The psychological effect of police strength through unity and organization is best transmitted to a mob by surprise and by formidable appearance of police. To gain this advantage, the following procedures are recommended:

      a. Police should dismount and assemble at some point out of sight of the mob. This assembly position should be as close to the mob as possible.

b. Police officers should conduct final equipment checks at this forward assembly position.

c. Upon completion of final equipment checks, the police unit should be moved by organized march formation into view of the rioters.

d. The police unit should be advanced to within a reasonably safe position of the rioters. From this position members of the unit may either be deployed into a riot control formation and halted, or halted in march column. Prior to further application of force, the police commander should deliver the proclamation and necessary instructions to the mob. If the mob fails to obey, the commander must immediately apply the measure of force required.

58. BASIC WEAPONS.

The most practical weapon for general use by police in a riot control operation is the riot baton. The riot baton is normally 26 to 36 inches long and constructed of dense wood. If the riot baton is not available for use, a hand weapon should be selected that gives the individual police officer confidence, power, and an extended reach. The riot baton is discussed fully in Chapter 11.

59. AUXILIARY WEAPONS.

The riot control unit should be equipped with certain auxiliary type weapons.

a. Shotgun. One shotgun, riot type, should be issued to each squad and should be carried by the assistant squad leader. It is employed to cover breaches in a formation until supporting police can be committed. It is also used to fire at selected targets when a short-range weapon is needed. Ammunition should be carefully selected. (See Figure 15.)

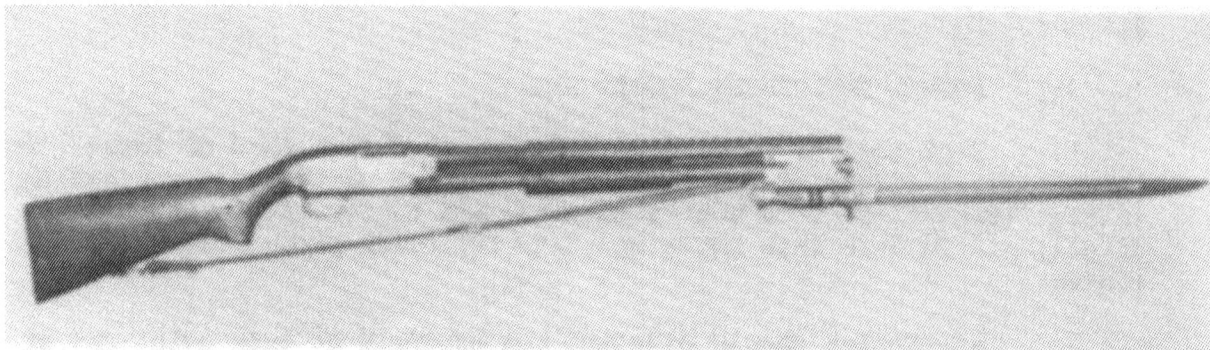

Figure 15. Riot type shotgun.

ST 19-180; 102

b. Sniper rifle. Normally, each platoon has one sniper rifle which is carried by a sharpshooter to fire at selected targets as directed by the platoon leader or company commander. The sniper rifle may be issued to selected marksmen. (See Figure 16.)

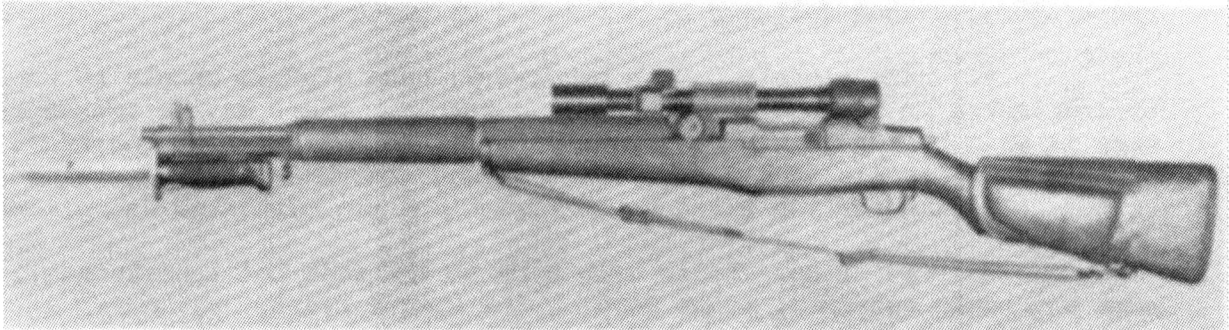

Figure 16. Sniper rifle.

c. Submachine gun or automatic rifle. Generally, one per platoon is issued and is carried by a member of platoon headquarters. It is used for psychological effect and to fire at selected targets as directed by the platoon leader or company commander.

d. Hand weapons. Hand weapons may be carried by commanders, drivers, grenadiers, members of crew-served weapons, and other personnel when it is impractical to carry rifles. They are used primarily as defensive weapons.

e. Machine guns. These weapons may be used to protect barriers, bivouacs, assembly and detrucking areas, and police on motor marches. Machine guns can be mounted on vehicles for use in riot control formations.

f. Riot control agents. For a detailed discussion of riot control agents and their employment, see Chapter 10.

g. Portable fire extinguisher. A portable fire extinguisher inside the formation can be used to extinguish fires on the clothing of members of the formation caused by "molotov cocktails" or other burning liquids hurled at the unit by the mob.

60. UNIT ORGANIZATION FOR RIOT CONTROL FORMATIONS.

The formations covered in this chapter (12 man squad, 4 squad platoon, 3 squad platoon, 3 platoon company with 4 squad platoons) are for illustration and are not intended to require unit reorganization. Any size squad, platoon, or larger unit can be employed and riot control formations can be adapted to fit the organization.

61. COMMANDS.

    a. <u>Oral commands</u>.

      (1) All commands for the riot baton are given in one count.

      (2) All other commands are given in two counts, with a preparatory command followed by a command of execution.

    b. <u>Hand signals</u>. When necessary, hand signals should be used by commanders in conjunction with oral commands. There may be occasions when it will be impossible to communicate with oral commands; therefore arm and hand signals should be well rehearsed and understood by all concerned. Signals for the three basic formations are described as follows:

      (1) <u>Line</u>. Raise both arms to the side until horizontal, arms and hands extended, palms down. (See Figure 17a.)

      (2) <u>Echelon right (left)</u>. Face the unit being signaled and extend the arm downward to the side at an angle of 45° below the horizontal in the direction in which the unit is to echelon, palm to the front; extend the other arm upward and to the side at an angle of 45°, palm to the front. (See Figure 17b.)

Figure 17a. Line formation.   Figure 17b. Echelon formation

(3) <u>Wedge</u>. Extend both arms downward and to the sides at an angle of 45° <u>below</u> the horizontal, arms and hands extended, palms down. (See Figure 17c.) Arm and hand signal for the diamond, a modification of the wedge, is also illustrated in Figure 17d.

Figure 17c. Wedge formation.   Figure 17d. Diamond formation.

62. CADENCES.

a. The normal cadence for movement into and assembly from all riot control formations is double time (180 steps per minute).

b. The normal cadence for movement of police while in any riot control formation is at quick time (120 steps per minute).

c. Cadence for the "on-guard" position is approximately 60 steps per minute. Instead of a normal walking step, the left foot is deliberately placed about one-half step forward and then the right foot is deliberately brought alongside the left. Better balance, ease in maintaining step, and the psychological effect produced by the deliberate drumming of the feet are considered the main advantages of this step.

d. Cadence may be increased or decreased at the discretion of the unit commander to meet varying situations.

e. A unit may be ordered into or assembled from riot control formations from the halt or while marching. As each man reaches his proper position, he automatically faces in the direction of the unit's intended advance and comes to a halt. He remains at the halt in the high port position and awaits further orders.

63. POSITION OF COMMANDER AND LEADERS.

a. When in column, the commander at each echelon normally assumes his position at the head of the column.

b. When in riot control formations, squad leaders and their assistants, platoon leaders and their assistants, and the company commander take positions in the rear of the assault elements of their respective units where they can best direct and control their unit. In the illustrations of riot control formations, the platoon and squad leaders are not shown uniformly in order to illustrate the flexibility of their positions behind the formations.

c. When in column, messengers (radio operators), sharpshooters, automatic weapons men, and other members of platoon headquarters normally take positions at the front of the column.

d. When a unit is in a riot control formation, headquarters personnel, at the discretion of the unit commander, are positioned near the commander. If the situation precludes this, they may be positioned anywhere behind the assault element.

64. INTERVAL AND DISTANCE.

a. Interval is the space between men, animals, vehicles, or units in a formation placed side to side, measured abreast. Distance is the space between men, animals, vehicles, or units in a formation measured from front to rear. The normal interval and distance between men in riot control formations are 30 inches (one pace). (See Figure 18.)

b. The interval and distance may be adjusted to meet particular situations.

c. In any echelon formation with normal interval and distance, the angle made by the formation and the route of advance will be approximately 45°. The angle formed by the two wings of any wedge formation will be approximately 90° when normal interval and distance are used.

Distance

1 Pace

Interval and Distance

1 Pace

Interval and Distance

1 Pace

Interval

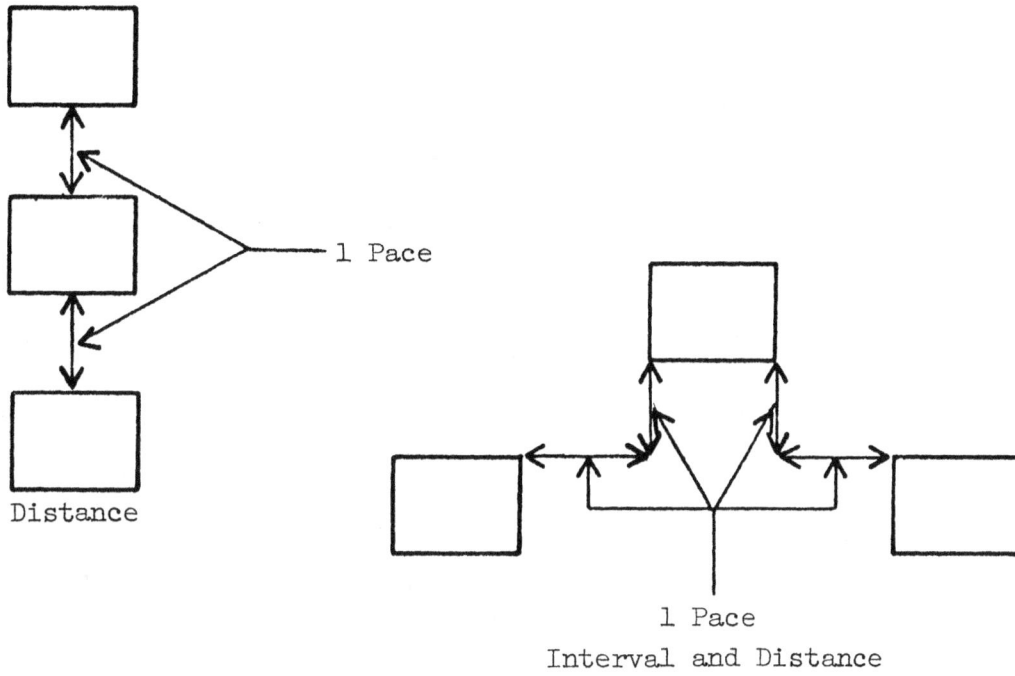

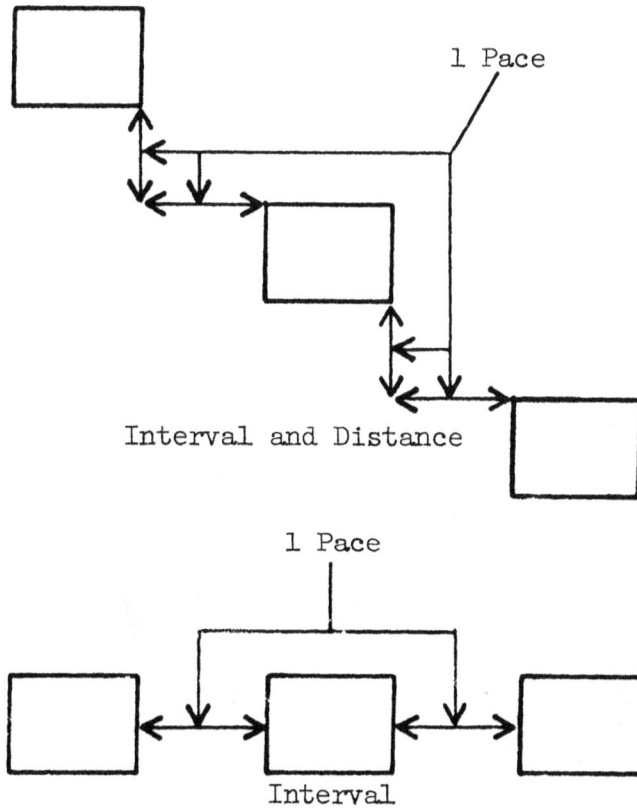

Figure 18.   Interval and distance.

ST 19-180; 107

Section II

SQUAD FORMATIONS

65. GENERAL.

When executing squad riot control formations from the column, the squad leader takes one or more steps to the right and faces his squad. As he gives his preparatory command he gives the arm and hand signal for the formation. At the command of execution, he points to the location at which he desires the number-two man to go. If he does not point, the squad will assume the present position of the number-two man of the squad to be the desired location for the formation.

66. SQUAD WEDGE.

a. Command. "SQUAD WEDGE ---- MOVE."

b. Execution. At the command of execution, the base man (Number 2) advances to the position designated by the squad leader. Even numbered men aline themselves in sequence on the number-two man, one pace to the right and one pace to the rear of each preceding man. Odd numbered men aline themselves in sequence on the number-two man, one pace to the left and one pace to the rear of each preceding man. (See Figures 19a & b.) The wedge may be modified into a diamond formation. (See Figures 20a & b.)

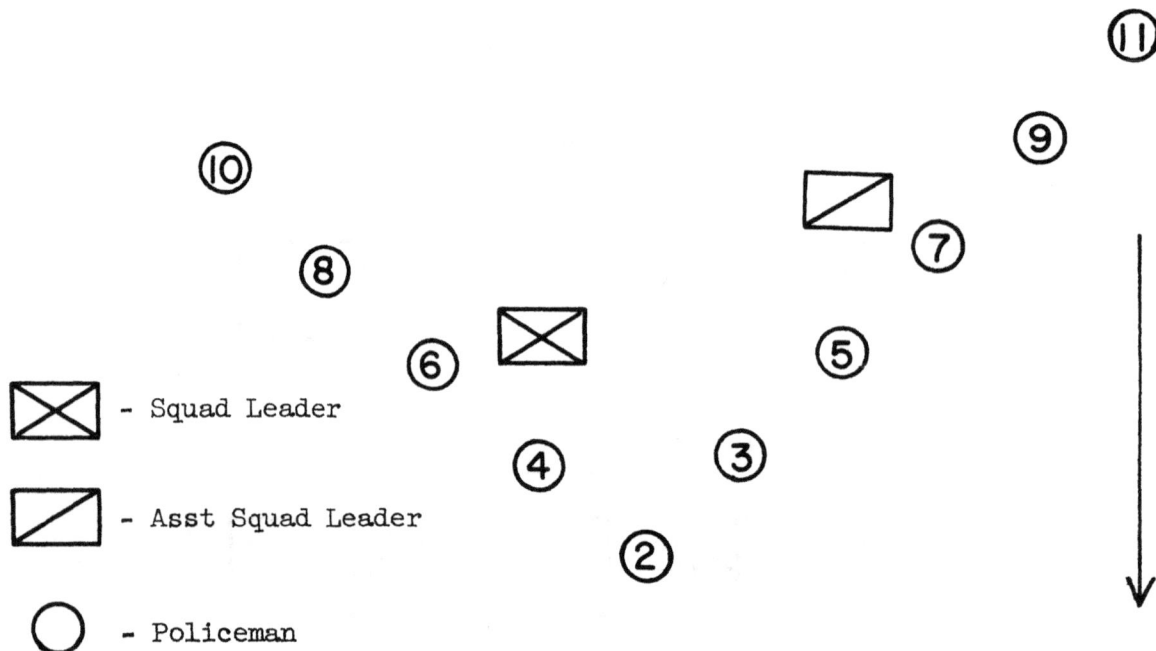

⊠ - Squad Leader

◪ - Asst Squad Leader

○ - Policeman

Figure 19a. Squad wedge formation.

ST 19-180; 108

Figure 19b. Squad wedge formation, position of attention

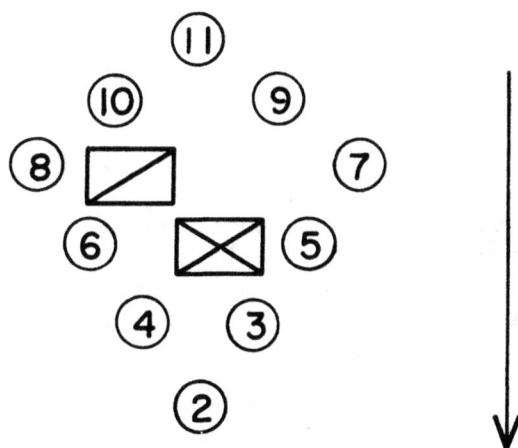

Figure 20a. Squad diamond.

ST 19-180; 109

Figure 20b. Squad diamond formation, position of attention.

67. SQUAD ECHELON RIGHT (LEFT).

   a. Command. "SQUAD ECHELON RIGHT (LEFT) ---- MOVE."

   b. Execution. At the command of execution, the base man
(number 2) advances to the position designated by the squad leader.
The men aline themselves in sequence on the base man, one pace to the
right (left) and one pace to the rear of each preceding man. (See
Figures 21a,b and 22a,b.)

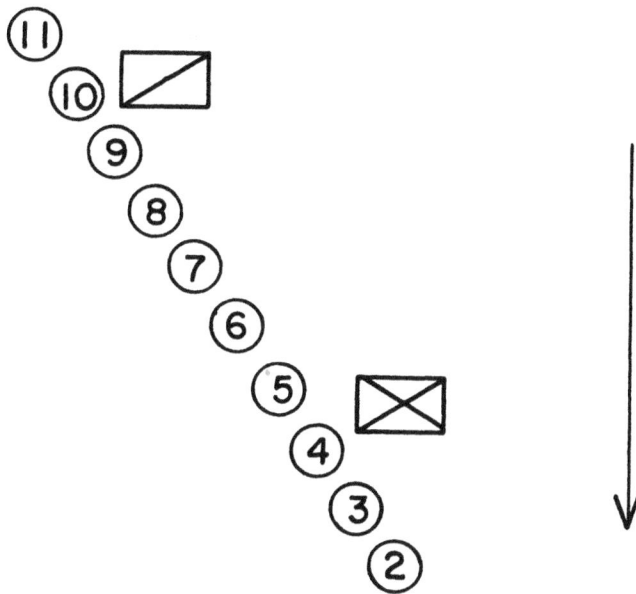

Figure 21a.   Squad echelon right formation.

Figure 21b.   Squad echelon right formation.

ST 19-180; 111

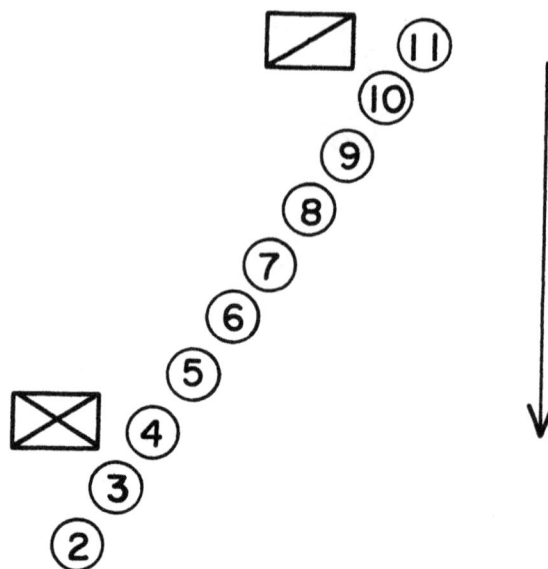

Figure 22a. Squad echelon left formation.

Figure 22b. Squad echelon left formation.

ST 19-180; 112

68. SQUAD LINE.

    a. Command. "SQUAD AS SKIRMISHERS ---- MOVE."

    b. Execution.

        (1) At the command of execution, men aline themselves in sequence on line with the base man, one pace to the right (or left) of each preceding man. The odd-numbered men aline themselves in sequence on line with the base man, one pace to the left of each preceding man - even number on the right. (See Figures 23a & b.)

        (2) If the commander desires and the situation required, he may designate a specified number of paces between men in the formation by so indicating in his preparatory command. For instance - "SQUAD AS SKIRMISHERS, TWO PACES ---- MOVE." If no interval is specified in the command, the unit will assume that a one-pace interval is desired. (See Figure 23a.)

Figure 23a. Squad line formation.

Figure 23b. Squad line formation, "on-guard" position.

69. ASSEMBLY FROM SQUAD FORMATIONS.

    a. <u>Command</u>. "SQUAD ASSEMBLE ---- MOVE."

    b. <u>Execution</u>. The squad leader moves in front of his squad As he gives his preparatory command, he gives the arm and hand signal for assembly. On the command of execution, he points to the location at which he desires the squad assembled. If he does not point, the squad will assume the present position of the number-two man to be the desired assembly point. At the command of execution, the base man (Number 2) advances to the position designated by the squad leader. The other men form the column in proper sequence behind the number-two man. The squad leader then takes his position at the head of the column.

Section III

PLATOON FORMATIONS

70. GENERAL.

Platoon headquarters should, as a minimum, consist of a leader, platoon sergeant, sharpshooter, automatic weapons man and a messenger (radio operator). Consideration should be given to equipping one man inside the formation with a portable fire extinguisher. In forming riot control formations from the column, the platoon leader moves out to the right or left front of his platoon and faces it when giving his commands. As he gives the command of execution ---- "MOVE," he will point to the approximate location at which he desires the platoon to form. If he does not point, it is assumed that the formation is to be formed immediately in front of the column. The platoon leader must pause between his preparatory command and command of execution a sufficient time to permit squad leaders to issue preparatory commands to their respective squads.

71. PLATOON WEDGE.

a. Command. "PLATOON WEDGE ---- MOVE."

b. Execution. Immediately following the platoon leader's preparatory command, the squad leaders of the 1st and 4th squads command, "FOLLOW ME." At the same time, the squad leaders of the 2d and 3d squads command, "STAND FAST." On the platoon leader's command of execution, the 1st and 4th squads move directly to the front. When the men of the 1st and 4th squads have cleared the front of the 2d and 3d squads, the squad leaders of the 1st and 4th squads command "SQUAD ECHELON LEFT ---- MOVE" and "SQUAD ECHELON RIGHT ---- MOVE," respectively. The number-two man of the 4th squad becomes the base man for the platoon, and the 4th squad executes an echelon right. The 1st squad executes its echelon left using the number-two man of the 4th squad as its base man. When this movement is completed, the squad leaders of the 2d and 3d squads command "SQUAD ECHELON LEFT ---- MOVE" and "SQUAD ECHELON RIGHT ---- MOVE," respectively, pointing to the rear elements of the wedge which has just been formed by the 1st and 4th squads. On the command of execution, the 2d and 3d squads move out and complete the formation. (See Figures 24a & b.) The platoon wedge may be modified into a diamond. (See Figure 25a & b.)

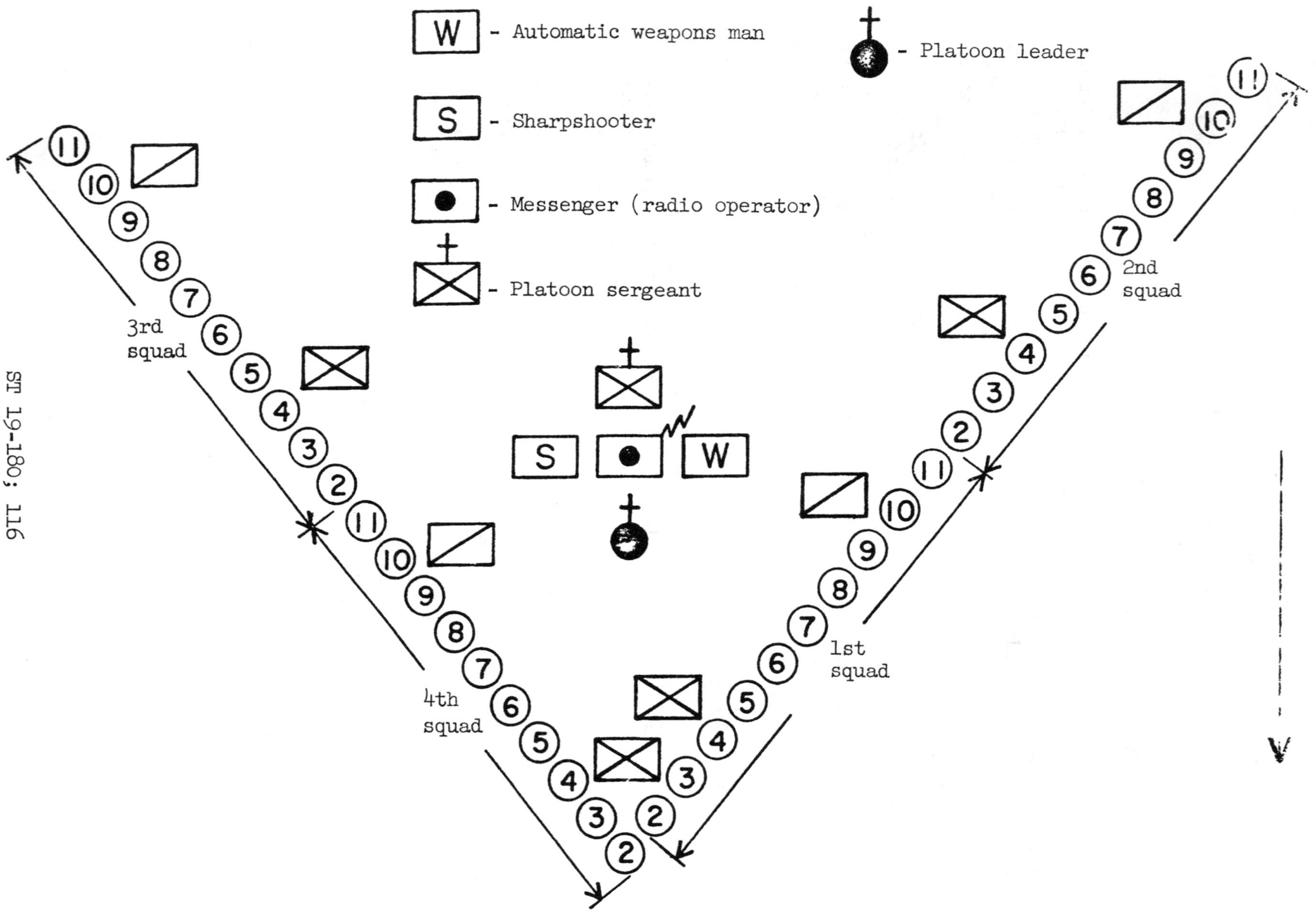

Figure 24a. Platoon wedge.

- Platoon leader

W - Automatic weapons man

S - Sharpshooter

- Messenger (radio operator)

- Platoon sergeant

2nd squad

1st squad

3rd squad

4th squad

Figure 24b.   Platoon wedge formation.

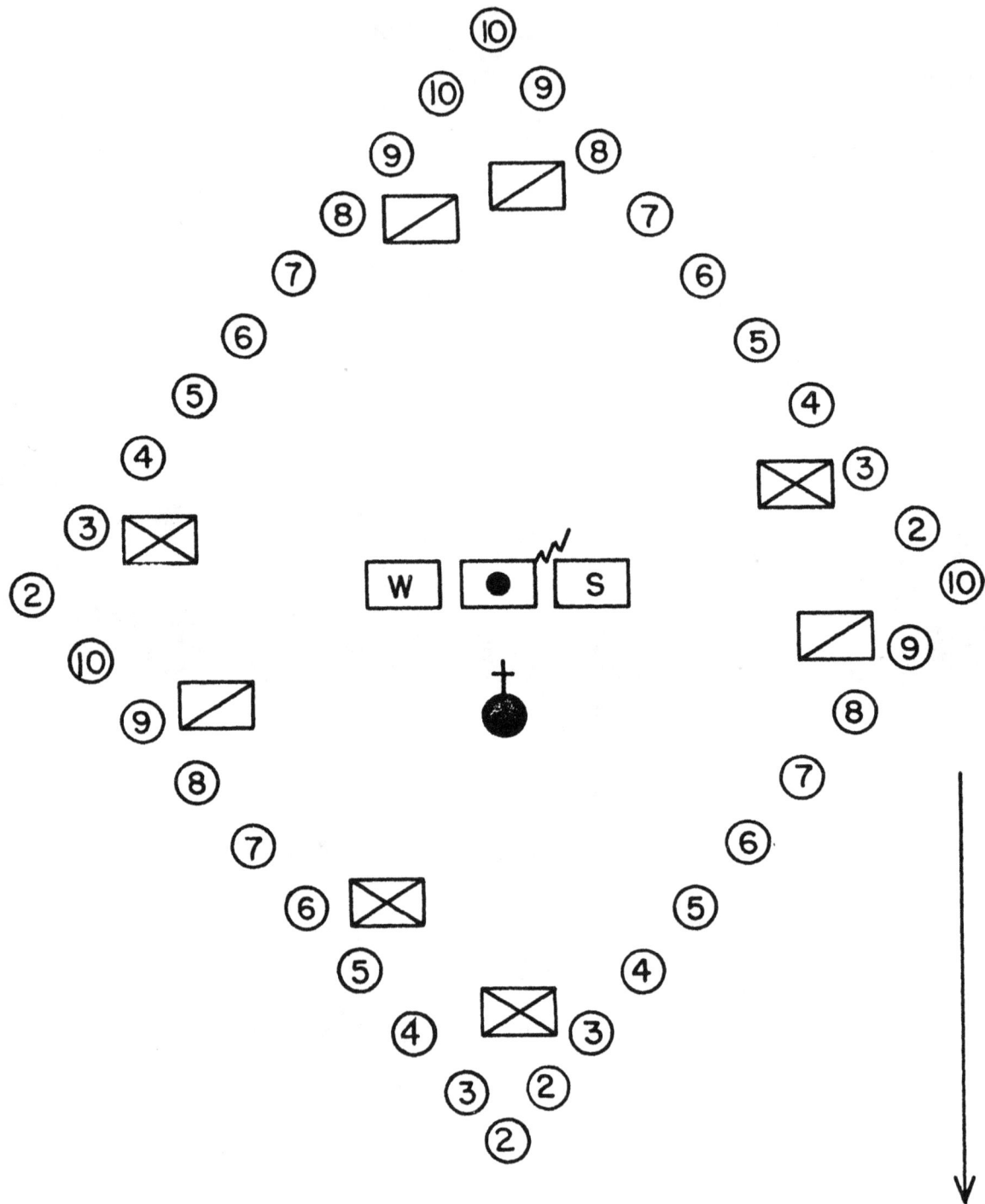

Figure 25a. Platoon diamond formation.

ST 19-180; 118

Figure 25b. Platoon diamond formation.

3 72. PLATOON WEDGE WITH TWO SUPPORT SQUADS.

   a. General support.

       (1) Command. "PLATOON WEDGE, 2D AND 3D SQUADS IN
SUPPORT ---- MOVE."

       (2) Execution. The 1st and 4th squads execute the wedge
as in paragraph 71, while the 2d and 3d squads remain in the column.
(See Figures 26a & b.)

   b. Lateral support.

       (1) Command. "PLATOON WEDGE, 2D AND 3D SQUADS IN
LATERAL SUPPORT ---- MOVE."

       (2) Execution.

           (a) The 1st and 4th squads execute the wedge as
before, while the 2d and 3d squads stand fast. After the wedge has

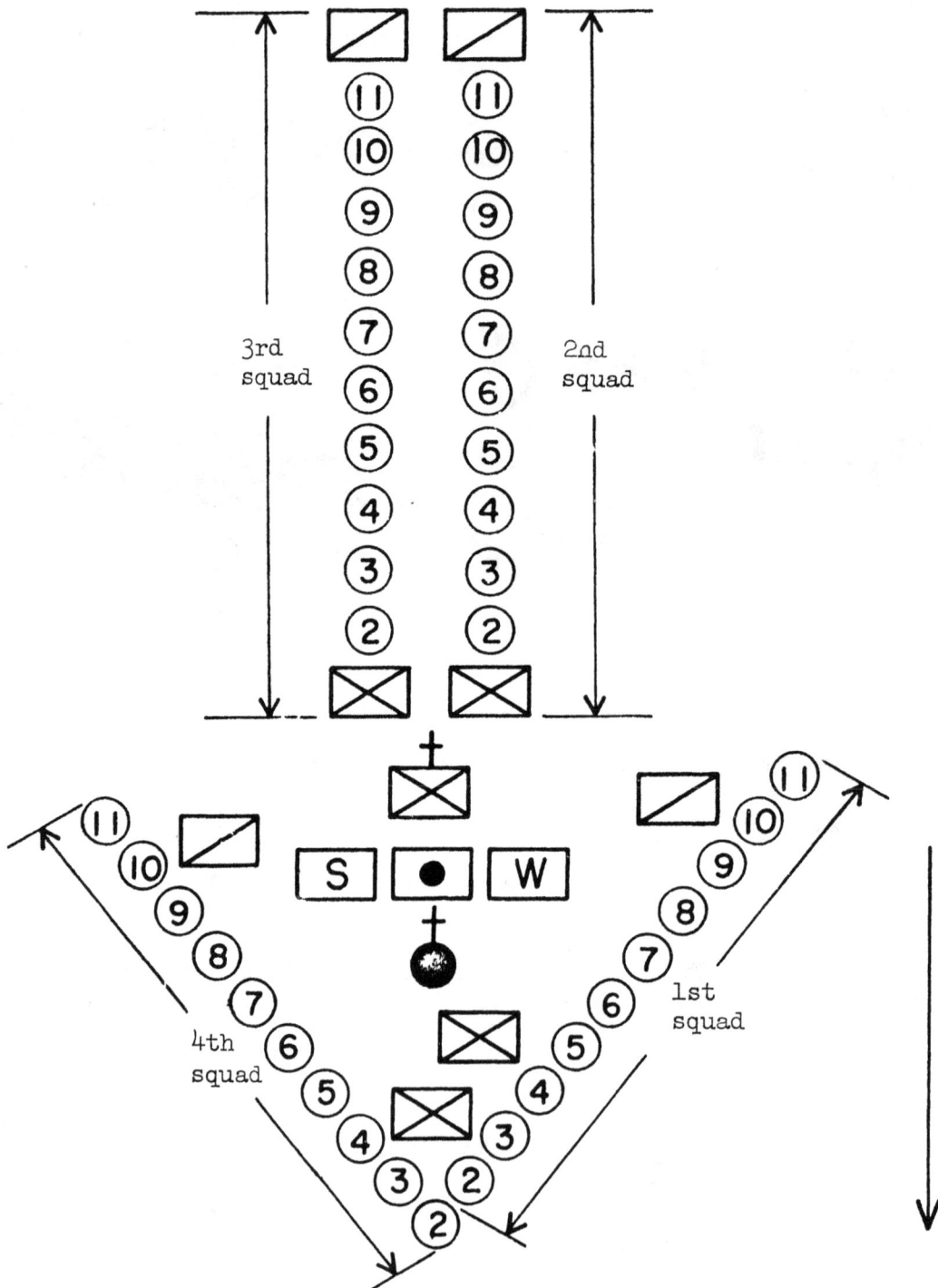

Figure 26a.   Platoon wedge, 2d & 3d squads in support.

ST 19-180; 120

Figure 26b. Platoon wedge formation, with 2 squads in support.

been formed by the 1st and 4th squads, the squad leaders of the 2d and
3d squads command "LEFT FLANK" and "RIGHT FLANK," respectively. At the
command of execution, "MOVE," the 2d and 3d squads move out to their
flanks, close in on the rear echelons of the wedge already formed and
automatically face in the direction of the platoon's advance. Support
elements remain at port arms or high port when leading elements are in
"en guard position." (See Figures 27a & b.)

       (b) The 2d and 3d squads can be committed from gen-
eral to lateral support at any time by the commander. He merely commands "2D AND 3D SQUADS, LATERAL SUPPORT ---- MOVE."

       (c) To have the 2d and 3d squads join the wedge
from either general or lateral support the platoon leader commands,
"2D AND 3D SQUADS, EXTEND THE WEDGE ---- MOVE." The 2d and 3d squad
commanders will command "SQUAD ECHELON LEFT" and "SQUAD ECHELON RIGHT,"
respectively and the platoon is restored to a single complete wedge.

   c. Close support.

    (1) Command. "PLATOON WEDGE, 2D AND 3D SQUADS IN CLOSE
SUPPORT ---- MOVE."

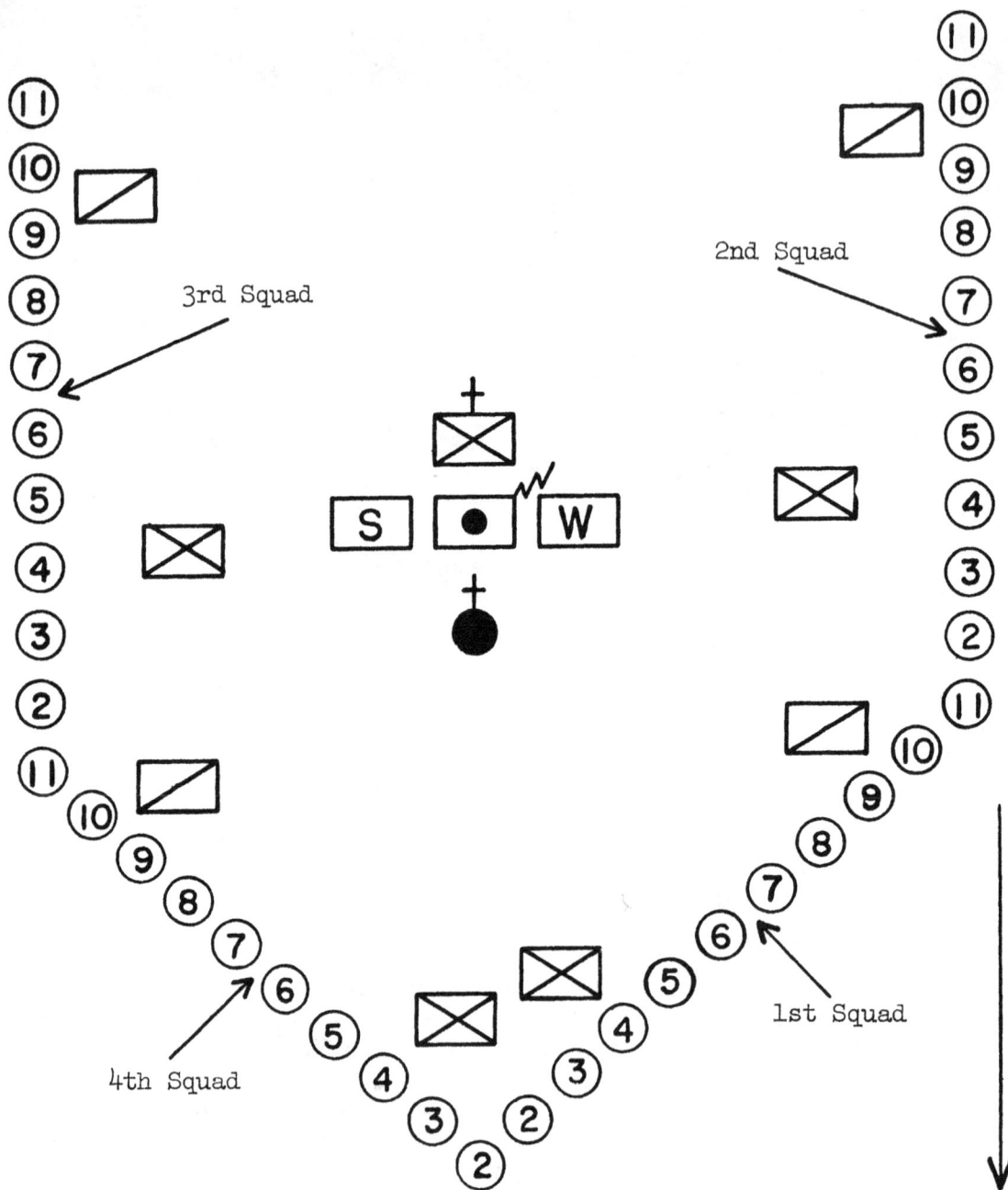

Figure 27a. Platoon wedge, two squads in lateral support.

Figure 27b. Platoon wedge formation,
with 2 squads in lateral support.

(2) Execution. The 1st and 4th squads execute a wedge
as before. The 2d and 3d squads execute a similar wedge and close in
on the leading wedge. The men in the supporting wedge cover the intervals between men in the leading wedge. (See Figures 28a & b.)

d. Assembling the support squads. To assemble the supporting squads from any position to gain general support, the commander
will command "2D AND 3D SQUADS, ASSEMBLE ---- MOVE." The 2d and 3d
squads then return to the column in rear of the wedge formed by the
other two squads.

73. PLATOON WEDGE WITH ONE SUPPORT SQUAD.

a. Command. "PLATOON WEDGE, 3D SQUAD IN SUPPORT ---- MOVE."

b. Execution. The 2d squad moves out and executes a squad
wedge. The 1st and 4th squads form echelons left and right respectively
on the 2d squad. The 3d squad remains in the column. (See Figure 29.)

c. Support squad. The support squad may be used as lateral
support on one or both sides of the formation or as close support for
any section of the wedge as necessary.

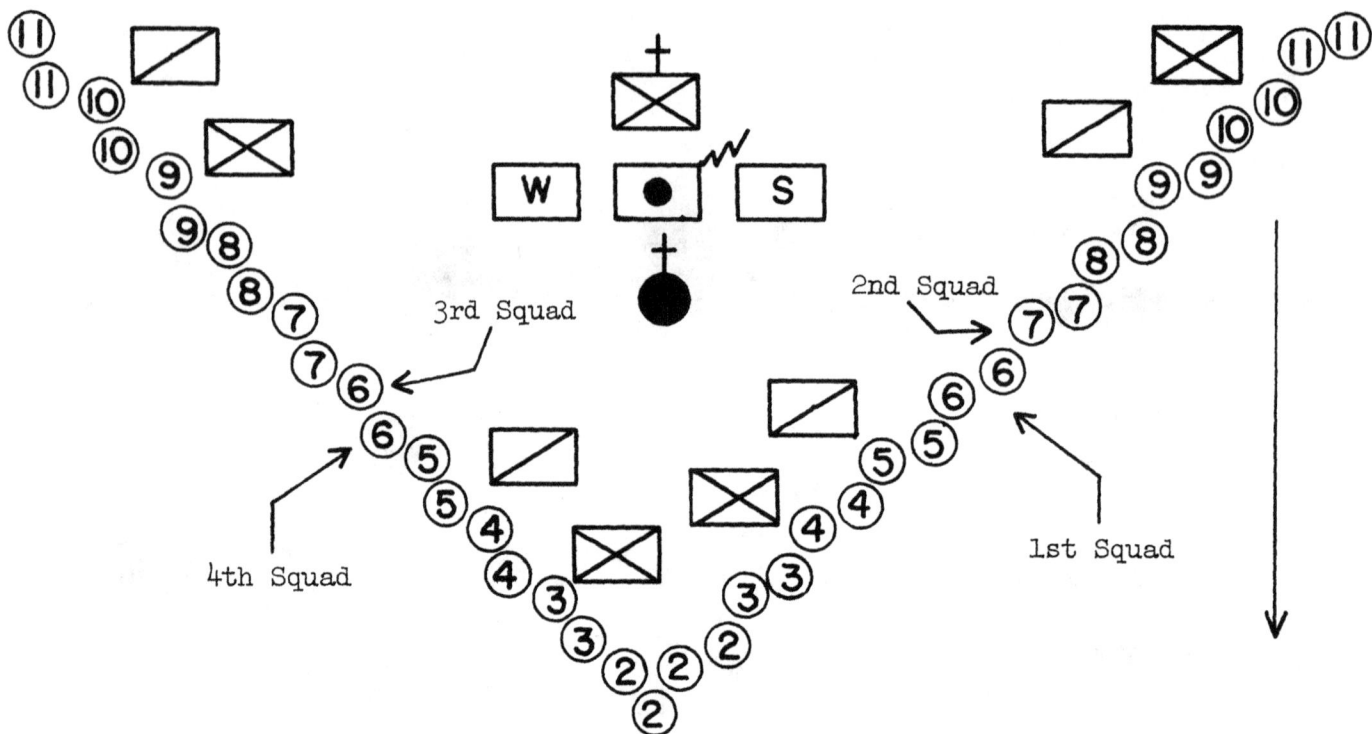

Figure 28a. Platoon wedge, 2d & 3d squads in close support.

Figure 28b. Platoon wedge formation, with 2 squads
in close support.

ST 19-180; 124

74. PLATOON ECHELON RIGHT.

    a.   Command.   "PLATOON ECHELON RIGHT ---- MOVE."

    b.   Execution.   Immediately following the platoon leader's preparatory command, the squad leader of the 1st squad commands "FOLLOW ME." The squad leaders of the 2d, 3d, and 4th squads command "STAND FAST." At the command of execution, the 1st squad moves out and executes an echelon right at the location designated by the platoon commander. As each squad clears the column, each successive squad moves out individually and extends the echelon already formed by the preceding squad(s). (See Figure 30.)

75. PLATOON ECHELON LEFT.

    a.   Command.   "PLATOON ECHELON LEFT ---- MOVE."

    b.   Execution.   The platoon echelon left is formed in the same manner as the echelon right except in inverse order (the 4th squad is the base squad and the remaining squads extend the echelon in inverse sequence) (See Figure 31.)

76. PLATOON ECHELON WITH SUPPORT.

    The 2d and 3d squads are in general, lateral, and close support with the echelon right and left in the same manner as with the wedge. (See Figures 32, 33, 34, and 35.)

77. PLATOON LINE.

    a.   Command.   "PLATOON AS SKIRMISHERS ---- MOVE."

    b.   Execution.   Immediately following the platoon leader's preparatory command, the squad leaders command "FOLLOW ME." At the platoon leader's command of execution, the 2d and 3d squads move to the front and spread out. At the same time, the 1st and 4th squads move forward and to their left and right flanks respectively. The squad leader of the 2d squad establishes a squad line at the position indicated by the platoon leader. The squad leaders of the 1st, 3d, and 4th squads establish squad lines individually and close and dress on the 2d squad or base squad. (See Figure 36.)

78. PLATOON LINE WITH SUPPORT.

    The two squads can be used in general, lateral, and close support with the line in the same manner as with the wedge and the echelon. However, when the 2d and 3d squads are used in support, the 4th squad then becomes the base squad for the line. (See Figures 37a, b; 38a, b; 39 and 40.)

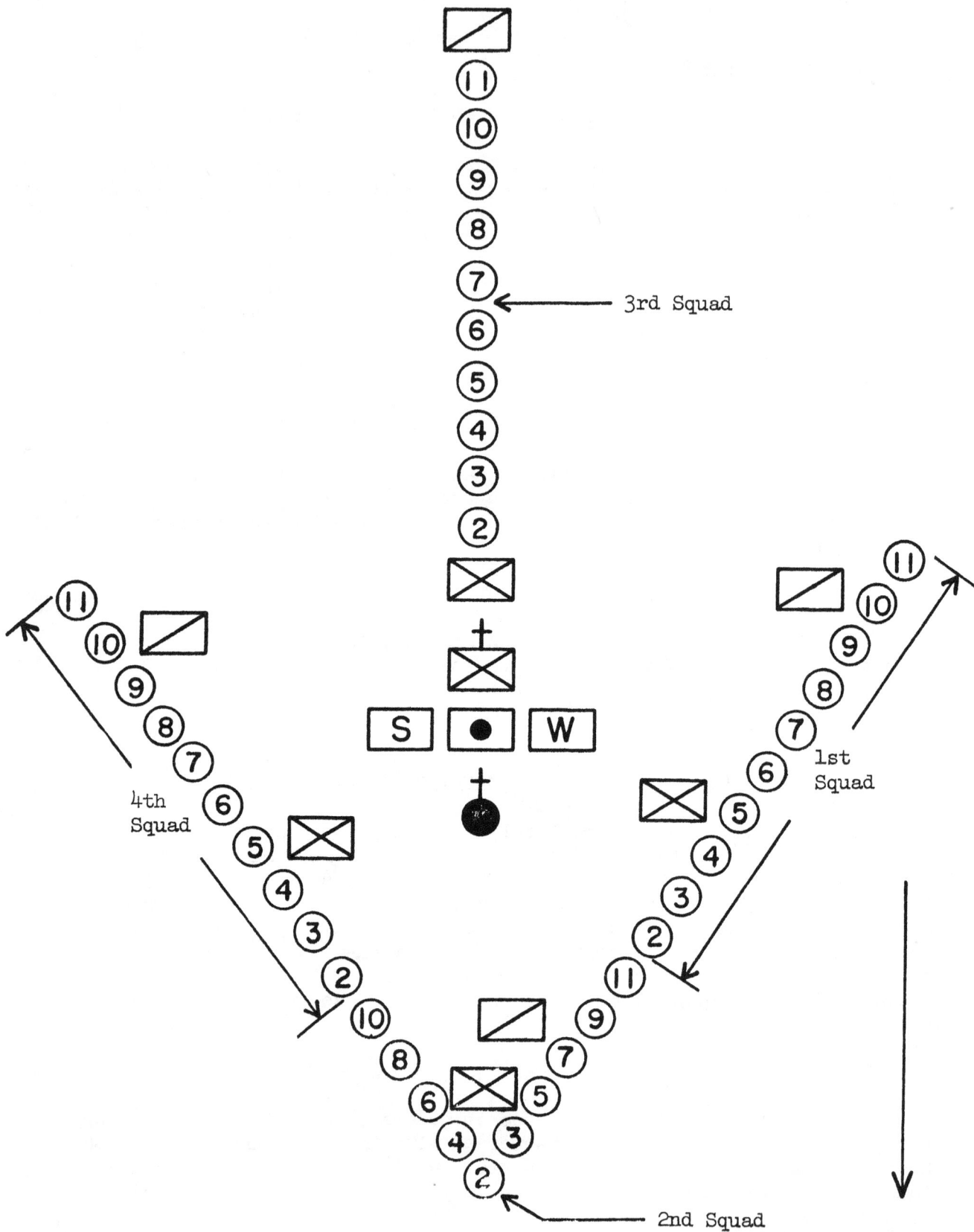

Figure 29. Platoon wedge formation, one squad in support.

ST 19-180; 126

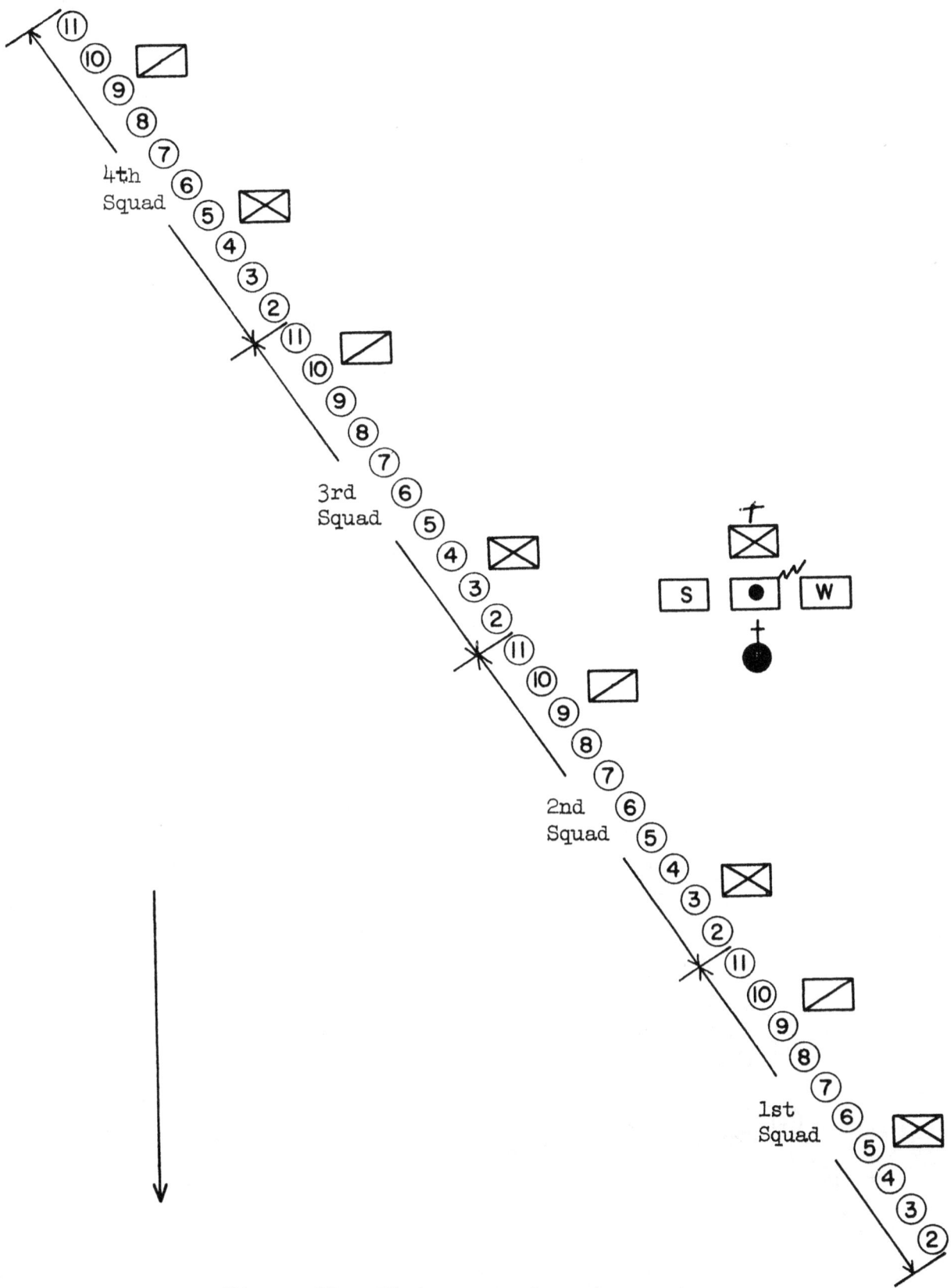

Figure 30. Platoon echelon right formation.

ST 19-180; 127

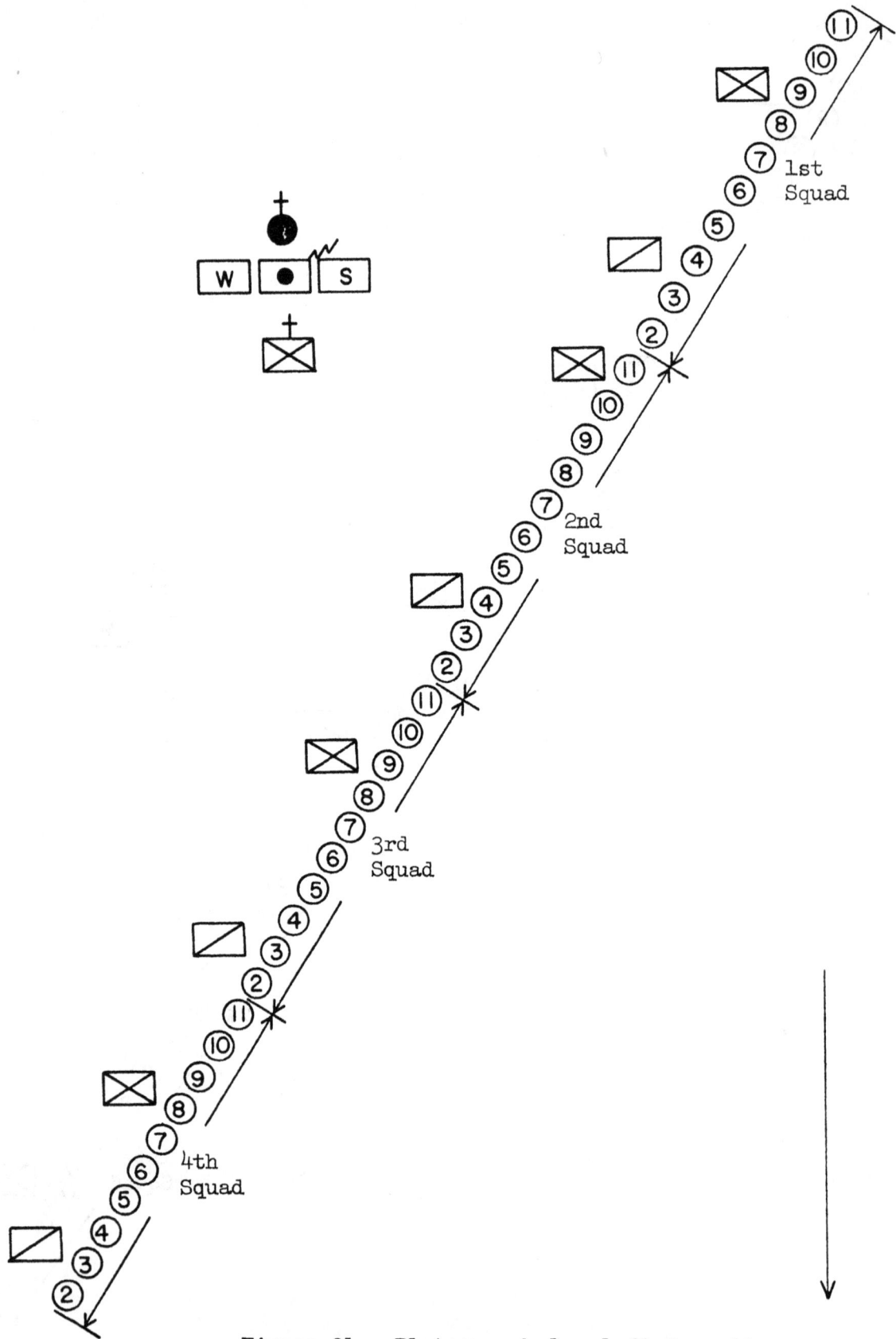

Figure 31. Platoon echelon left formation.

ST 19-180; 128

COMMAND: "PLATOON
ECHELON RIGHT,
2D AND 3D
SQUADS IN SUP-
PORT -- MOVE."

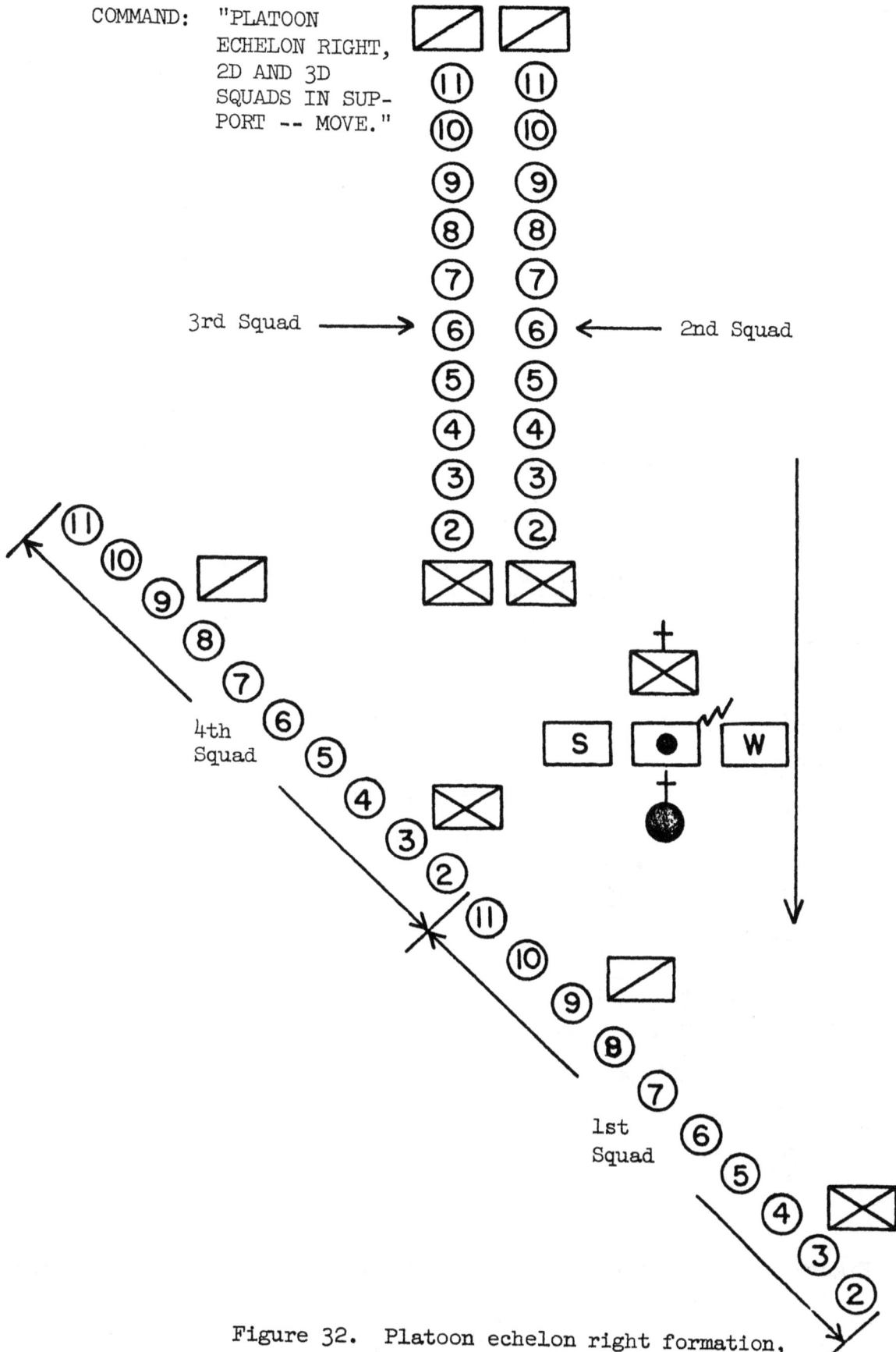

3rd Squad

2nd Squad

4th
Squad

S   W

1st
Squad

Figure 32.   Platoon echelon right formation,
two squads in support.

ST 19-180; 129

COMMAND: "PLATOON ECHELON LEFT, 2ND AND 3RD
             SQUADS IN LATERAL SUPPORT -- MOVE."

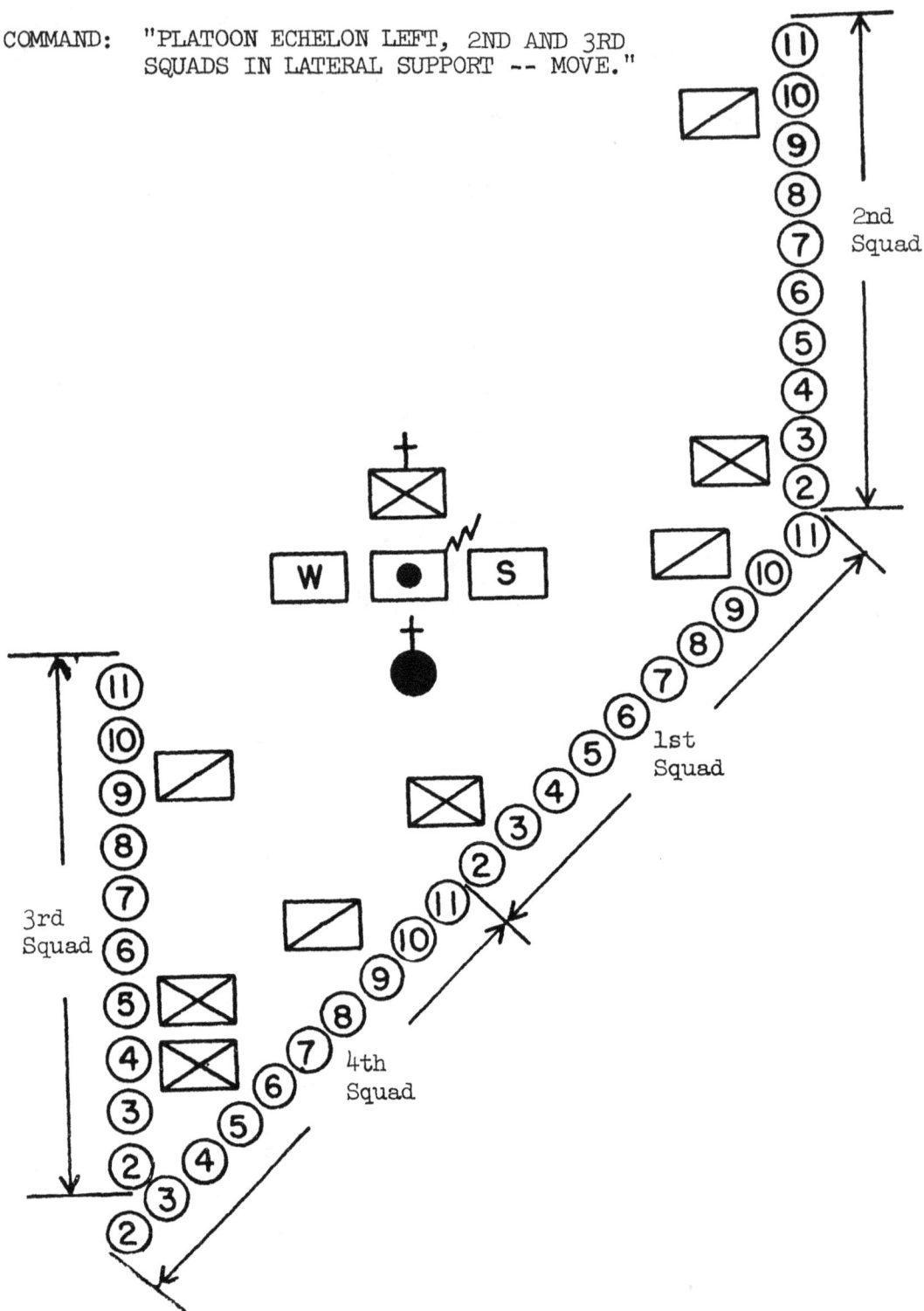

Figure 33. Platoon echelon left, with two squads in lateral support

COMMAND: "PLATOON ECHELON LEFT, 2ND AND 3RD
SQUADS IN CLOSE SUPPORT -- MOVE."

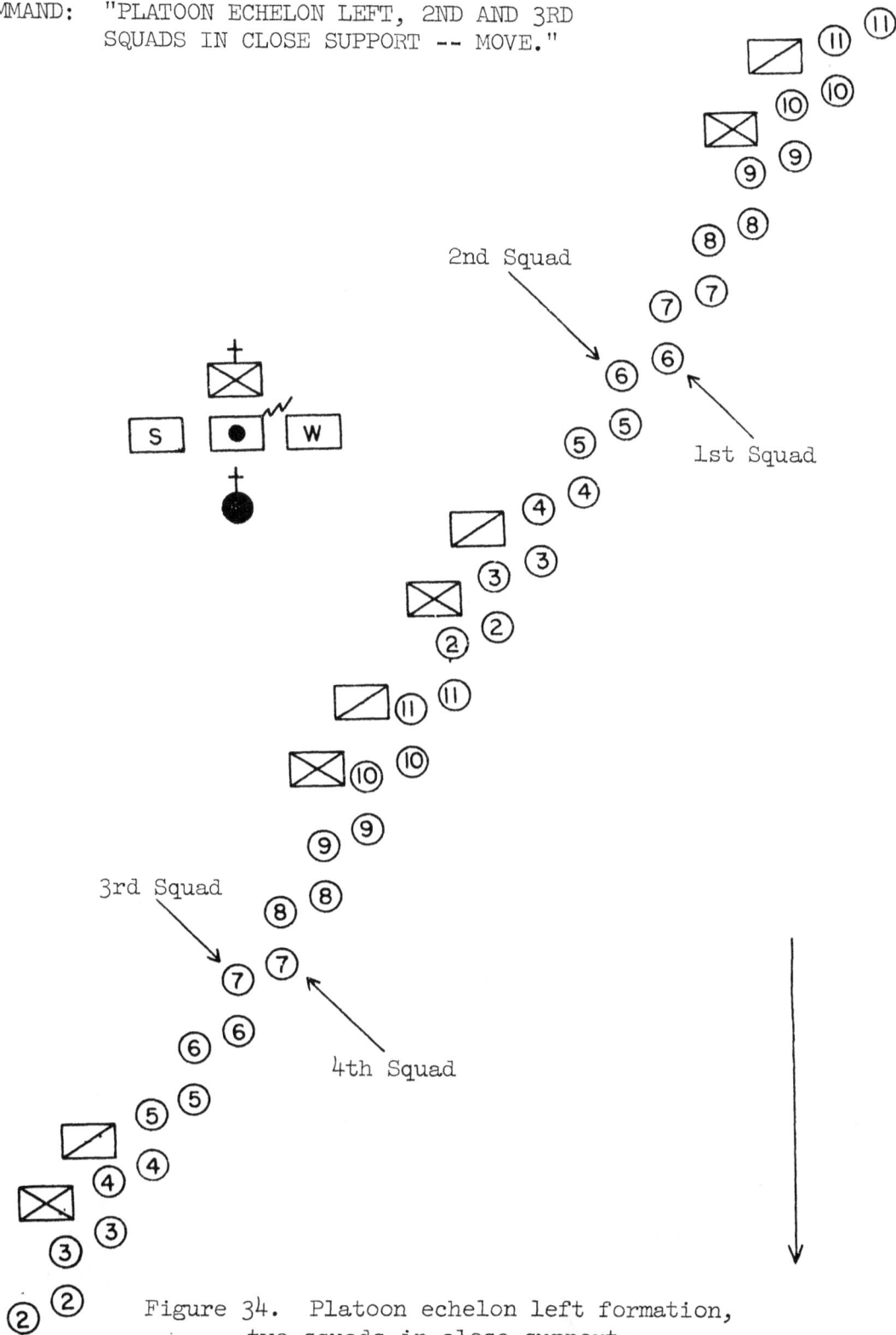

2nd Squad

1st Squad

S ● W

3rd Squad

4th Squad

Figure 34. Platoon echelon left formation,
two squads in close support.

ST 19-180; 131

COMMAND: "PLATOON ECHELON LEFT, 1ST SQUAD IN
LATERAL SUPPORT TO THE LEFT -- MOVE."

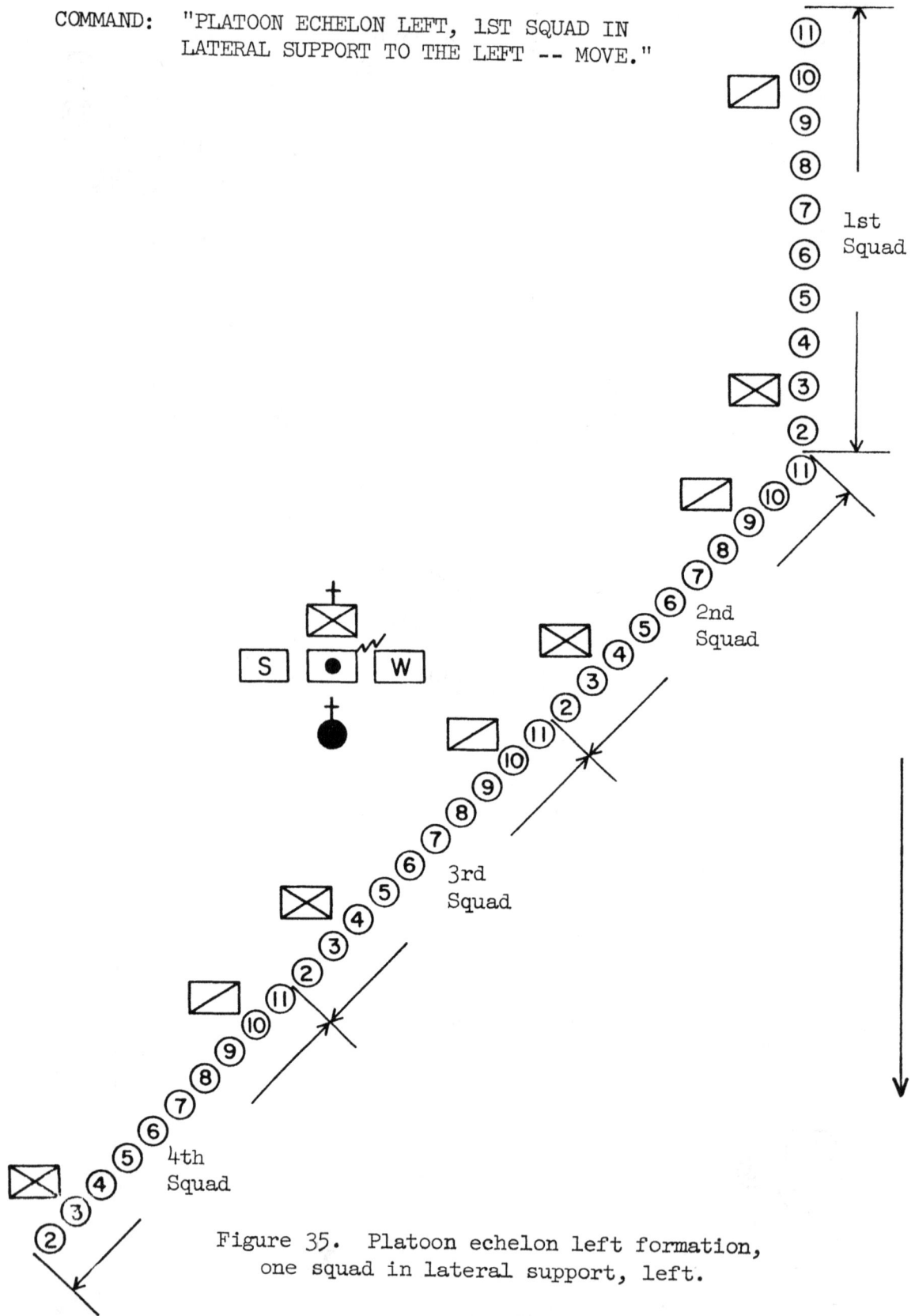

Figure 35. Platoon echelon left formation,
one squad in lateral support, left.

ST 19-180; 132

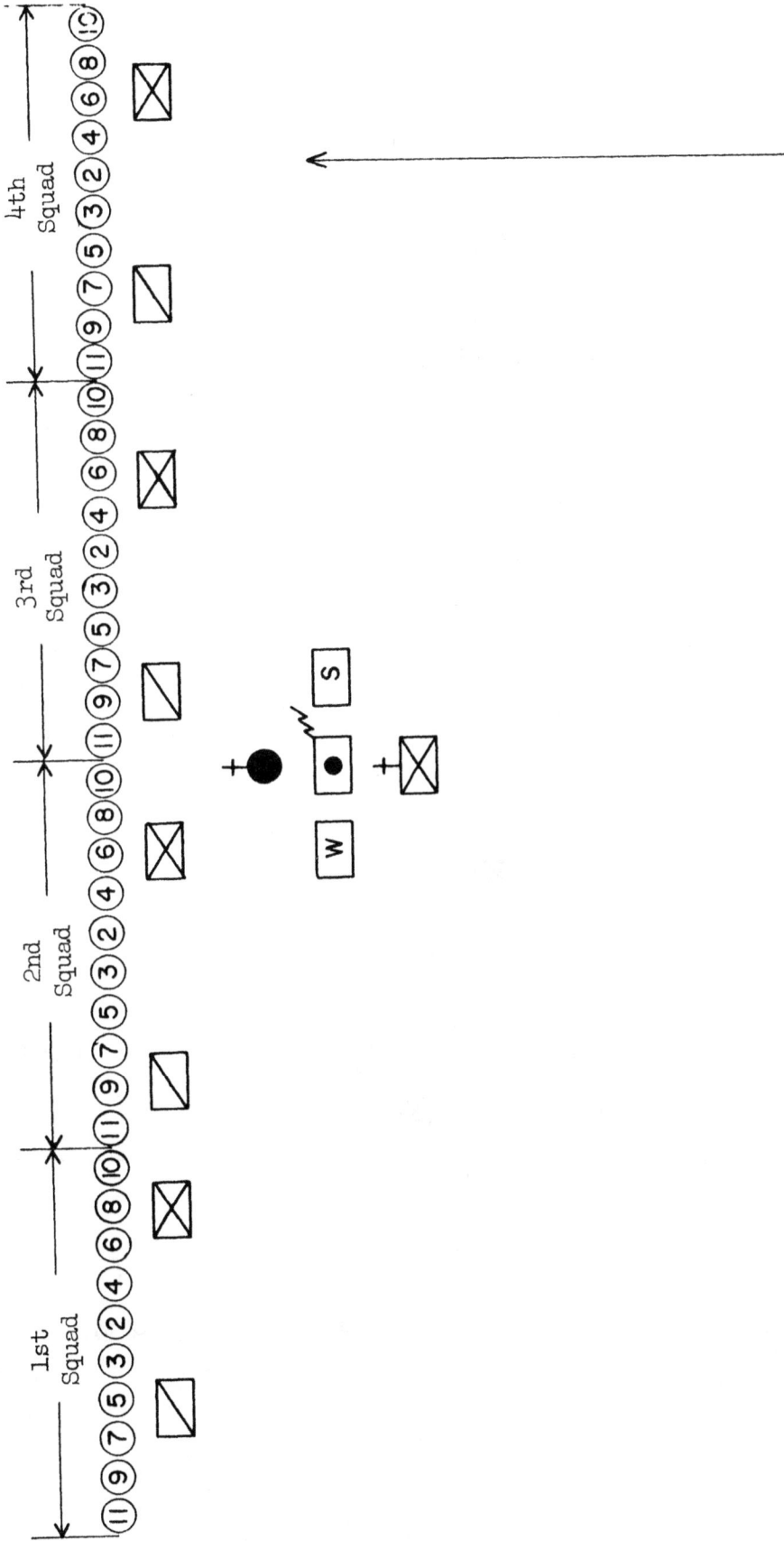

Figure 36. Platoon line.

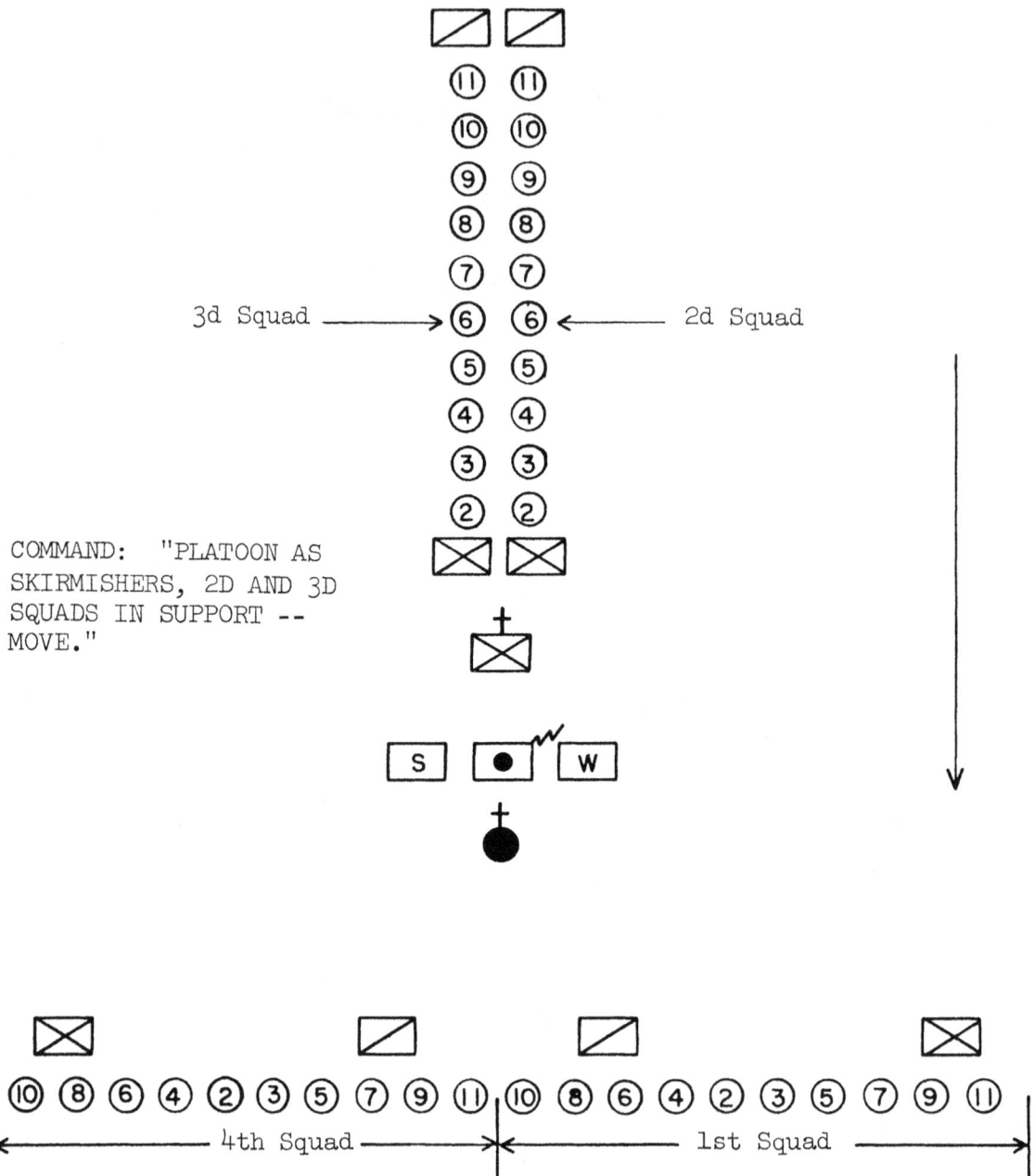

3d Squad ⟶

2d Squad ⟵

COMMAND: "PLATOON AS
SKIRMISHERS, 2D AND 3D
SQUADS IN SUPPORT --
MOVE."

4th Squad

1st Squad

Figure 37a. Platoon line, two squads in support.

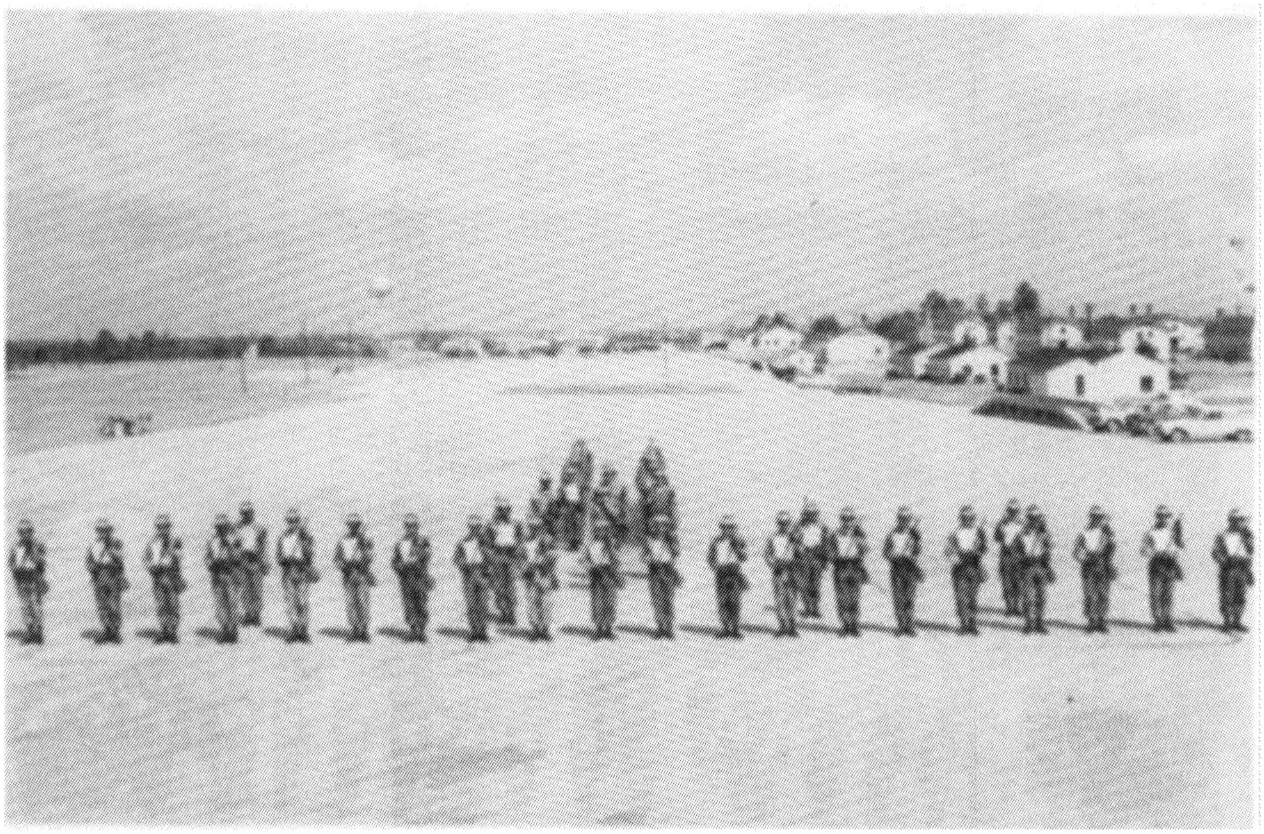

Figure 37b. Platoon line formation, two squads in support

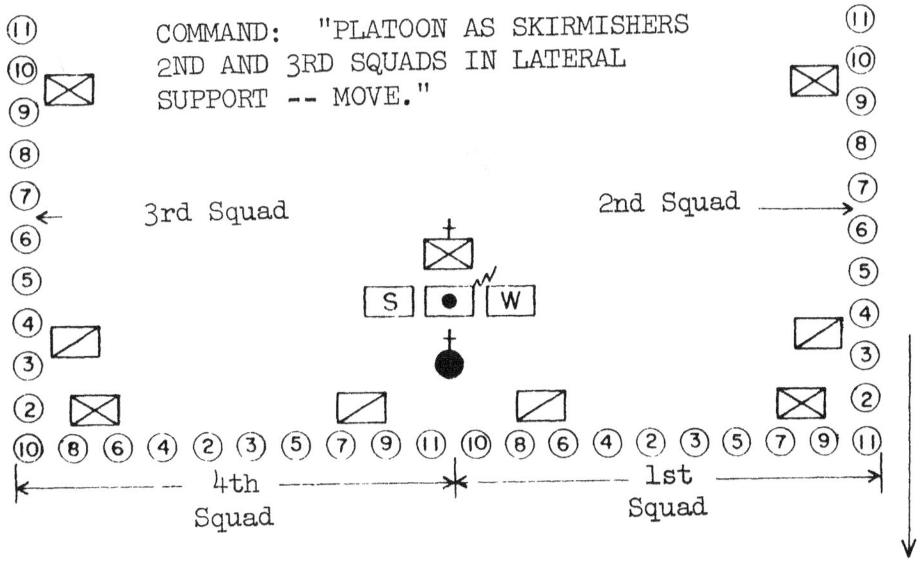
COMMAND: "PLATOON AS SKIRMISHERS
2ND AND 3RD SQUADS IN LATERAL
SUPPORT -- MOVE."
3rd Squad
2nd Squad
S
W
4th
Squad
1st
Squad
11
10
9
8
7
6
5
4
3
2

Figure 38a. Platoon line, two squads in lateral support.

Figure 38b.   Platoon line formation, two squads
in lateral support.

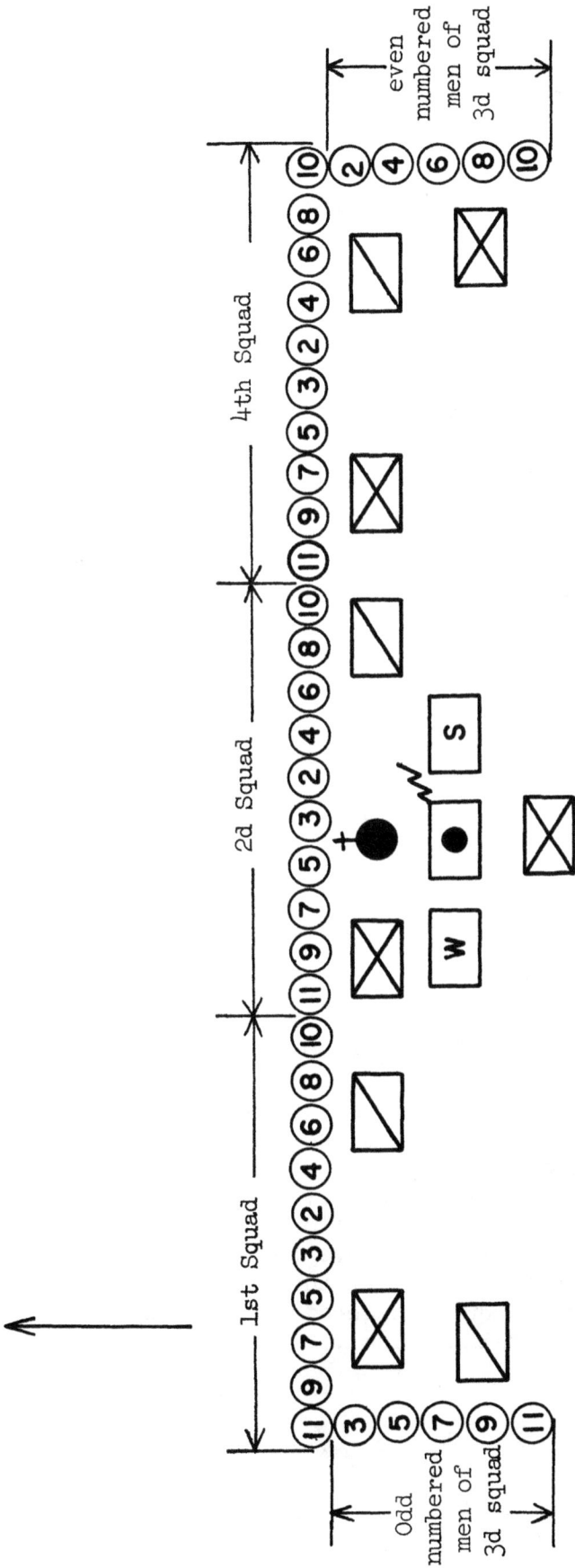

COMMAND: "PLATOON AS SKIRMISHERS, 3RD SQUAD IN LATERAL SUPPORT ---- MOVE."

Figure 39. Platoon line, one squad in lateral support.

COMMAND: "PLATOON AS SKIRMISHERS, 2ND AND 3RD SQUADS
           IN CLOSE SUPPORT ---- MOVE."

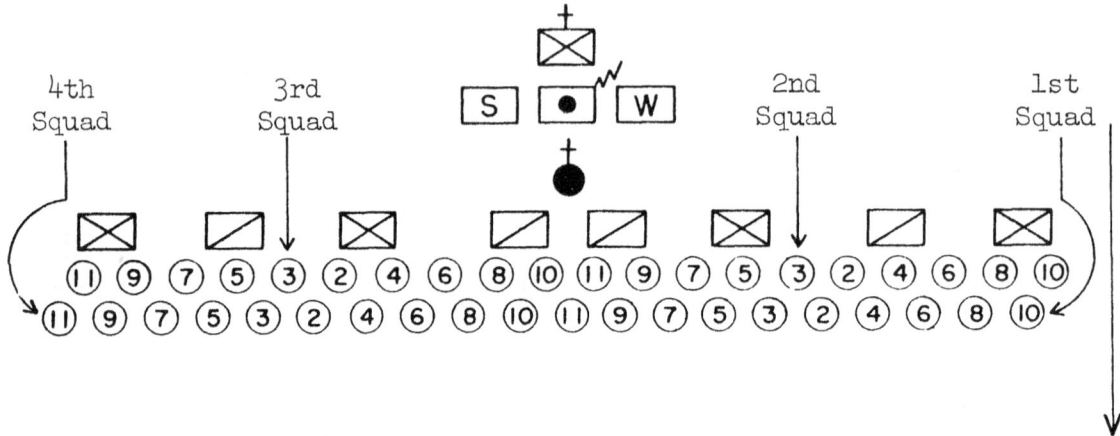

Figure 40. Platoon line, two squads in close support.

79. ASSEMBLING FROM PLATOON FORMATIONS.

    a. Command. "PLATOON ASSEMBLE ---- MOVE."

    b. Execution. The platoon leader moves out in front of his
platoon. As he gives his preparatory command, he will point to the location at which he desires the platoon assembled. If he does not point,
the platoon will assume that the desired assembly point is directly in
front of its present location. Immediately following the platoon leader's
preparatory command, the squad leaders will move to the head of their
respective squads and command "FOLLOW ME." At the command of execution,
the squads follow their respective squad leaders to their appropriate
positions as the platoon returns to the column.

80. VARIATIONS OF PLATOON FORMATIONS.

During riot control operations, the platoon leader may desire to rotate his squad in the assault element of the formation to give any squad or squads a rest. He is not bound to use only those squads specified in the preceding paragraphs in the leading or assault element of his platoon formations. By merely changing his preparatory command, he may select the squads he desires to lead his unit. For example, if he desires to use the 1st and 3d squads to lead his platoon wedge, he would issue the command "PLATOON WEDGE, 2D AND 4TH SQUADS IN SUPPORT ---- MOVE. By designating the support squads in the preparatory command, the platoon leader is also telling the other two remaining squads that they are to lead the assault. The platoon leader may also relieve any two squads from the assault element by forming a like formation with the supporting squads and have the supporting element pass through the leading element. This procedure is frequently used when it becomes necessary to put on gas masks for a chemical attack.

81. EXECUTION OF FORMATIONS (THREE-SQUAD PLATOON).

The execution of riot control formations using a three-squad platoon is essentially the same as that used with a four-squad platoon with the following exceptions:

a. The 1st and 3d squads are normally used as the assault or leading element in all formations in which one squad is used as general or lateral support. (See Figure 41.)

b. The 2d squad is the base squad in a platoon line formation when all three squads are committed initially to the assault element.

c. The support squad (usually the 2d squad) may be held in general support in single column or in column of twos, for example:

(1) Platoon wedge, 2d squad held in general support in single column.

(a) Command. "PLATOON WEDGE (ECHELON RIGHT OR LEFT, OR LINE), 2D SQUAD IN SUPPORT ---- MOVE."

(b) Execution. The 1st and 3d squads move out and form the formation while the 2d squad remains in place in column.

(2) Platoon wedge, 2d squad held in general support in column of twos.

(a) Command. "PLATOON WEDGE (ECHELON RIGHT OR LEFT, OR LINE), 2D SQUAD IN SUPPORT IN COLUMN OF TWOS ---- MOVE."

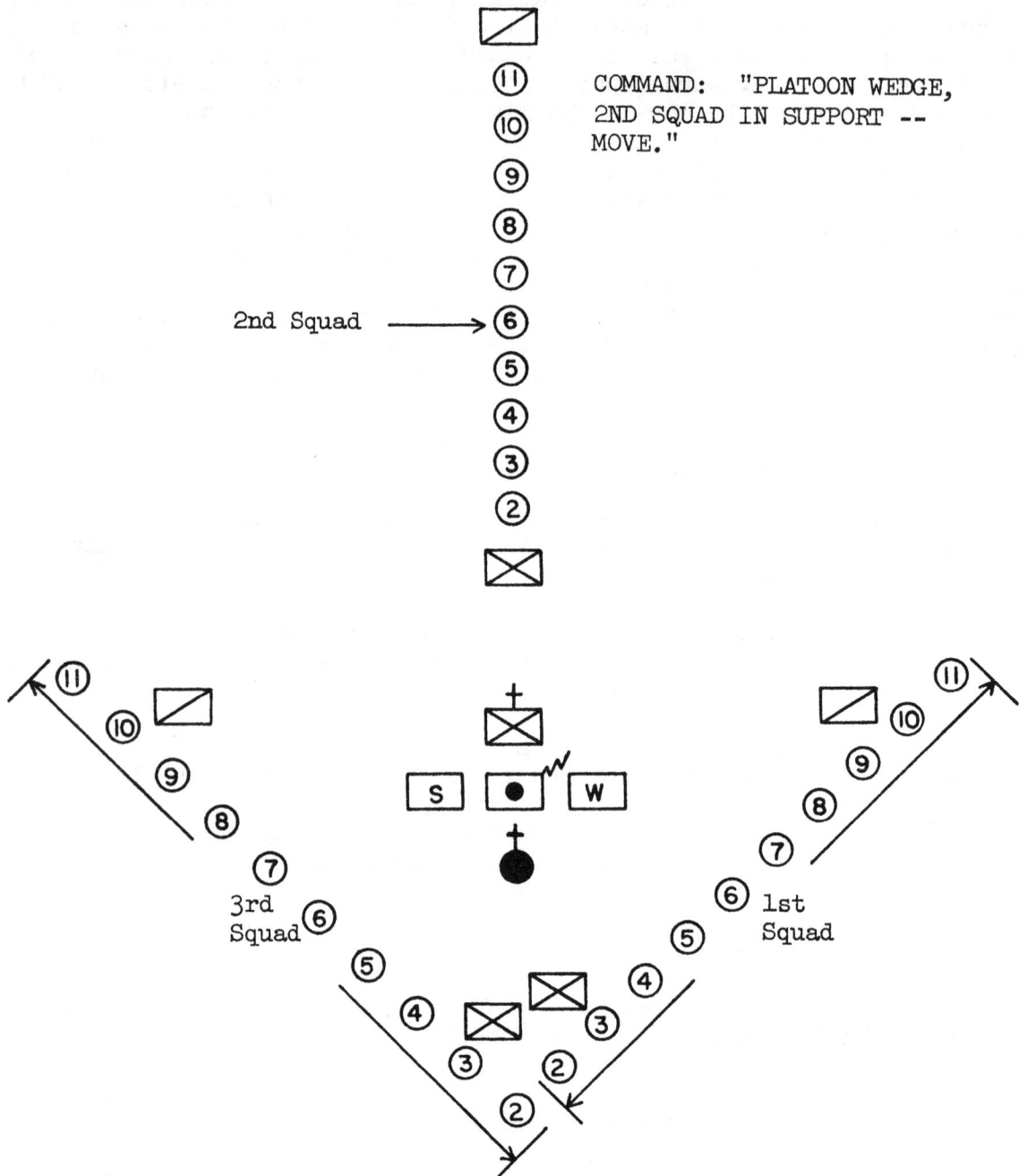

COMMAND: "PLATOON WEDGE, 2ND SQUAD IN SUPPORT -- MOVE."

2nd Squad →

3rd Squad

1st Squad

Figure 41.   Platoon wedge, one squad in support
3-squad platoon.

ST 19-180; 140

(b) Execution.

1. The 1st and 3d squads move out and establish the formation. The second squad, at the command of the squad leader, executes a column of twos to the right.

2. When the support squad is committed to either lateral support or to extend the existing formation, the even numbered men move to the right and the odd numbered men to the left. They will execute these movements in the same manner as the support squads in a four-squad platoon.

3. The squad leader will normally take control of the even numbered men and the assistant squad leader the odd numbered men. (See Figures 42 and 43.)

82. ASSEMBLY FROM FORMATIONS.

The 3-squad platoon is assembled in the same manner as the 4-squad platoon.

Even numbered men
of 2nd Squad →

Odd numbered men
← of 2nd Squad

S   ●   W

3rd
Squad

1st
Squad

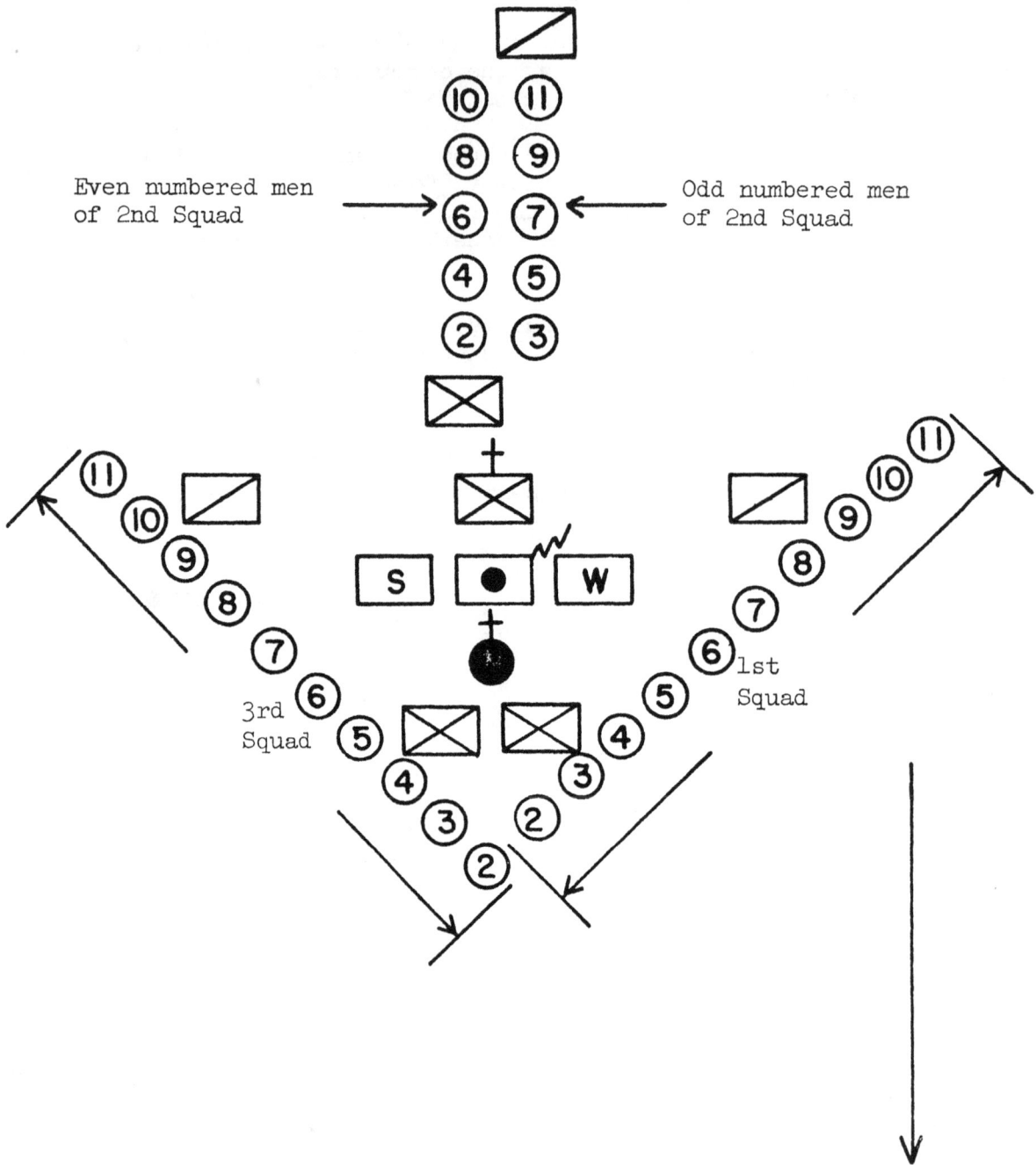

Figure 42. Platoon wedge, one squad in support in
column of two's, 3-squad platoon.

ST 19-180; 142

COMMAND: "PLATOON WEDGE, 2ND SQUAD IN LATERAL
SUPPORT -- MOVE."

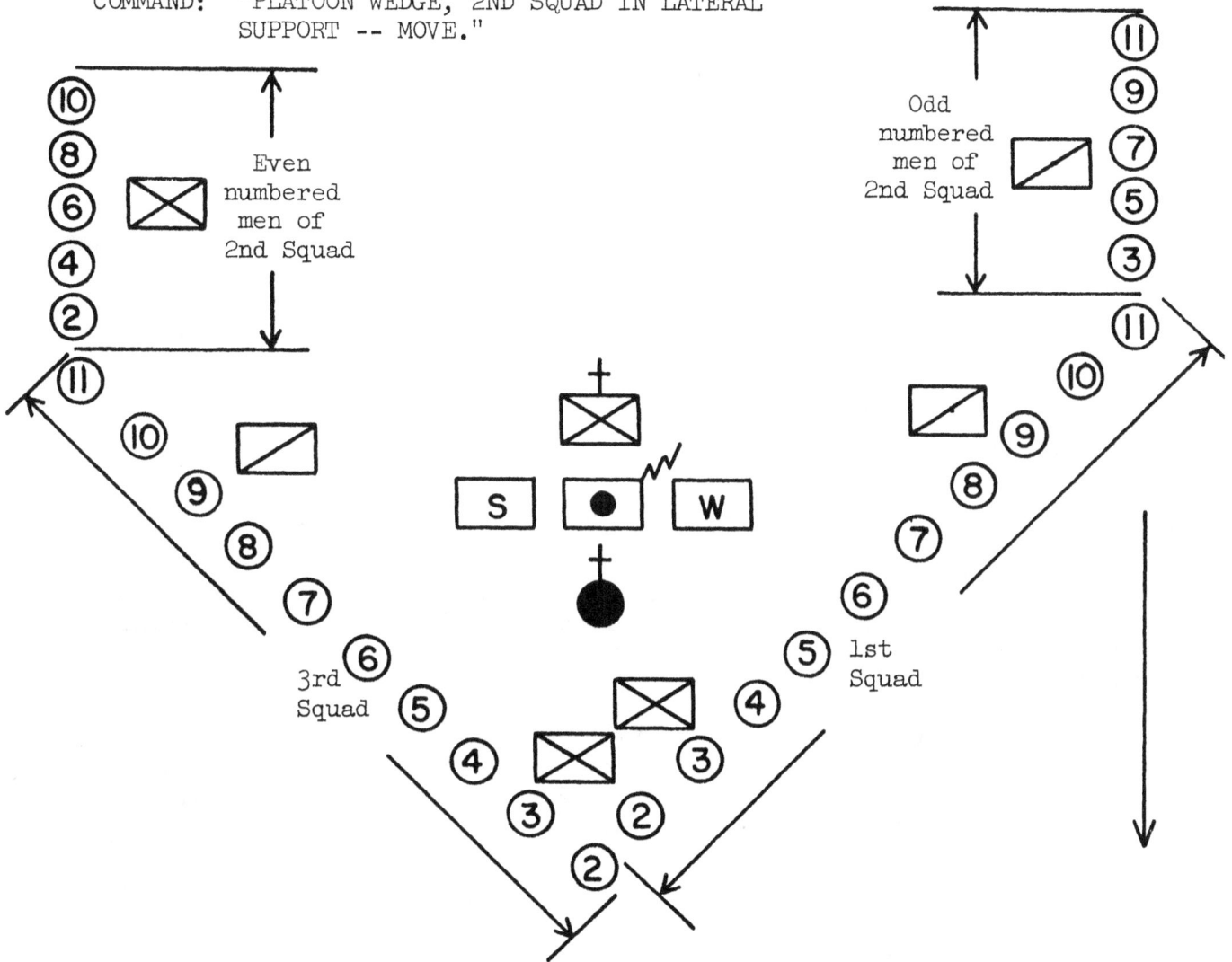

Even
numbered
men of
2nd Squad

Odd
numbered
men of
2nd Squad

S · W

3rd
Squad

1st
Squad

Figure 43. Platoon wedge, one squad in lateral support,
3-squad platoon.

Section IV

COMPANY FORMATIONS

83. GENERAL.

    a. <u>Company headquarters</u>. The company commander can use as many personnel as needed for his headquarters. He has, however, the complete resources of his platoons and will normally find it advantageous to use as few persons as possible for the company headquarters.

        (1) The following support, if possible, should be available:

           (a) Communications to maintain radio control with his, or next higher headquarters.

           (b) Transportation to keep available an adequate supply of chemical munitions.

    b. <u>Designation of location of formations</u>. When the commander orders his company into riot control formations from the column, he will move out to the left or right and near the head of the column where he can be seen by his platoon leaders and face the company. As he gives the preparatory command, he will give the appropriate arm and hand signal. On the command of execution, he will point to the approximate location at which he desires the formation formed. If he does not indicate a location, it will be assumed that the formation is to be formed immediately to the front of the leading platoon.

84. COMPANY WEDGE IN DEPTH.

    a. <u>Command</u>. "COMPANY WEDGE IN DEPTH ---- MOVE."

    b. <u>Execution</u>. Immediately following the company commander's preparatory command, each platoon leader will give the command "PLATOON WEDGE." The squad leaders will follow with their respective commands to their squads to form the platoon wedge. At the company commander's command of execution, each platoon will establish a platoon wedge immediately to its front. (See Figure 44.)

    c. Should the company commander desire a more formidable formation, he may give the command "2D PLATOON, SUPPORT THE WEDGE ---- MOVE. The men of the 2d platoon will move forward and cover the intervals between the men of the leading platoon and automatically assume the same position as the men of the leading platoon, which will normally be the "ON GUARD" position. The platoon leader of the 3d platoon will then move his platoon forward to occupy the position formerly held by the 2d platoon. (See Figure 45.)

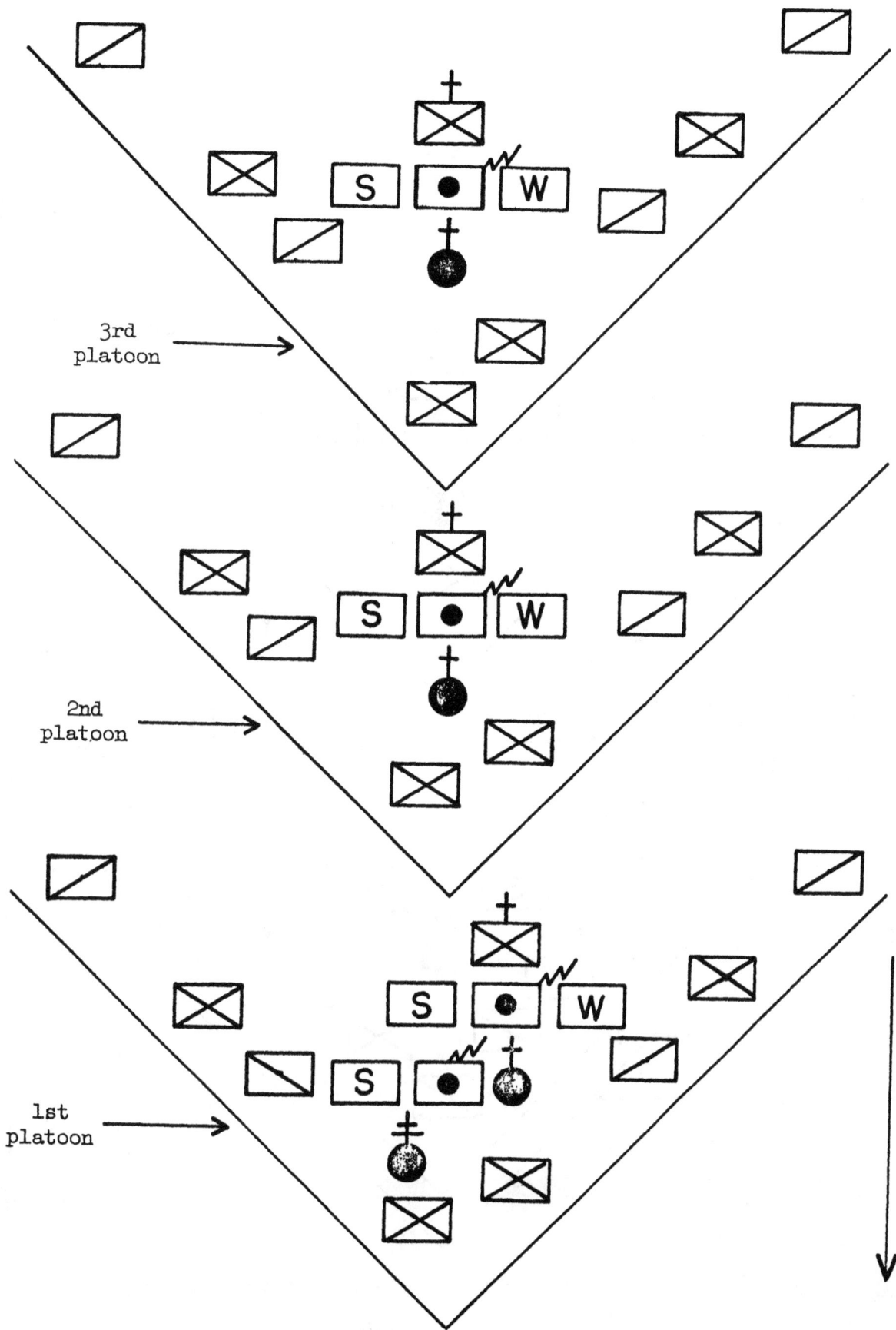

Figure 44. Company wedge formation in depth.

ST 19-180; 145

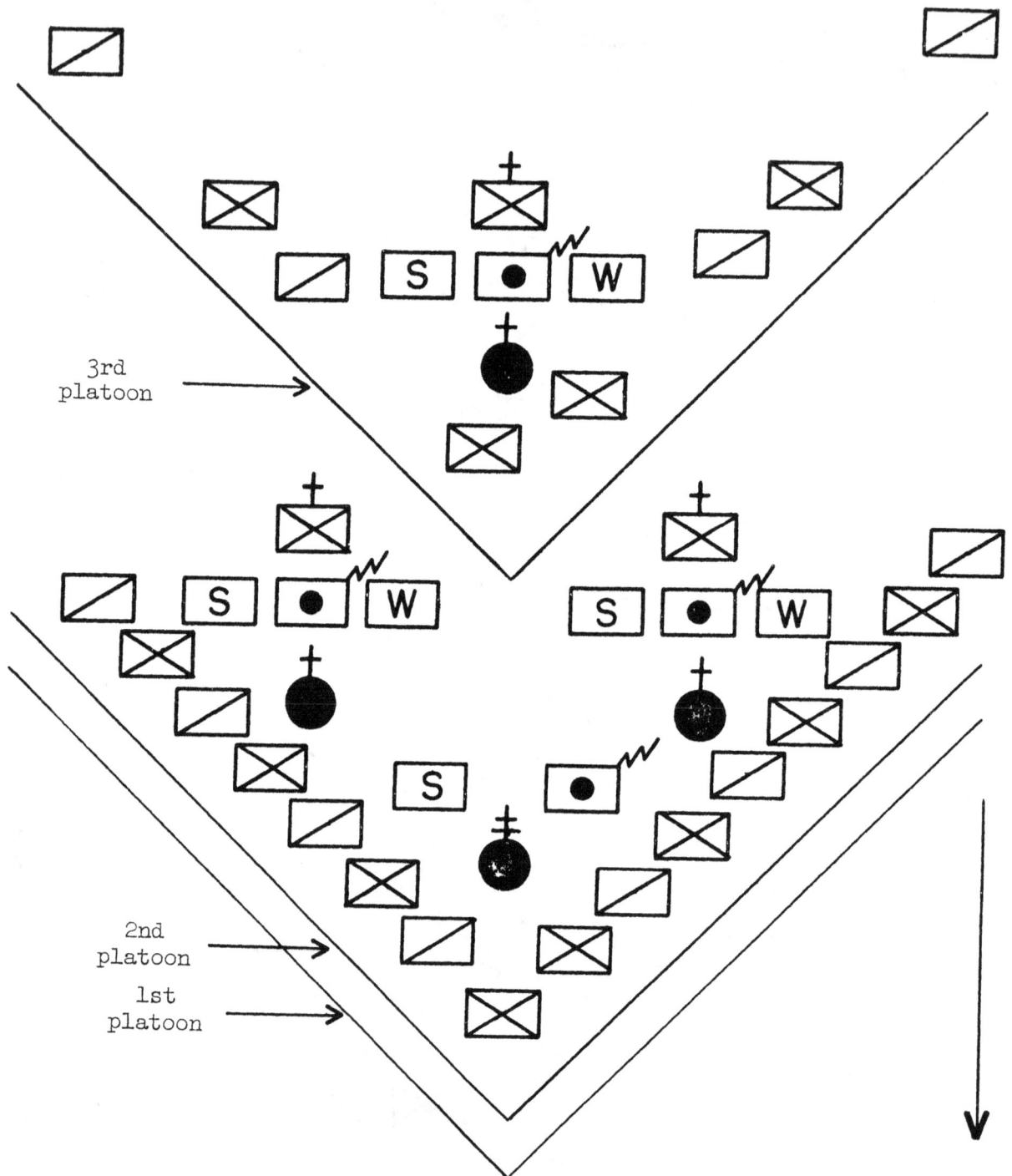

Figure 45. Company wedge in mass, 3rd platoon in depth.

ST 19-180; 146

d. If the 3d platoon is called upon to support the wedge, it will move forward and take up a position directly behind the 2d platoon. The men of the 3d platoon will remain at the "high port" position. All key personnel will step to the rear and inside the formation. Platoon and squad leaders and their assistants will mutually assist each other in controlling the unit. (See Figure 46.)

85. COMPANY WEDGE IN MASS.

a. Command. "COMPANY WEDGE IN MASS ---- MOVE."

b. Execution. The company wedge in mass is the same formation as formed above (Figure 46), with the 2d and 3d platoons supporting the 1st platoon. However, in this case, the company commander indicates his desire for this formation in his initial command. The platoons each form a wedge individually and the 2d and 3d platoons close on the 1st platoon without further command.

86. COMPANY WEDGE WITH SUPPORT.

a. In company formations, the 1st platoon will normally form the assault element, with the 2d and 3d platoons used in support. The support platoons can be employed in the same manner as the support squads in platoon formations. Several variations of a company wedge with support are illustrated in Figures 47 through 50 with appropriate commands for their execution.

b. When the company commander desires to rotate his assault platoon, he merely moves another platoon up to the head of the column prior to issuing his command for the formation to be employed. One platoon can be relieved from the assault element by another platoon while in riot control formation by merely having a support platoon pass through the assault platoon. This procedure can be used effectively when it becomes necessary to put on gas masks in preparation for the employment of chemicals.

87. COMPANY ECHELON AND LINE.

The company echelon (right or left) and company line are formed in the same manner and with the same variations as the company wedge. (See Figures 51 through 57.)

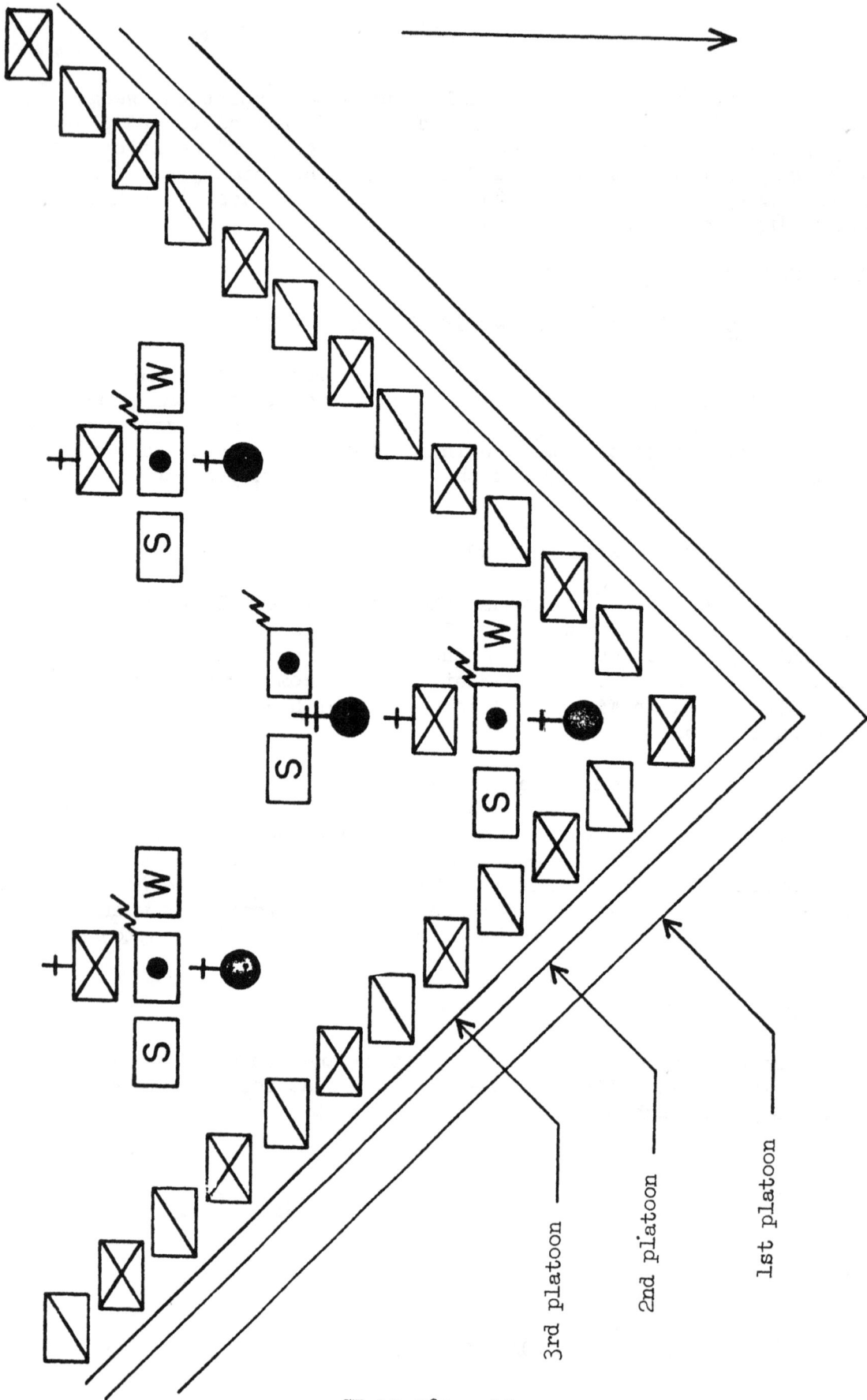

Figure 46. Company wedge in mass.

3rd platoon

2nd platoon

1st platoon

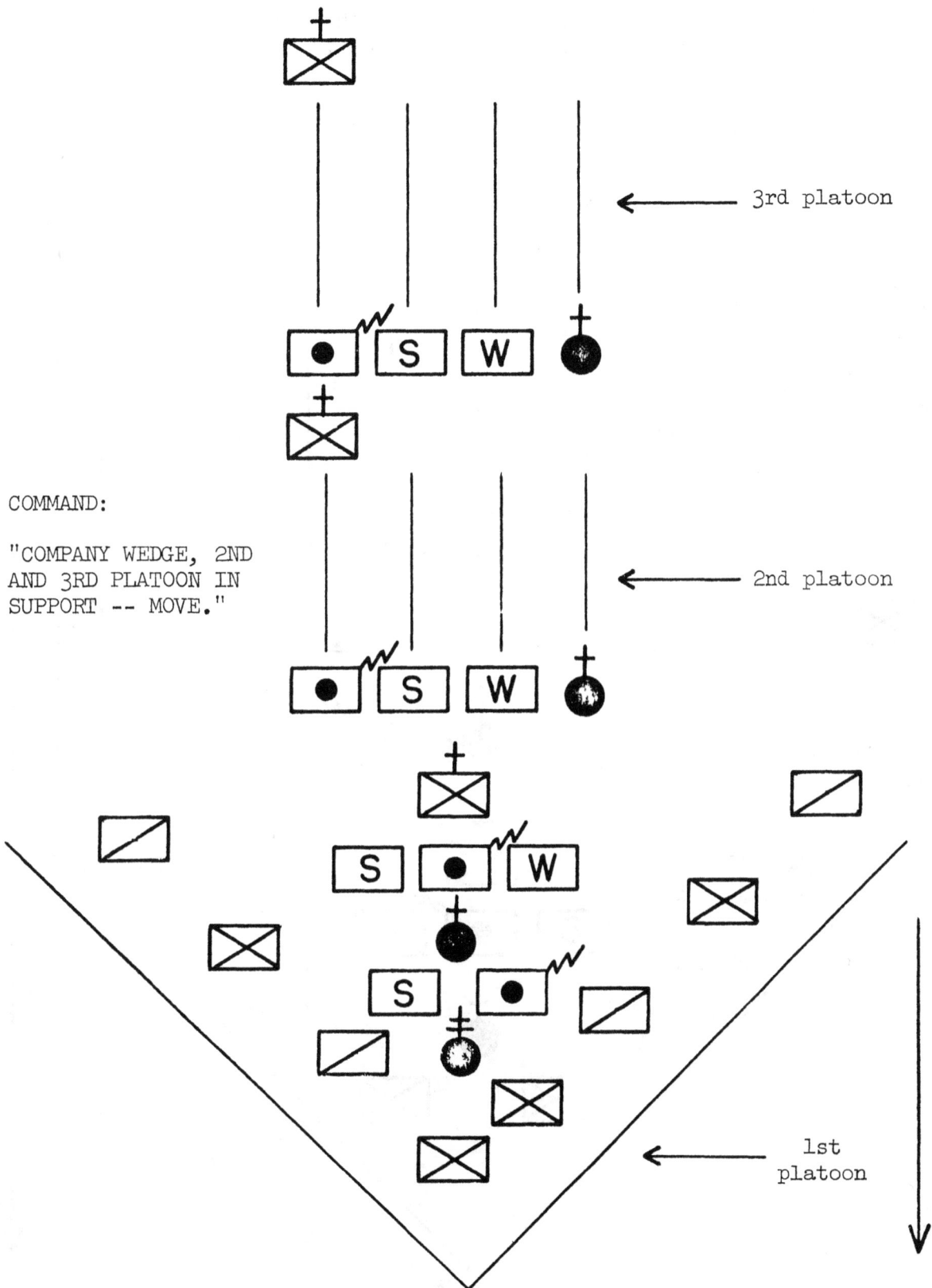

COMMAND:

"COMPANY WEDGE, 2ND AND 3RD PLATOON IN SUPPORT -- MOVE."

3rd platoon

2nd platoon

1st platoon

Figure 47.   Company wedge, two platoons in support.

ST 19-180; 149

COMMAND: "COMPANY WEDGE, 2ND PLATOON IN LATERAL SUPPORT,
          3RD PLATOON IN SUPPORT -- MOVE."

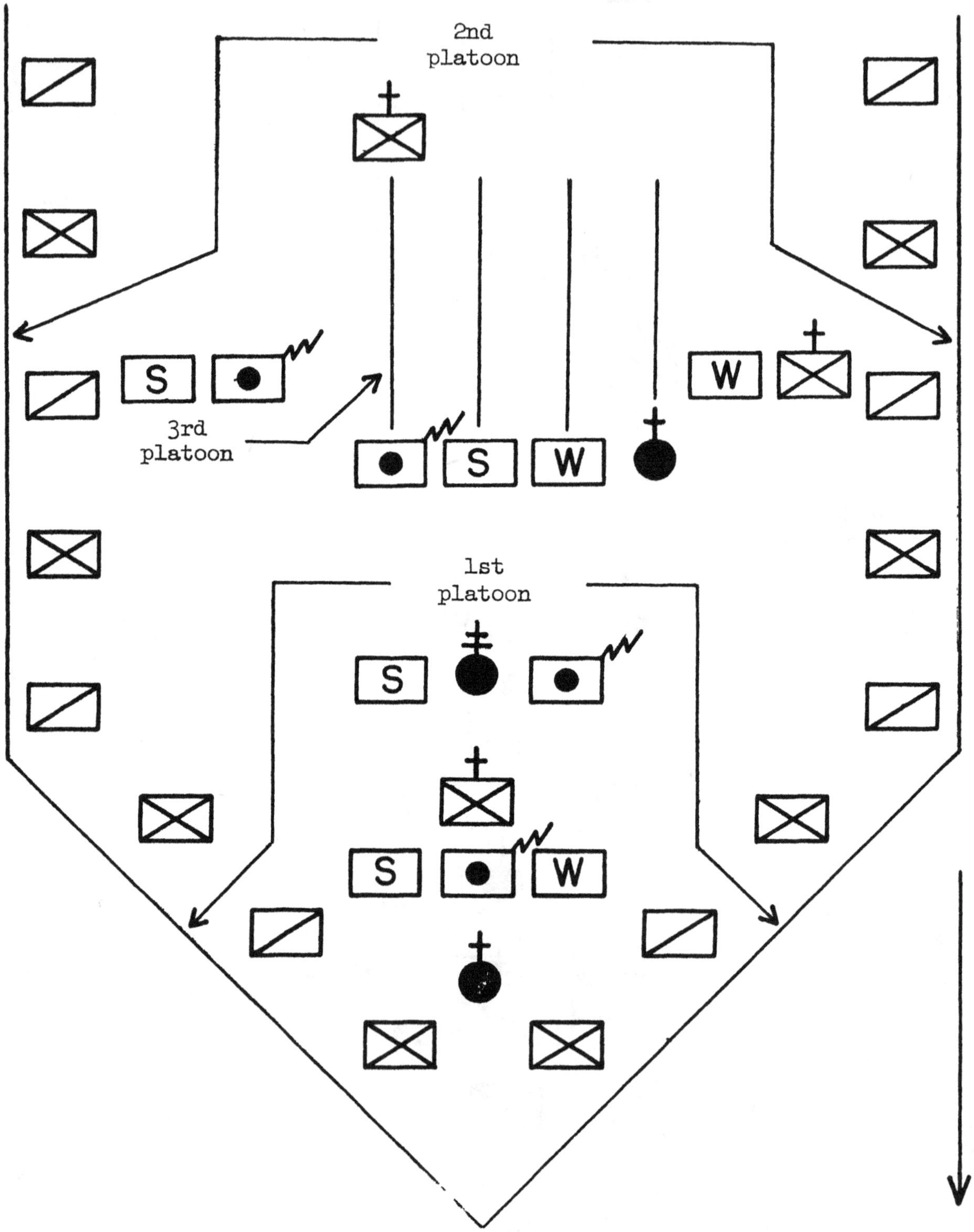

Figure 48. Company wedge, one platoon in lateral support,
            one platoon in support.

ST 19-180; 150

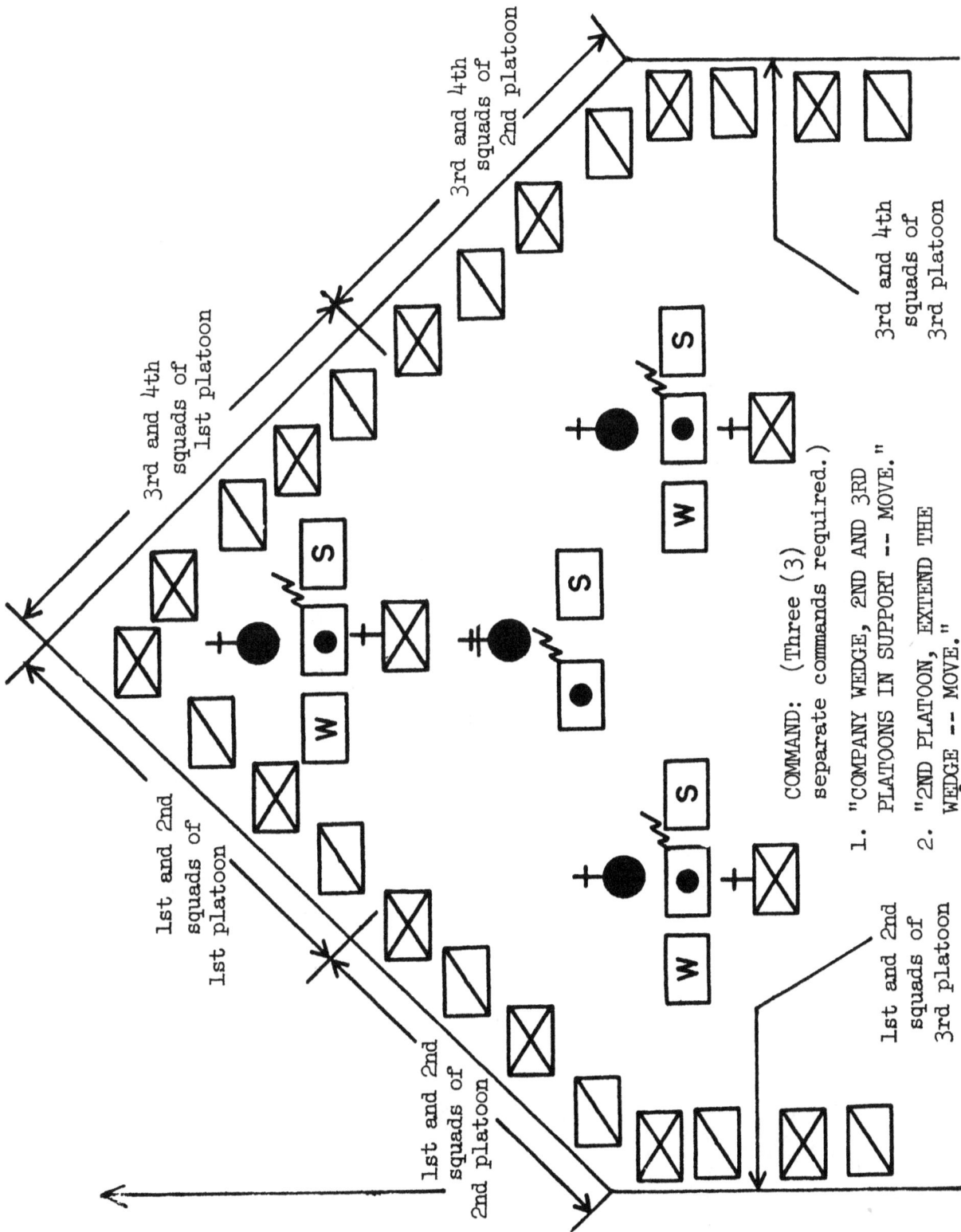

3rd and 4th squads of 2nd platoon

3rd and 4th squads of 1st platoon

3rd and 4th squads of 3rd platoon

1st and 2nd squads of 1st platoon

1st and 2nd squads of 2nd platoon

1st and 2nd squads of 3rd platoon

COMMAND: (Three (3) separate commands required.)

1. "COMPANY WEDGE, 2ND AND 3RD PLATOONS IN SUPPORT -- MOVE."

2. "2ND PLATOON, EXTEND THE WEDGE -- MOVE."

3. "3RD PLATOON, LATERAL SUPPORT -- MOVE."

Figure 49. Company wedge, one platoon in lateral support.

COMMAND: "COMPANY WEDGE IN MASS, 3RD PLATOON
IN LATERAL SUPPORT IN COLUMN OF
TWOS -- MOVE."

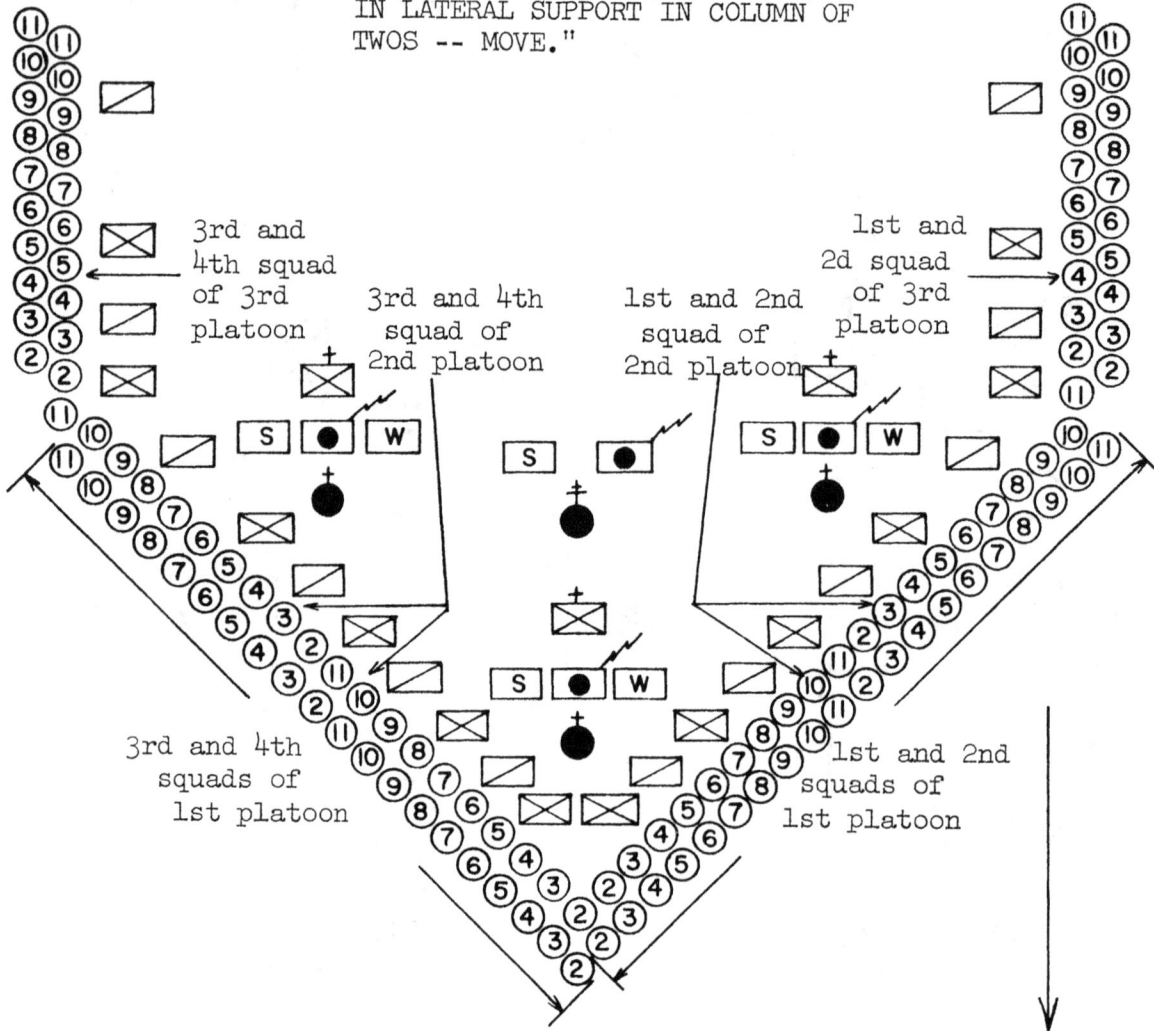

3rd and
4th squad
of 3rd
platoon

3rd and 4th
squad of
2nd platoon

1st and 2nd
squad of
2nd platoon

1st and
2d squad
of 3rd
platoon

3rd and 4th
squads of
1st platoon

1st and 2nd
squads of
1st platoon

Figure 50. Company wedge in mass, one platoon in lateral
support in column of twos.

COMMANS:

"COMPANY ECHELON
LEFT, 2ND PLATOON
IN LATERAL SUPPORT,
3RD PLATOON IN SUP-
PORT -- MOVE."

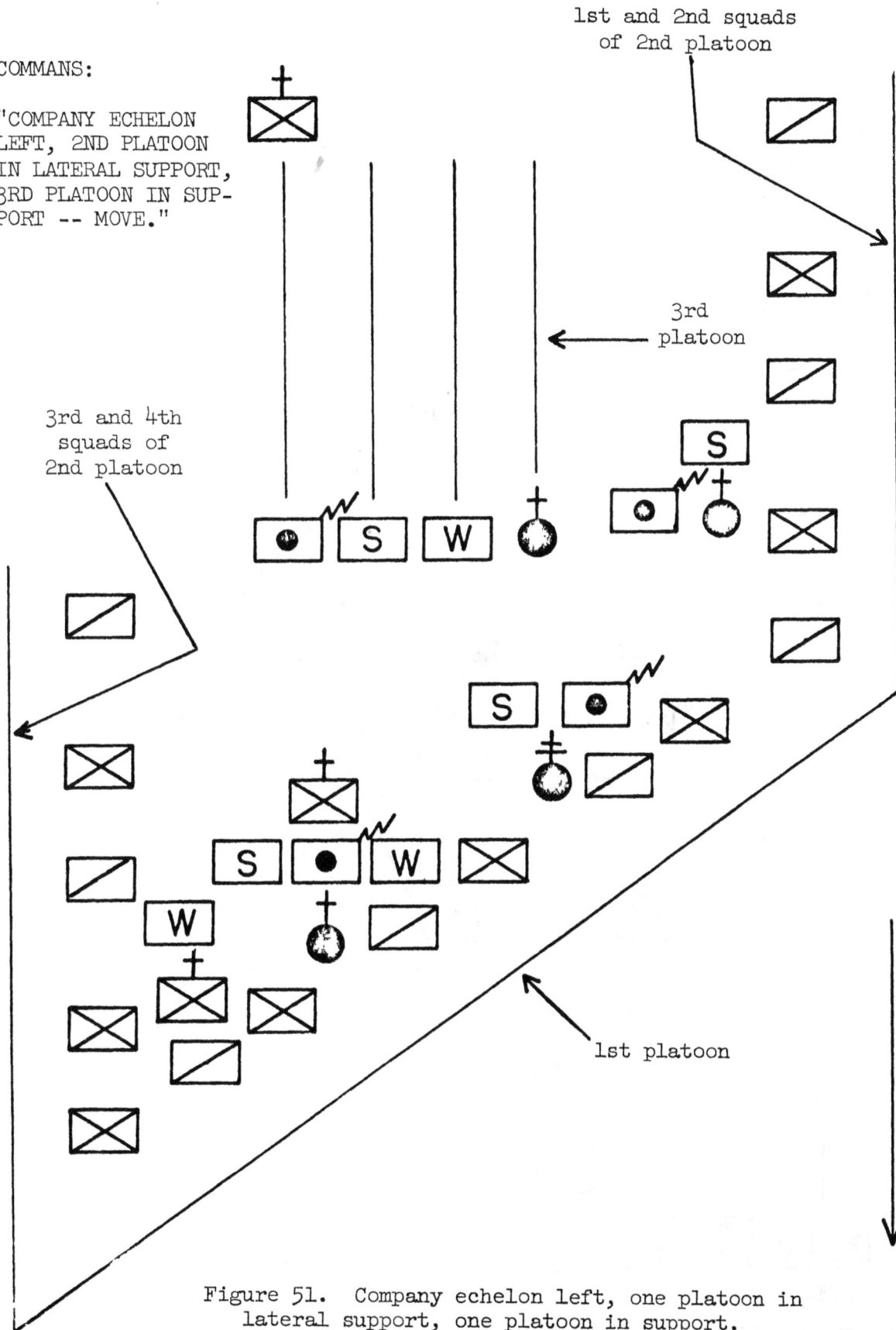

1st and 2nd squads
of 2nd platoon

3rd and 4th
squads of
2nd platoon

3rd
platoon

1st platoon

Figure 51.   Company echelon left, one platoon in
lateral support, one platoon in support.

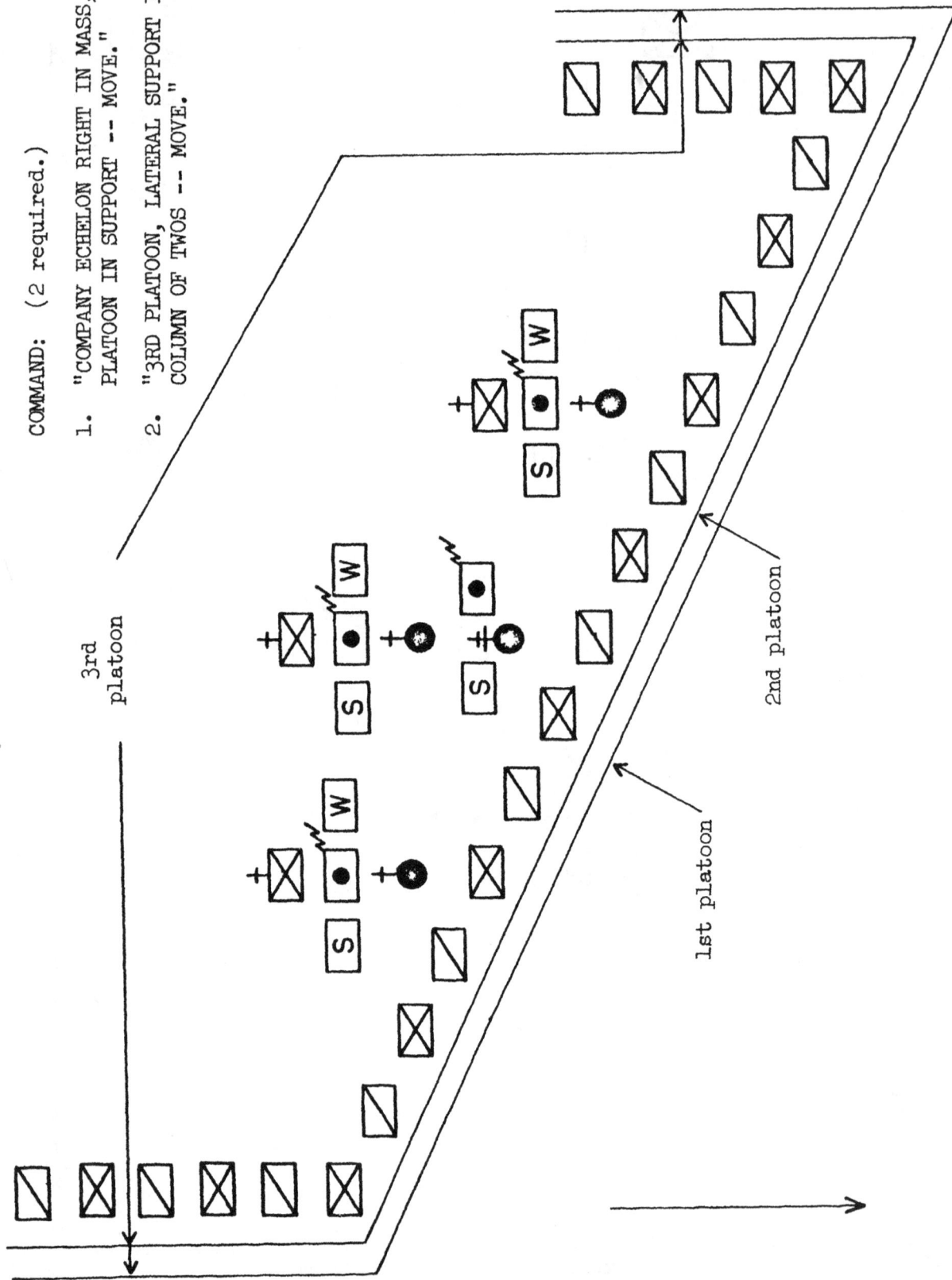

COMMAND: (2 required.)

1. "COMPANY ECHELON RIGHT IN MASS, 3RD PLATOON IN SUPPORT -- MOVE."

2. "3RD PLATOON, LATERAL SUPPORT IN COLUMN OF TWOS -- MOVE."

Figure 52. Company echelon right in mass, one platoon in lateral support in column of twos.

3rd platoon

COMMAND:

"COMPANY ECHELON LEFT
IN DEPTH, 3RD PLATOON
IN SUPPORT -- MOVE."

2nd platoon

1st
platoon

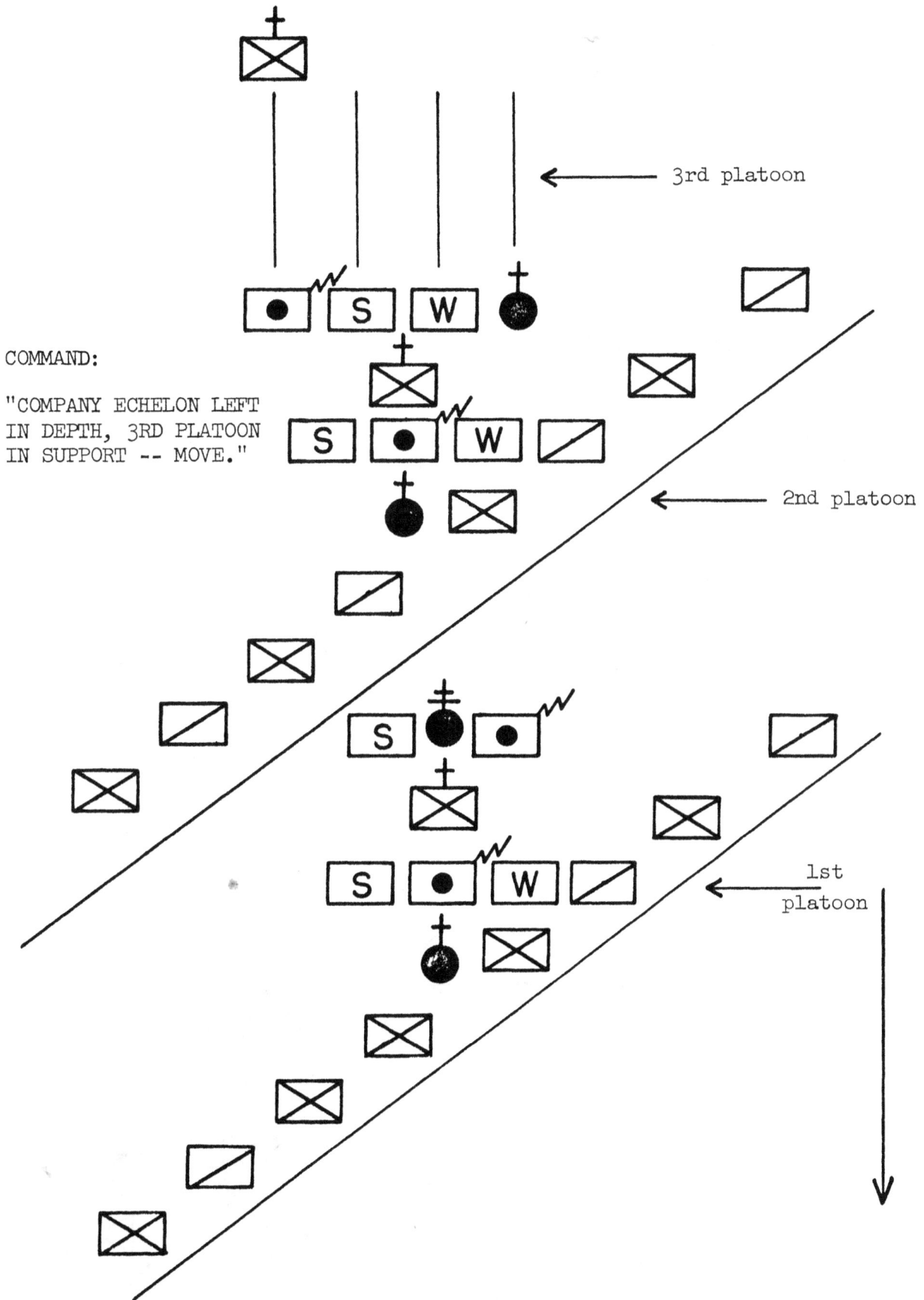

Figure 53. Company echelon left in depth,
one platoon in support.

ST 19-180; 155

COMMAND: "COMPANY ECHELON
RIGHT IN MASS, 3RD PLATOON
IN SUPPORT -- MOVE."

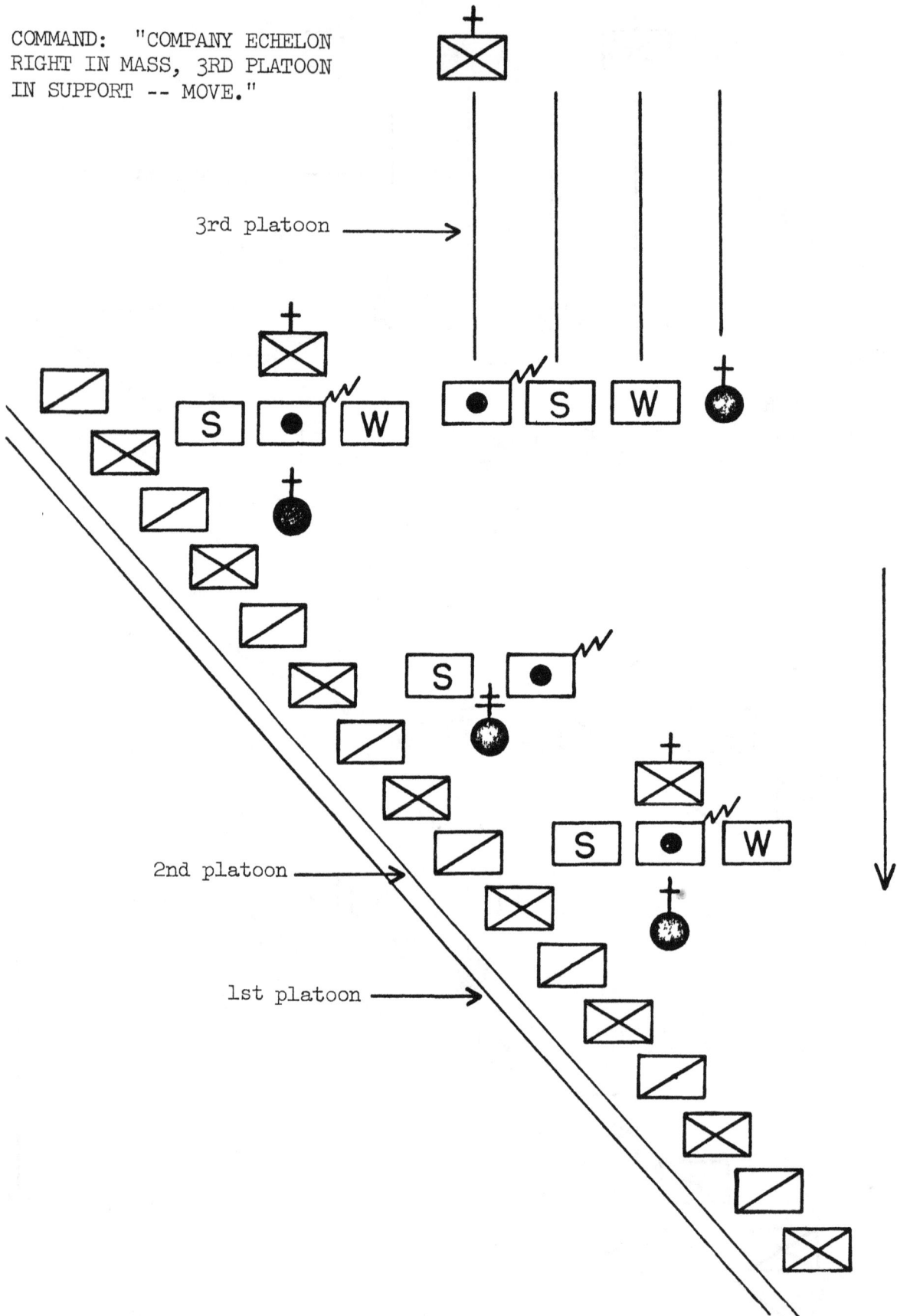

3rd platoon

S ● W

● S W

2nd platoon

S ● W

S ●

1st platoon

Figure 54. Company echelon right in mass,
one platoon in support.

ST 19-180; 156

COMMAND:

"COMPANY AS SKIRMISHERS, 2ND PLATOON IN LATERAL SUPPORT, 3RD
PLATOON IN SUPPORT -- MOVE."

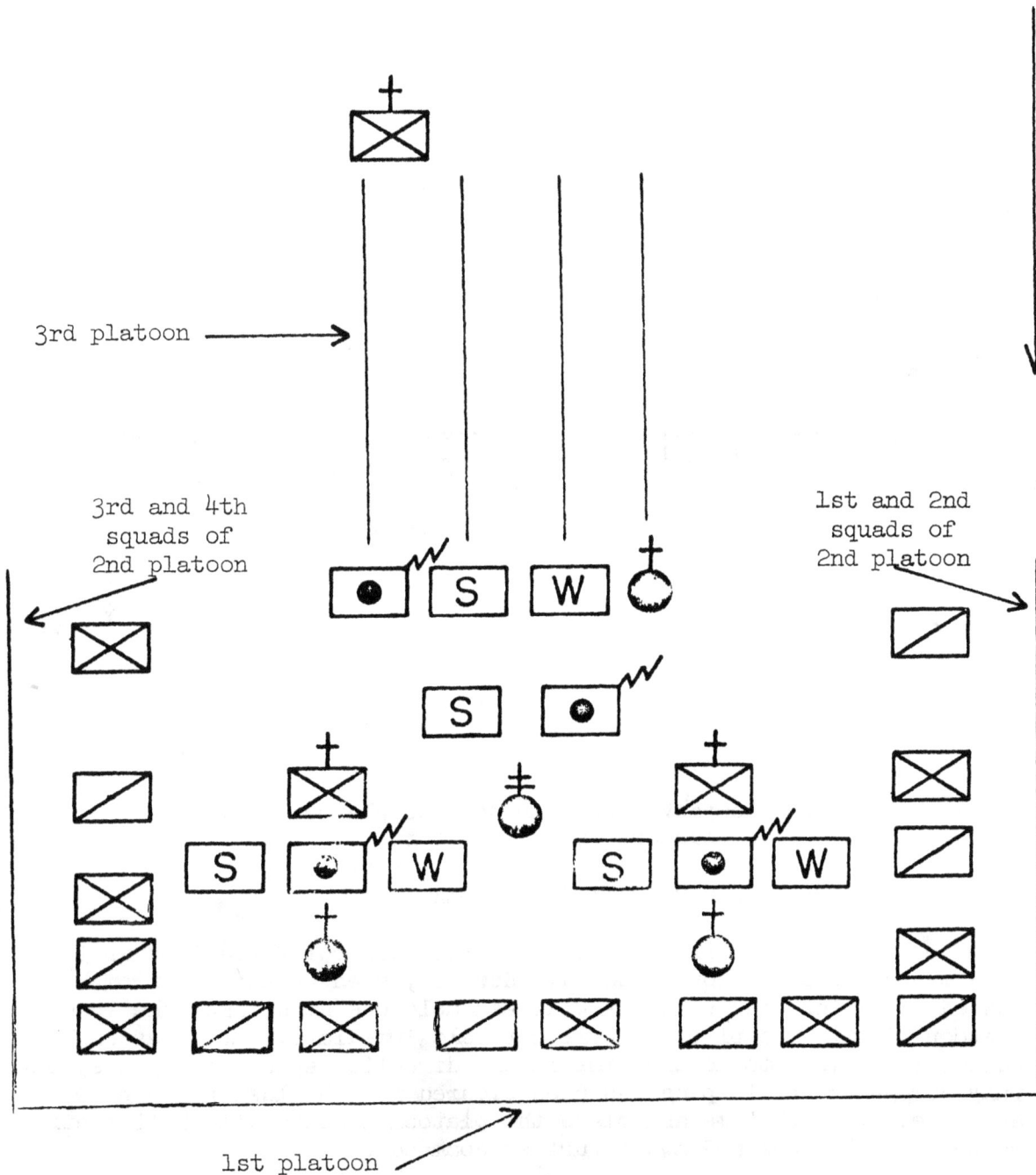

3rd platoon

3rd and 4th
squads of
2nd platoon

1st and 2nd
squads of
2nd platoon

1st platoon

Figure 55. Company line, one platoon in lateral support,
one platoon in support.

ST 19-180; 157

COMMAND: "COMPANY AS SKIRMISHERS IN MASS, 3RD PLATOON IN LATERAL
SUPPORT IN COLUMN OF TWOS ---- MOVE."

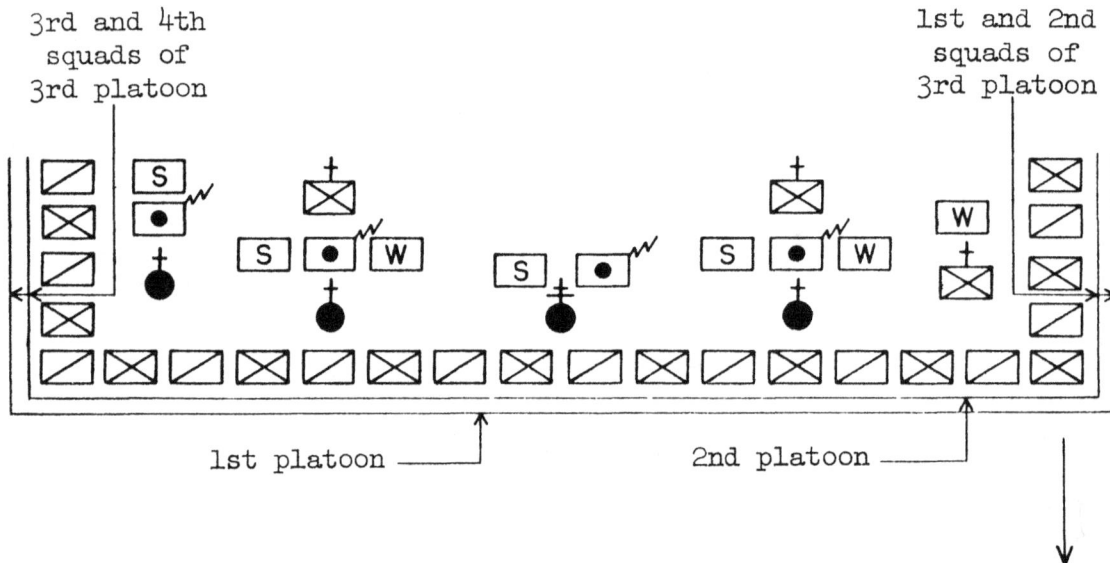

Figure 56. Company line in mass, one platoon in lateral
support in column of twos.

88. ASSEMBLY FROM COMPANY FORMATIONS.

A company will assemble from riot control formations in the
same manner as a platoon or squad. However, when assembling from a
massed formation, the platoons will assemble one at a time, the leading
platoon first. The platoons will not halt immediately after assembling,
but will continue to double time in the direction specified by the company commander until space has been cleared for the last platoon to
assemble, at which time and place the platoon leaders will halt their
respective platoons and await further commands.

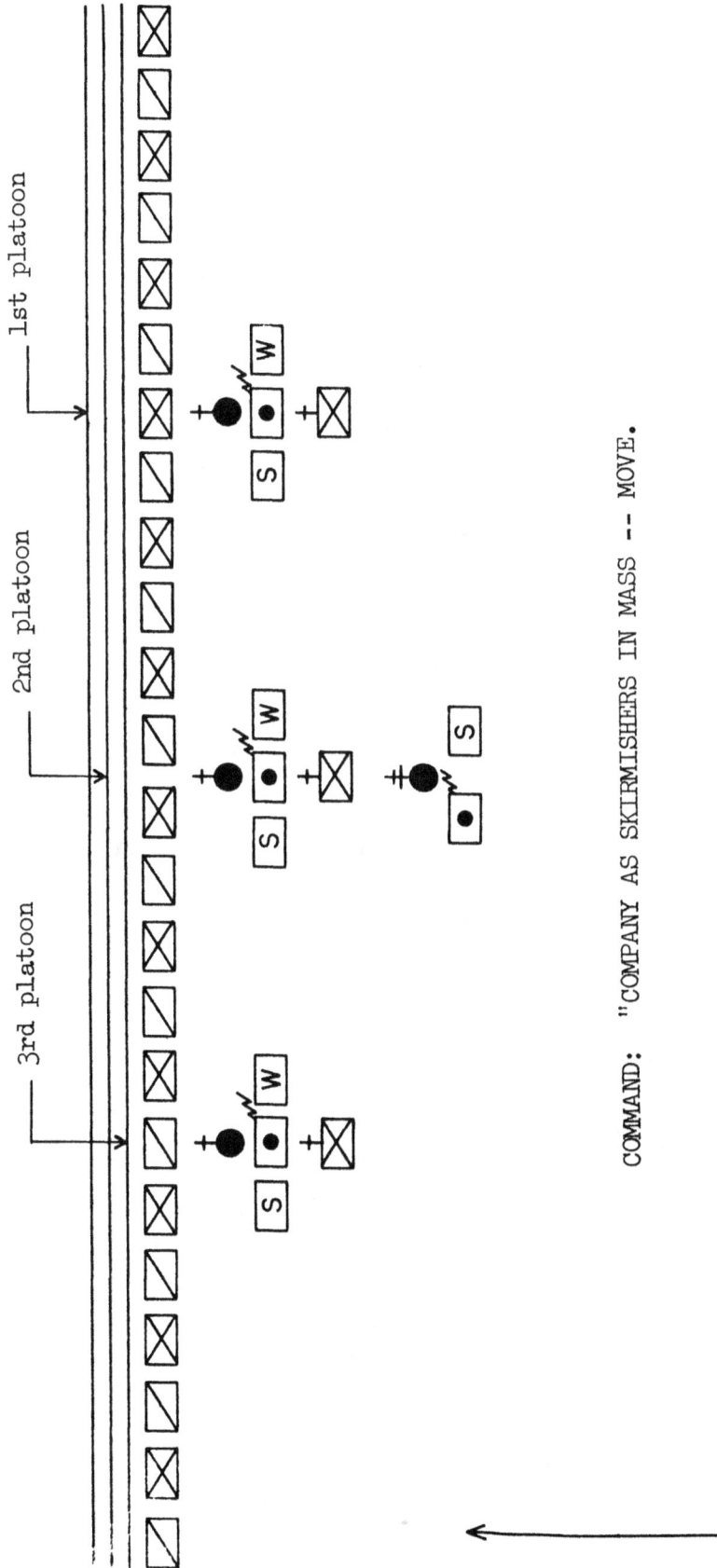

COMMAND: "COMPANY AS SKIRMISHERS IN MASS -- MOVE.

Figure 57. Company line in mass.

Section V

VEHICLES AND POLICE FORMATIONS

89. GENERAL.

a. Employment of vehicles. In meeting crowds and mobs on a large scale, it may be advantageous to employ vehicles with police in riot control formations. By using vehicles, we gain three distinct advantages over the crowd or mob--mobility, fire power, and shock action. While vehicles add strength to any formation, they have certain vulnerable characteristics that cannot be overlooked. A formation with vehicles is executed from the column when possible. (See Figure 58.)

(1) Vulnerable characteristics.

(a) Tracked vehicles can be disabled by jamming iron bars and similar weapons in the "bogie wheels."

(b) Tires of wheeled vehicles can be punctured or slashed with pointed or sharp instruments.

(c) Headlights and windshields can easily be smashed and radiators punctured with numerous weapons.

(d) Brake and fuel lines can be cut or broken with numerous weapons.

(e) Open or unguarded areas on vehicles can be attacked with homemade bombs, stones, "molotov cocktails," and other missiles.

(2) Precautionary measures.

(a) Windshields of vehicles should be removed or completely depressed to horizontal position.

(b) Shields or mobile barriers can be constructed of wooden or metal frame strung with barbed wire and mounted across the front of vehicle.

(c) Police in the formation should be pressed tightly against the front corners of each vehicle to prevent rioters from attacking the sides and rear of the vehicles.

b. Armored vehicles. These should be employed when available and practical because of their much greater psychological effect as well as the greater protection they will afford the occupants.

ST 19-180; 160

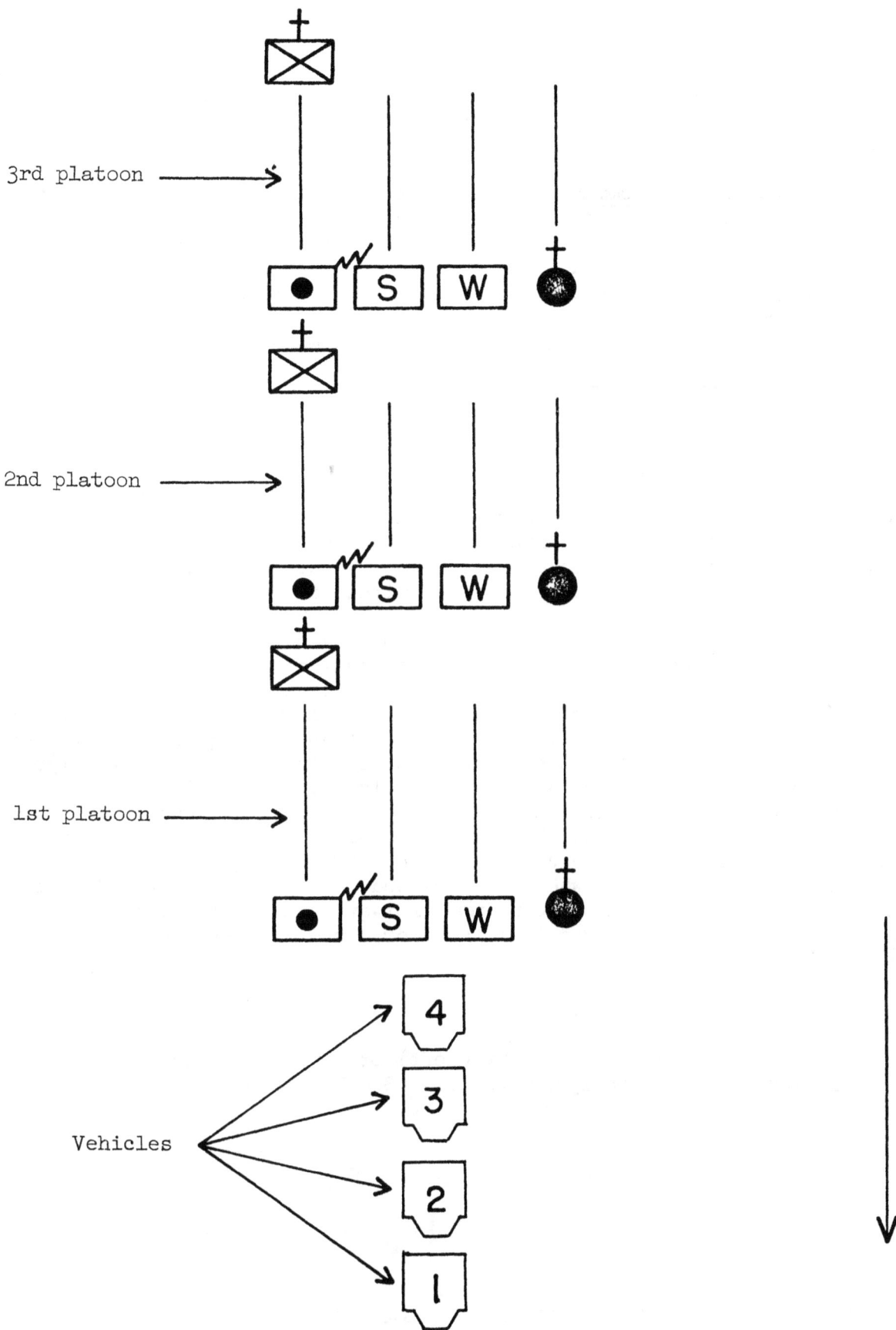

Figure 58. Company column, with motor vehicles.

ST 19-180; 161

c. <u>Protection</u>. Vehicles should always be used in conjunction with foot troops--never alone. They should be employed only over terrain for which they are suited.

d. <u>Police commander</u>. Whenever a combination of vehicles and police are employed, the commander of the police will command the unit. He will join the leader of the motor section in the command vehicle. From this position he has a position of vantage and can survey the situation and direct the disposition of police and vehicles by radio, oral commands and hand and arm signals. In every instance, however, the commands are executed through the subordinate leaders.

90. COMPANY WEDGE WITH SUPPORT.

a. <u>Command</u>. The same commands are used as in the case of foot troops alone. In addition, because of the increased noise and distances involved, the company commander from his position in the lead vehicle will give the arm and hand signal for the wedge. Because of the rather complicated maneuver involved, the command and/or signal will be construed to apply to the lead platoon only. The other platoons will remain in general support until further directed. (See Figure 59.)

b. <u>Execution</u>. The motor section moves out first. The number two vehicle, driving to the right, passes the lead vehicle and establishes the position designated for the point of the wedge. At the same time, the 3d and 4th vehicles swing out to the left and right respectively and form a wedge with the number two vehicle. The 1st and 4th squads form respectively on the front end of the number two vehicle. As soon as the troops are in position, the 3d and 4th vehicles close in on the left and right and tighten the formation. The 2d and 3d squads of the lead platoon will then form left and right echelons respectively on the 3d and 4th vehicles to complete the wedge. The command vehicle (Number 1) will take up a position inside the wedge where the commander can best direct and control the unit. The 2d and 3d platoons move forward and remain in general support or they can be employed in lateral or close support. (See Figures 60 and 61.)

91. ECHELON AND LINE.

To form an echelon right (left) or line, the same procedure is followed as when forming the wedge. (See Figure 62.)

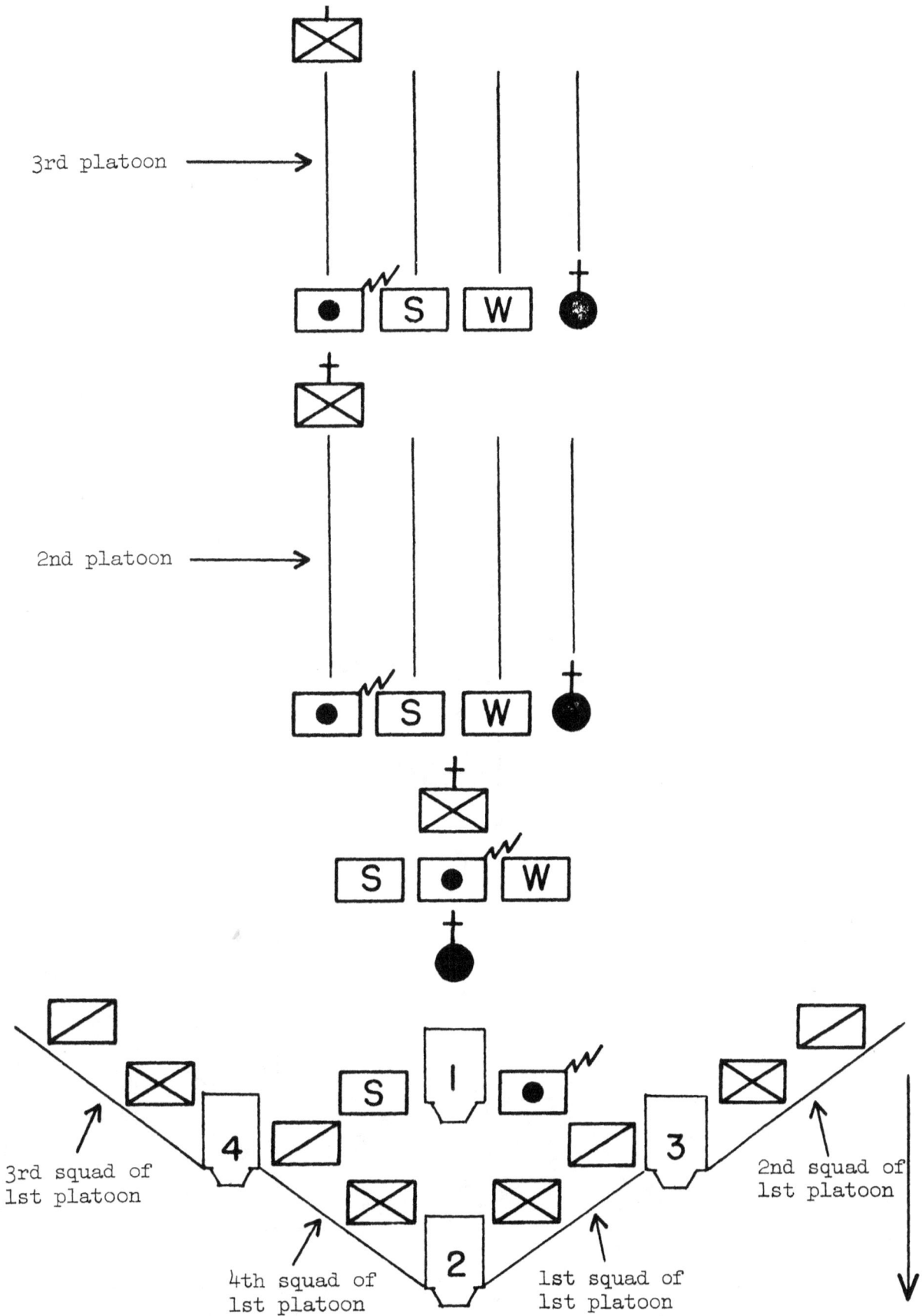

3rd platoon

2nd platoon

3rd squad of
1st platoon

4th squad of
1st platoon

1st squad of
1st platoon

2nd squad of
1st platoon

Figure 59. Company wedge formation, two platoons in
support (with motor vehicles).

ST 19-180; 163

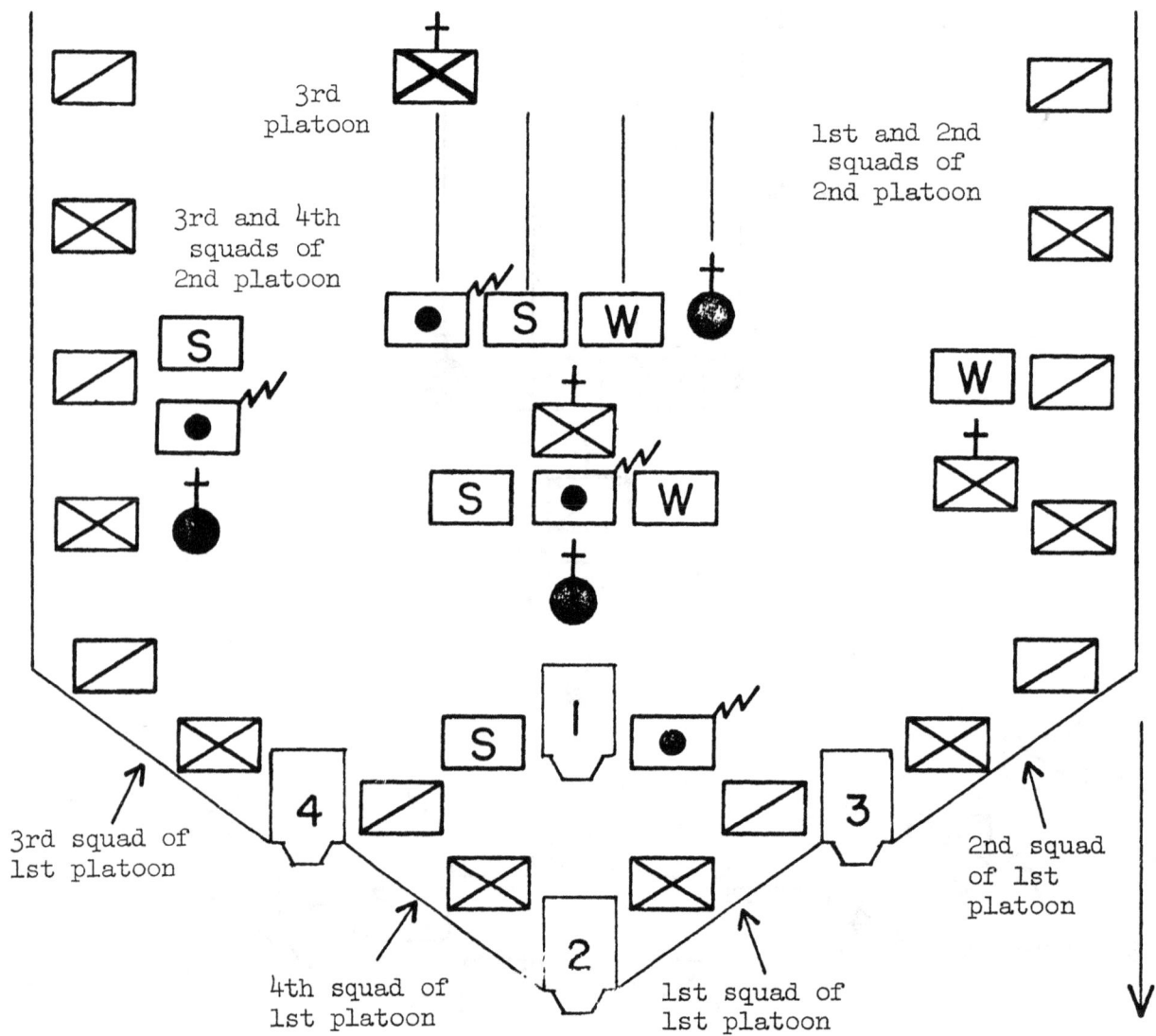

Figure 60. Company wedge formation, 2nd platoon in lateral
support, 3rd platoon in support (with motor vehicles).

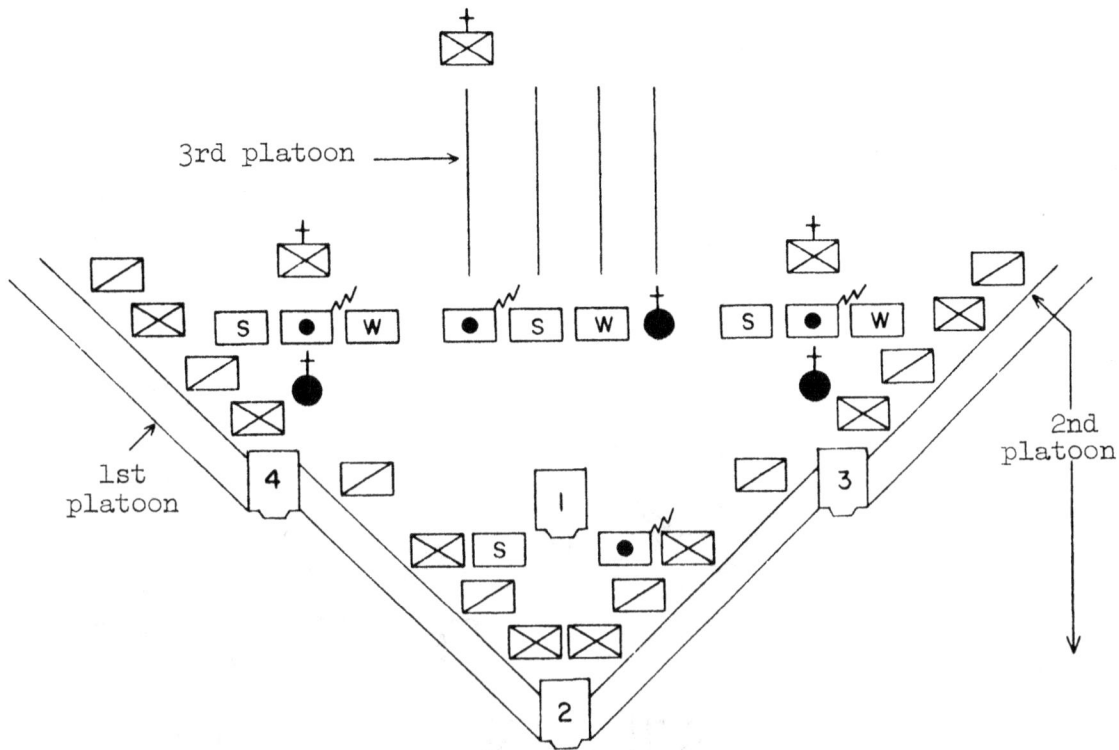

Figure 61.   Company wedge in mass, 3rd platoon in support
(with motor vehicles).

92.   ASSEMBLY FROM FORMATION.

The command vehicle moves forward through the formation and
upon taking up a position in advance of the formation, the commander,
facing the formation, gives the motor section the hand signal for assembly.   Immediately, the other vehicles break away and return to their
proper positions in column behind the lead vehicle, while the troops
stand fast.   The second in command will then assemble the foot troops
in the usual manner.

93.   VARIATIONS OF FORMATION.

Many suitable variations to the formations described and illus
trated above may be employed and appropriate commands and signals can be
devised to execute them.   However, because of the somewhat complicated
nature and coordination required in these formations, new variations
should be practiced extensively, if possible, before they are used in
actual riot situations.

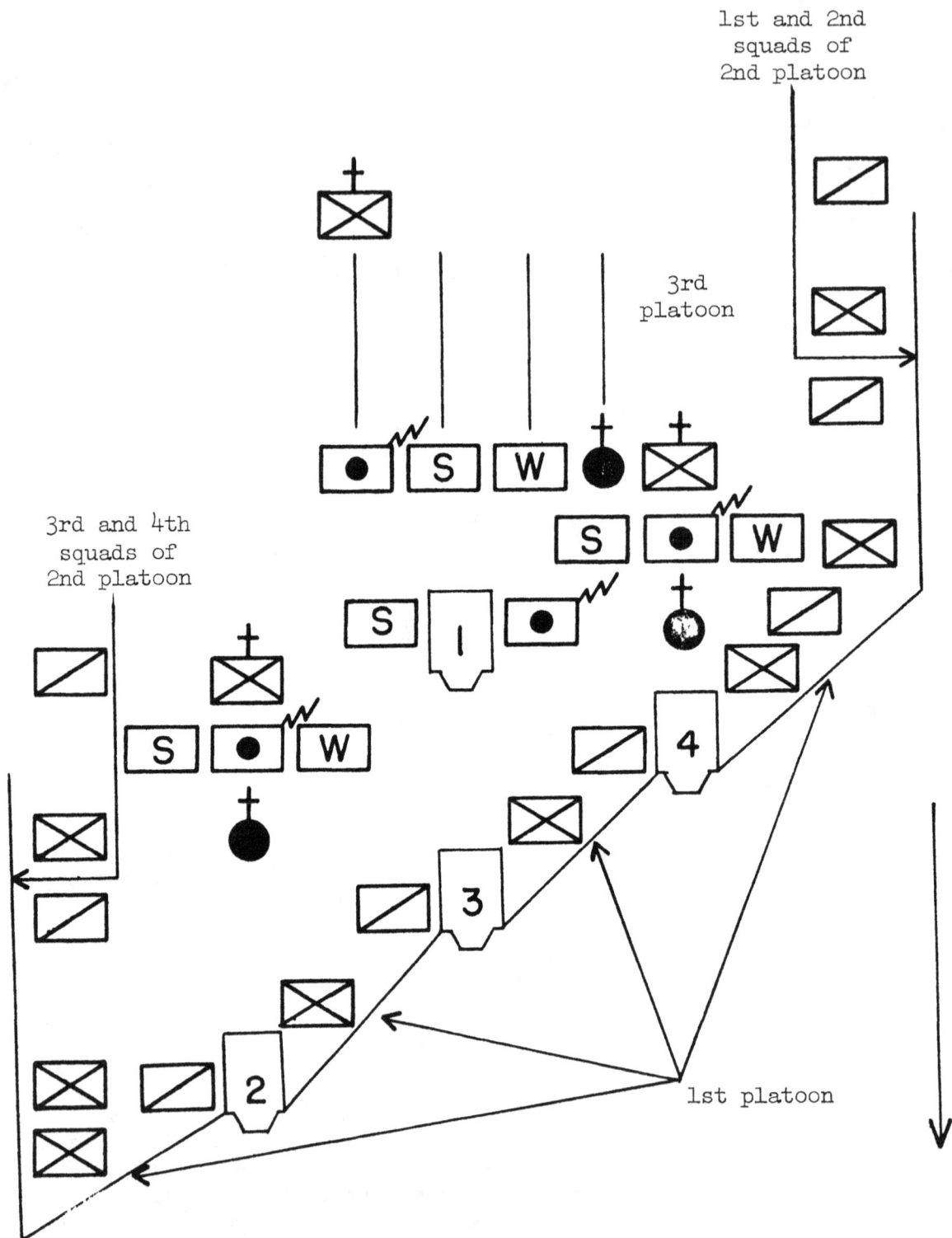

Figure 62. Company echelon left, 2nd platoon in lateral support,
3rd platoons in support (with motor vehicles).

ST 19-180; 166

CHAPTER 10

USE OF RIOT CONTROL AGENTS

Section I

USE OF RIOT CONTROL AGENTS IN CONTROLLING CIVIL DISORDERS

94.   INTRODUCTION.

Riot control agents provide the commander of a committed police unit with a distinct advantage in combatting civil disorder. Riot control agents are the most effective means of achieving temporary neutralization of a mob commensurate with the requirement of minimum permanent injury. Effective employment of riot control agents limits unnecessary casualties among police forces. The task of police in civil disorders is to restore order with the minimum amount of force necessary. This chapter will discuss the types, characteristics, and tactical employment of munitions used in the control of riotous situations.

95.   IMPORTANCE OF RIOT CONTROL AGENTS.

Riot control agents are important weapons when effectively employed. The advantages obtained through their proper utilization include those indicated below:

a.   They are capable of producing an immediate effect on a mob.

b.   They are effective over widespread areas.

c.   They achieve the largest percentage of temporary incapacitation with the least amount of injury.

d.   They facilitate economy of force.

96.   CHARACTERISTICS OF RIOT CONTROL AGENTS.

a.   Nonpersistent agents. Nonpersistent agents remain effective in the open for a period of ten minutes or less at the point of release.

b.   Persistent agents. Persistent agents remain effective in the open for a period exceeding ten minutes at the point of release.

c.   Use in riot control. Riot control agents suitable for use in riot control operations include tear gas (CN), a more severe tear agent (CS), Adamsite, a vomiting agent (DM), and CN-DM combination. CS is not found in combination with other agents; however, it may be employed with other separate munitions. Although CN, CS, and DM are classified as non lethal, they must be employed with caution due to their psychological effects on individuals. DM (Adamsite) munitions are toxic and should not be used in closed areas or in mechanical dispersers. DM, either singly or in combination with another agent will poison open food and water supplies. The micropulverized powdered form of this agent is particularly dangerous. A type of smoke referred to as HC is commonly used in civil disorders.

97. TYPES OF MUNITIONS USED IN CIVIL DISTURBANCES.

    a. <u>Smoke pot, HC M1.</u> (See Figure 63a.)

      (1) Weight of complete munition - 12 lbs.

      (2) Time of functioning - 5-8 minutes.

      (3) Persistency in open - variable according to wind, maximum ten minutes.

      (4) Minimum protection - none needed.

      (5) Physiological action - negligible.

      (6) First aid - none.

      (7) In closed areas - can be dangerous.

    b. <u>Smoke pot, HC M5.</u> (See Figure 63b.)

      (1) Weight of complete munition - 33 lbs.

Figure 63a.
Smoke pot, HC M-1.

      (2) Time of functioning - 12-22 minutes.

      (3) Persistency in the open - variable according to the wind conditions, maximum ten minutes.

      (4) Minimum protection - none needed.

(5) Physiological action -
negligible.

(6) First aid - none.

(7) In closed areas -
can be dangerous.

c. Grenade, Hand Smoke, HC,
AN-M8. (See Figure 64a.)

(1) Weight of complete
munition - 25.5 oz.

(2) Time of functioning -
2-2½ minutes.

(3) Persistency in open -
variable according to wind conditions,
maximum ten minutes.

(4) Physiological ac-
tion - negligible.

(5) First aid - none.

(6) Minimum protection - none necessary.

d. Grenade, hand, riot, CN, M7A1 (CN, M7).

(1) Weight of complete munition - 19.02 oz.

(2) Time of functioning - 20-60 seconds.

(3) Persistency in open - maximum ten minutes.

(4) Minimum protection - gas mask; tight fiting goggles
offer limited protection to eyes.

(5) Physiological action - lacrimation, mild skin itch-
ing.

(6) First aid - flush eyes with water. If available,
use boric acid or sodium sulfite (1/4% solution). Keep eyes open and
face into direction of uncontaminated wind.

(7) Time for maximum effect - immediate.

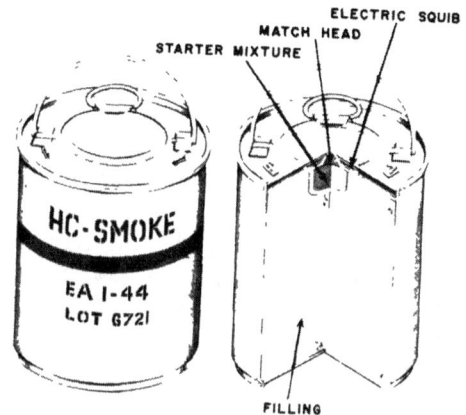

Figure 63b.
Smoke pot, HC M5.

e. <u>Grenade, hand, riot, CS, M7A2 (CS M7A1)</u>. (See Figure 64b.)

    (1) Weight of complete munition - 19 oz.

    (2) Time of functioning - 15-35 seconds.

    (3) Persistency in open - variable according to wind conditions.

    (4) Minimum protection - protective mask; field clothing.

    (5) Physiological action - extreme burning sensation of the eyes; copious flow of tears; coughing; difficult breathing and chest tightness; involuntary closing of the eyes; stinging action on moist skin areas; concentrations (via ingestion) produce nausea and vomiting.

    (6) First aid treatment - remove to uncontaminated air; face into wind; caution against rubbing eyes; keep affected persons well spaced; shower after 6 hours.

    (7) Time for maximum effect - 20-60 seconds.

Figure 64a.
Hand grenade, HC.

Figure 64b.
Hand grenade, CS.

f. Grenade, hand riot, CN-DM, M6A1 (CN DM M6).

(1) Weight of complete munition - 17 oz.

(2) Time of functioning - 20-60 seconds.

(3) Persistency in open - variable according to wind conditions, maximum ten minutes.

(4) Minimum protection - best commercial mask.

(5) Physiological action - lacrimation; irritation of the mucous membranes; viscous discharge from the nose; sneezing and coughing; severe headaches; acute pain in the chest; cramps; nausea with vomiting; involuntary anal evacuation.

(6) First aid - flush eyes with boric acid; inhale chloroform frequently; take aspirin for headaches; leave contaminated area.

NOTE: Grenade launchers. These launchers are designed for use with the rifle or carbine. When used with the chemical projection adapter and special cartridges, the M6, M7, and M8 grenades may be launched at distances up to 200 yards. (See Figures 65a & b; 66a & b.)

g. Grenade, hand, riot, CN M25A1 (baseball grenade). (See Figure 67.)

(1) Weight of complete munition - 8 oz.

(2) Time of functioning - immediate (bursts).

(3) Filling - 3.5 oz. CN powder, micropulverized chloraceto phenone, magnesium oxide.

(4) Persistency in open - variable according to wind conditions.

(5) Minimum protection - protective mask; tight fitting goggles offer limited protection to eyes.

(6) Physiological action - lacrimation, skin stinging or burning; no permanent irritation.

(7) First aid - flush eyes with water. If available, use boric acid or sodium sulfite 1/4% solution. Keep eyes open and face into uncontaminated wind.

(8) Time for maximum effect - immediate.

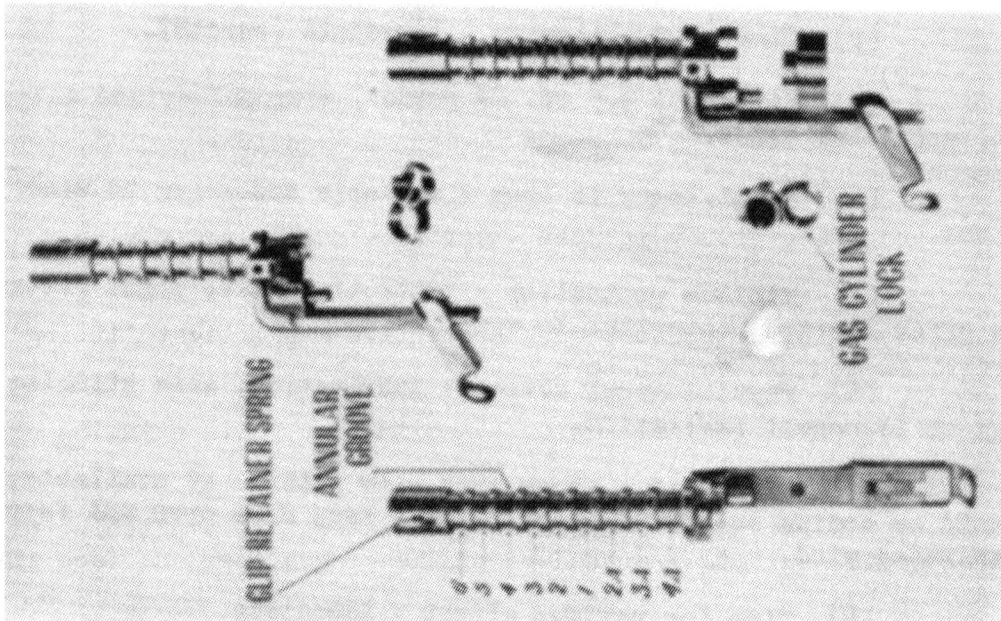

AUXILIARY
GRENADE CARTRIDGE
M7

CARBINE
GRENADE CARTRIDGE
CAL. .30, M6

RIFLE
GRENADE CARTRIDGE
CAL. .30, M3

Figure 65b. Grenade cartridges.

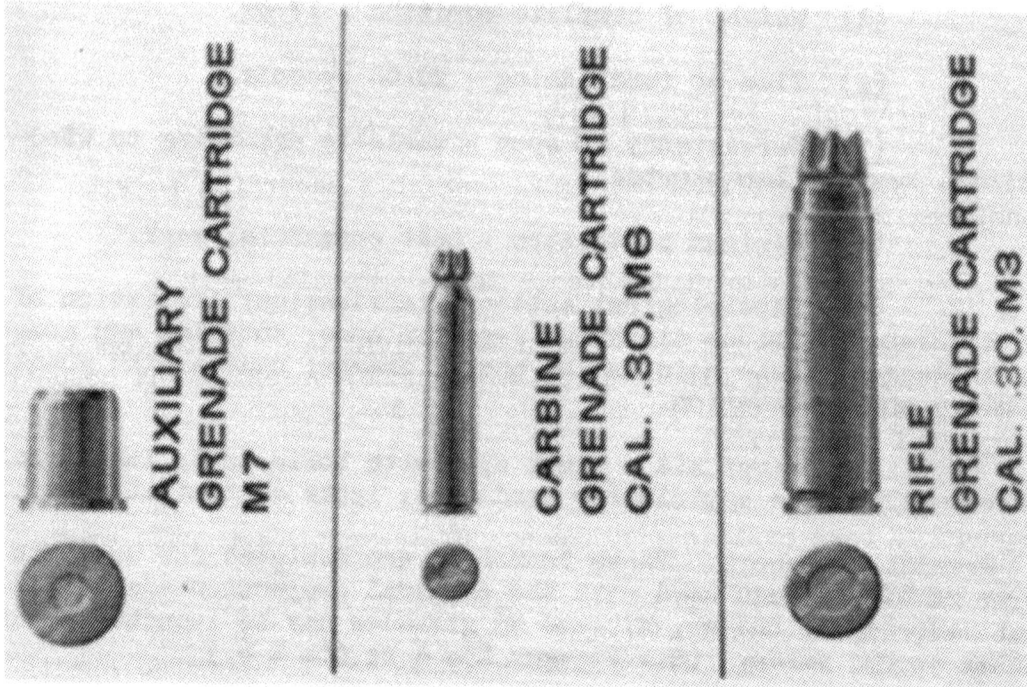

CLIP RETAINER SPRING

ANNULAR GROOVE

GAS CYLINDER LOCK

Figure 65a. Grenade launcher.

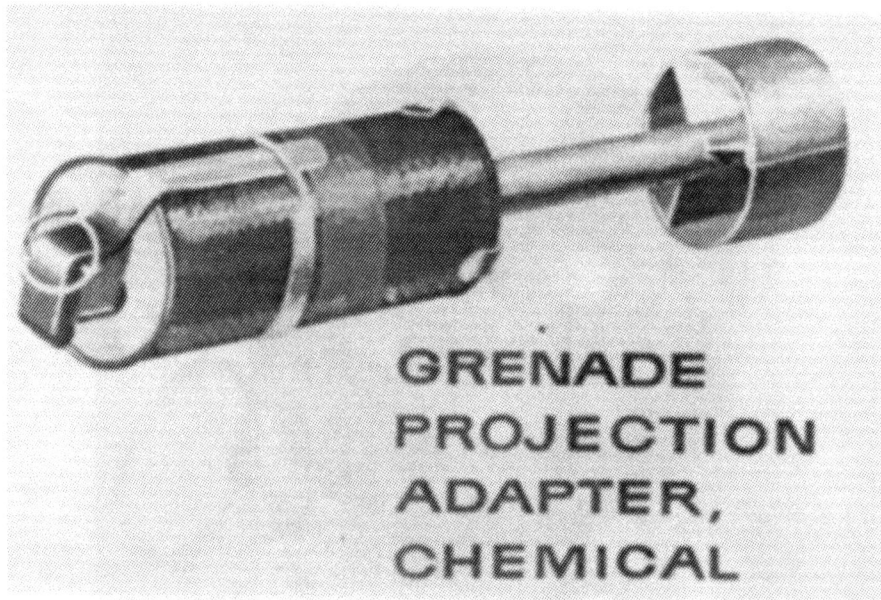

Figure 66a. Grenade, projection adapter, chemical.

Figure 66b. Release of riot control agent by grenade launcher.

Figure 67.   Baseball grenade, M25A1.

h.   Grenade, hand, riot, CN1 M25A2, CS1 M25A2, DM1 M25A2 (baseball grenades).

(1)   Weight of complete munition - 8 oz.

(2)   Time of functioning - immediate (bursts).

(3)   Filling approximately 2.25 oz. of CN1 or CS1, or DM1 (95% CN, CS, or DM plus 5% silica aerogel).

(4)   Persistency (in open) - variable according to wind conditions.   Greater in wooded terrain.

(5)   Minimum effective protection - protective mask; field clothing.

(6)   Physiological action - extreme burning sensation of the eyes; copious flow of tears; coughing; difficult breathing and chest tightness; involuntary closing of eyes; stinging action on moist skin areas; nausea and vomiting on exposure to extreme concentrations (via ingestion).

(7)   First aid treatment - for CN, CS and DM see paragraphs d(6), e(6), f(6), respectively.

(8) Time for maximum effect - for CN1, CS1, and DM1 see above paragraphs d(7), e(7), and f(7), respectively.

i. Other grenades. Other hand grenades that are commercially manufactured and considered effective for use in riot control operations include the following:

(1) Federal Laboratories Spedeheat Grenade (CN). This grenade emits CN from holes in the side, top, and bottom for 25 to 35 seconds. The CN begins discharging after the grenade is thrown. There is no explosion or danger of fragmentation. The agent is emitted in a visible cloud.

(2) Federal Laboratories Triple Chaser Grenade (CN). Two seconds after thrown this grenade splits into three parts, each of which functions like a separate grenade. Each section gives off gas for 20-25 seconds. In using this grenade throw it as far as possible.

(3) Federal Blast Dispersion Grenade (CN). Two seconds after thrown this grenade opens up and discharges tear gas dust through slots in the sides. The aluminum container does not fragment. The dust is not as readily visible as the smoke in the previous grenades but it is extremely effective. This can be well illustrated by walking into the dust cloud after firing. WARNING. Do not relax grip on the fuze lever before throwing. This grenade will cause injury if it goes off in the hand. This grenade is safe to use even in conditions where it lands in extremely inflammable material.

(4) Lake Erie Chemical Company Jumper-Repeater (CN or CS). This grenade emits invisible agent in three separate discharges, coinciding with three jumps to change position and extend area of effectiveness. The instantaneous discharge leaves no time to pick up and throw back the device. This is a blast type grenade and is purportedly fireless.

(5) Lake Erie Chemical Company Instantaneous Single Blast Grenade (CN or CS). This grenade discharges contents in a single blast, 1-3/4 seconds after being thrown. This grenade is also purportedly fireless. Lake Erie Chemical Company also provides a grenade filling for both types of grenades which emits a combination of CN and a nauseating agent.

NOTE: GRENADE THROWING TECHNIQUE. To throw a hand grenade, the following procedure should be followed: With the wind blowing against your back, grasp the grenade firmly with the fingers of the throwing hand holding the fuze lever against the body of the grenade. Pull out the safety pin by grasping and pulling on the safety ring with the free hand. Throw the grenade. After the grenade is thrown the fuze or arming lever falls from the body of the grenade and permits the striker cap to fall forward and thus activate the primer. The primer in turn ignites the fuze delay and the grenade is subsequently activated.

98. TYPES OF MECHANICAL RIOT CONTROL AGENT DISPERSING UNITS.

The following mechanical devices have been developed for use in dispersing riot control agents; CN and CS in micropulverized form:

a. Riot control agent disperser, portable, M3. The device is capable of dispersing approximately 20 pounds of micropulverized DM or approximately 15 pounds of micropulverized CS in one continuous burst of 25 seconds or in intermittent bursts as desired. The agent is projected approximately 30 feet prior to billowing out into a cloud. This device can be used singly or in battery. (See Figure 68.)

Figure 68.   Portable mechanical riot control
agent disperser.

b. Riot control agent disperser, helicopter or vehicle-mounted, M4. Disperses the micropulverized powder form of CN and CS at the rate of 50 pounds per minute. (See Figure 69.)

c. Gas guns. Both the Federal Laboratories Company and the Lake Erie Chemical Company manufacture a 1-1/2 inch bore single-shot gun which is used for firing tear gas projectiles and shells.

Figure 69. Mechanical riot control agent disperser,
vehicle mounted.

      (1) Long range projectile. At maximum elevation (37-1/2°)
this projectile has a range of 200-225 yards. It should not be fired
directly into a group of persons. When the gun is fired the projectile
tumbles end over end in flight. This projectile is useful for releasing
a riot control agent to the rear of a mob.

      (2) Barricade piercing projectile. This projectile can
be fired at a maximum range of 300-325 yards. However, the range at
which it can be fired accurately is considerably less. For example, at
ranges up to 75 yards the projectile can achieve a fair percentage of
hits on window targets. As the projectile leaves the gun four fins
spring into position. These fins plus the weight in the nose of the
projectile give the projectile stability in flight. Available projectiles include both those which function on impact and those which function a few seconds after impact. The "barricade" projectile is designed
primarily for use against those persons who barricade themselves and resist attempts to arrest them. This projectile is not suitable for use
against mobs if serious injuries or deaths are to be avoided.

      (3) Short range shells. Upon discharge, the short range
shell discharges a heavy cloud of riot control agent from the muzzle of
the gun. There is no projectile and only a piece of wadding and the

ST 19-180; 177

agents are discharged from the gun. The maximum range of the agent
cloud is about forty feet. To avoid the possibility of blinding a person by part of the blast, the gun should be discharged by aiming below
the waist. For greatest effectiveness, the blast should be fired at the
target from a distance of not more than fifteen feet. This shell can be
used against front-line members of a mob or to seal off areas.

99. NATURAL FACTORS INFLUENCING BEHAVIOR OF RIOT CONTROL AGENT
CLOUDS IN THE FIELD.

Riot control agents can be used advantageously under favorable
conditions. If used improperly or under adverse weather conditions, these
agents can quickly render police personnel ineffective. The following are
some important considerations:

a. Lateral spread. When a riot control agent is released, the
cloud is blown from side to side by shifting air currents which cause a
lateral spread as the cloud moves downwind. (See Figure 70.)

Figure 70. Lateral spread.

ST 19-180; 178

b. Drag effect. Due to a greater wind velocity at higher elevations and to interference of vegetation and other ground objects, wind currents carry agent clouds along the ground with a rolling motion, causing the base of the cloud to be retarded and elongated.

c. Vertical rise. This is dependent on the variables of weather such as temperature, wind speed, and differences between temperatures, densities of the cloud, and the surrounding air. (See Figure 71.)

Figure 71. Vertical rise.

d. Obstacles. Obstacles such as buildings, large rocky structures, and trees affect the air in that they act as wind tunnels. They confine the force of the wind and reduce the wind's lateral spread; therefore, the wind velocity tends to increase. This interference is apparent for a distance equal to thirty times the height of the obstacle.

100. TACTICAL FACTORS TO CONSIDER IN THE USE OF RIOT CONTROL AGENTS.

a. Selection of proper riot control agent.

(1) Riot control agents. CN and CS produce a temporary effect and do not prevent a mob from reforming. An agent in the form of a micropulverized powder is more persistent than one in vapor form.

Powdered agents dispersed inside a building may remain persistent for days or even weeks. Persons exposed to a cloud of micropulverized CN or CS powder inhale it and the powder gets into their eyes, hair, and cloth ing and on their skin. Such persons may be affected for several hours. When a baseball grenade explodes, the area of intolerable concentration of the agent is about 10 yards in diameter which is larger than the area of the visible cloud.

(2) Tear agent--vomiting agent combination. It may be necessary to use grenades containing a combination of tear and vomiting agents (CN-DM) against a violent mob. To produce the maximum effect DM requires 15 to 30 minutes; therefore, it is usually combined with CN to produce an effect more quickly. The physical reaction to DM is suffi- ciently violent and lasting to incapacitate persons for several hours after exposure. If a CN-DM combination is employed, a chemical officer and medical personnel should be present.

(3) Smoke. Smoke may be used to determine the approxi- mate velocity of the wind and to provide concealment for the movement of police. (See Figure 72.) Police moving behind or through a smoke screen can approach a building or barricade close enough to throw gre- nades. Smoke separates members of a mob from one another, reduces the accuracy of their aimed fire, and causes confusion. However, it is not advisable to attempt to disperse a disorderly assemblage with smoke. Since smoke produces no physiological reaction, it will restrain a mob only momentarily and may be interpreted as a bluff.

Figure 72. Use of smoke to determine wind direction.

ST 19-180; 180

b. Governing tactical factors. The tactics and techniques of placing riot control agents are governed primarily by wind, area occupied by the mob, and munitions available.

(1) Wind. The direction of the wind fixes the general vicinity of the line from which the agent cloud must be released in order to drift across the occupied area. The direction and velocity of the wind are determined with the use of smoke both prior to and during the actual release of the agent cloud. Winds are subject to rapid changes in direction and velocity, especially on city streets and between tall buildings which form multiple thermals and cross currents. In view of this, prior to the use of a riot control agent, a careful evaluation of the possible effect of sudden changes in the direction of wind carrying the agent cloud into neutral zones, public utilities, hospitals, schools, etc., must be made. The velocity of the wind must also be considered in determining the distance between the line of release and the mob; strong winds indicate increased distance. This distance in turn affects the amount of riot control agents which must be released in order to place an effective concentration on the mob.

(2) Area occupied by the mob. The agent release line is usually at right angles to the direction of the wind. It should be long enough to insure the creation of a cloud which, when it reaches the mob, will include considerably more than the area actually occupied by the mob. Roughly, the length of the agent line should be equal to the average width of the target plus one-fifth of the distance from the agent line to the mob. (See Figure 73.)

(3) Munitions available. It is well to remember that riot control munitions are always to be used in sufficient quantities to produce an immediate and decisive effect. Sufficient munitions must be available to properly produce the agent cloud and maintain it until the mob has been dispersed.

(4) Temper and objectives of mob. The temper and objectives of a mob are other factors that must be evaluated before using agents Use of insufficient quantities may infuriate a mob to further acts of violence. It would be inadvisable to use riot control agents when less forceful means could be utilized to disperse the mob. However, when agents can be utilized to restore law and order with a minimum of damage to property and personnel it is advisable to use them.

c. Practical application.

(1) The quancity of munitions and their employment must be determined on the ground. Use ample quantities.

(2) It is desirable to set off a pilot smoke grenade to determine the direction and velocity of the wind.

Figure 73. Riot control agent release line.

(3) The line of release should be far enough to windward so that the smoke or other agents will have joined into one cloud before reaching the mob.

(4) Grenades and smoke pots are set off simultaneously and sustained or shifted as necessary.

(5) Combustion-type munitions should not be thrown into a crowd or mob since they can be thrown back.

(6) M25A1 or M25A2 grenades may be used to advantage regardless of direction of wind. The powder is more persistent than the vapor in buildings, vegetation, and in close contact with rioters. The vapor clouds have greater range in field concentrations. Release methods for M25 grenades are illustrated in Figures 74 and 75.

(7) The rioters must have ample avenues of escape from the advancing cloud.

ST 19-180; 182

Figure 75. Release of riot control agent, baseball grenade, by throwing underhand.

Figure 74. Release of riot control agent, baseball grenade, by throwing overhand.

ST 19-180; 183

(8) When attacking a building police should be careful in using the burning-type grenade where combustibles are present. In the interest of safety, combustion-type agents should not be used near combustible materials.

101. SUMMARY OF GENERAL TACTICAL CONSIDERATIONS AND PROCEDURES WHEN USING RIOT CONTROL AGENTS IN CIVIL DISTURBANCES.

  a. <u>Principal factors determining the tactics to be employed.</u>

   (1) Wind direction and velocity.

   (2) Area occupied by, or to be denied, rioters.

   (3) Type and quantity of munitions on hand.

   (4) Temper and objectives of the rioters.

  b. <u>Procedure for using riot control agents.</u>

   (1) Determine area to be covered.

   (2) Determine direction of wind.

   (3) Determine line of release of the riot control agent.

   (4) Use sufficient quantity of riot control agents.

   (5) Provide definite avenues of escape for the mob.

  c. <u>General tactical considerations.</u>

   (1) Where force is necessary, riot control agents frequently will accomplish the mission without permanent physical injury to rioters

   (2) Prompt action is essential.

   (3) Police must have protective masks on before the agent attack begins.

   (4) The grenadiers must be provided with adequate protection.

   (5) If CN-DM or CS-DM is used, the presence of the unit chemical officer is desirable.

   (6) If the supply of riot control agents is limited, a short heavy concentration should be placed on the most threatening point.

(7) When smoke is used care must be exercised to make sure that it does not benefit rioters by screening their movements to points of vantage.

Section II

PROTECTIVE MEASURES AND TRAINING

102. INTRODUCTION.

Police officers should be thoroughly oriented and trained in other aspects of riot control agents in addition to the techniques of employment. The effective utilization of riot control agents requires the individual officer to know certain protective measures, to include the use of the gas mask. He should also be aware of the characteristic effects that are induced among personnel subjected to exposure. This section is intended to assist the police official in obtaining a working knowledge of the use and characteristics of the gas mask and in the presentation of a gas perception training exercise.

103. GAS MASKS.

a. General. The M9A1 Protective Mask, developed for use by United States military forces is now used by many countries throughout the world. Other types of masks available to various agencies include the newer M17 and the M22. The M22 was developed primarily for use by civilian personnel. The material covered in this section is written primarily for the M9A1 Protective Mask; however, masking and unmasking techniques, inspections, and training exercises are adaptable to any type of gas mask. (See Figures 76, 77, 78, and 79.)

b. Functioning. The gas mask protects the face, throat, and lungs against injury from the effects of gas. The basic functioning of the mask includes four main points.

(1) The face piece covers the eyes, nose, mouth, and face

(2) When the wearer breathes in, the contaminated air is drawn through the canister where it is purified by chemicals and filters

(3) The purified air passes into the facepiece where it is breathed by the wearer. (See Figure 80.)

(4) Exhaled air passes through an outlet valve in the facepiece. The outlet valve is constructed so that it allows air to escape but prevents air from entering. NOTE: The canister does not provide oxygen and does not protect against nonriot type gases such as ammonia and carbon monoxide.

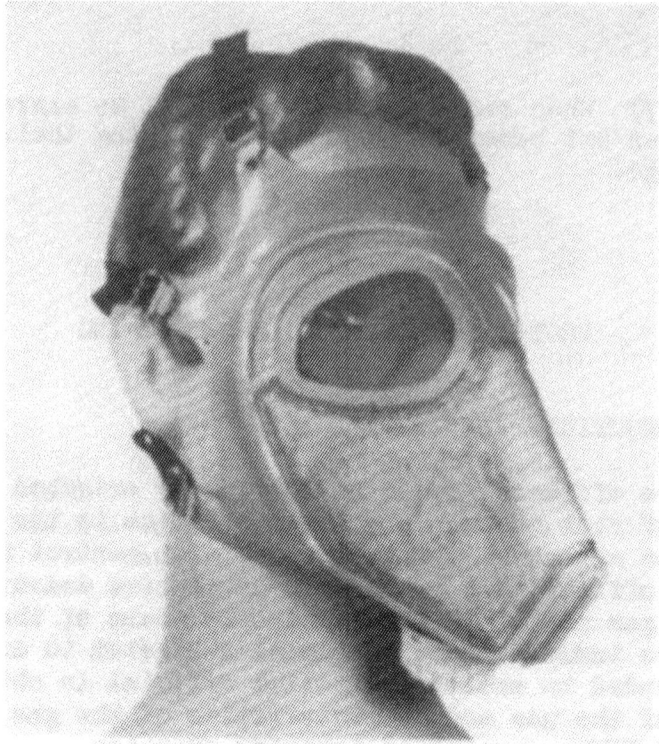

Figure 76. Civilian protective mask M22.

Figure 77. M17 protective mask.

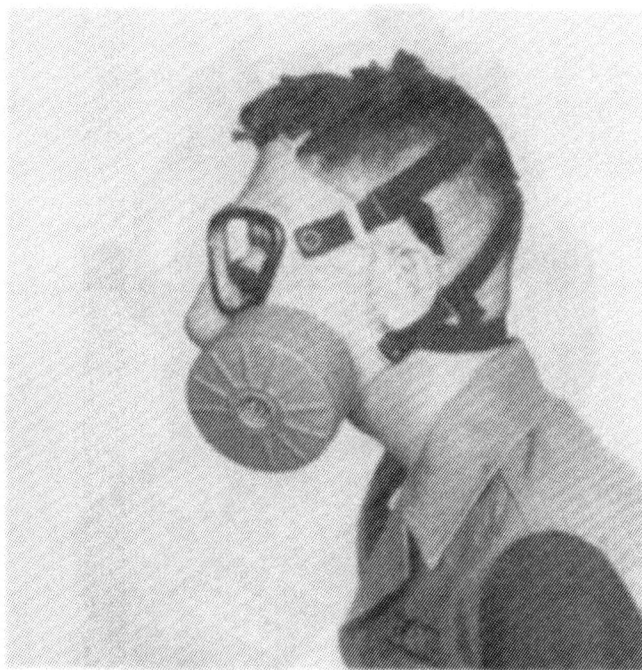

Figure 78. M9A1 protective mask, side view.

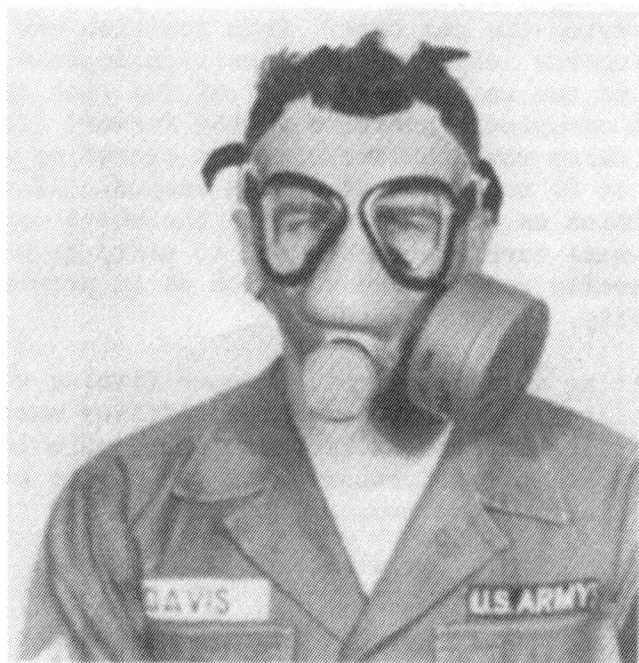

Figure 79. M9A1 protective mask, front view.

ST 19-180; 187

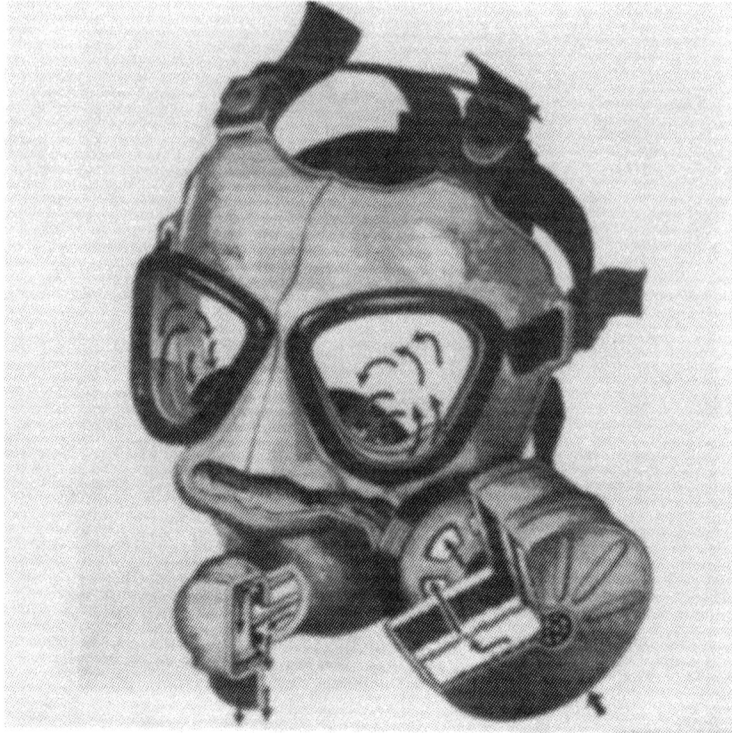

Figure 80. M9A1 protective mask air flow.

c. Carrying positions. Figures 81a and 81b show various
positions for carrying the gas mask. Each position has advantages as
well as disadvantages. Selection of a position depends upon the location or function of the individual member of the riot control formation.
If the individual occupies a position in the forward line, then the side,
front, and chest carry would hinder him when executing various riot control formations, or in the handling of his weapon. If a particular individual is to function as a grenadier, then the chest carry is recommended
as the empty gas mask carrier can be used to carry grenades. The leg
carry is the generally recommended position as it permits maximum movement and flexibility.

d. Fitting and adjustment. Proper fitting of the mask is a
command responsibility. A qualified police officer must supervise the
fitting. Proper fitting prevents restriction of circulation which causes
headaches and physical discomfort, reduced vision, or other interference
with riot control duties, and reduces the possibility of casualty.

e. Basic principles of fit.

(1) The mask must fit the contour of the face. When several sizes of masks are available, one which gives the most comfortable
gas-tight fit should be selected. Masks are made of flexible material

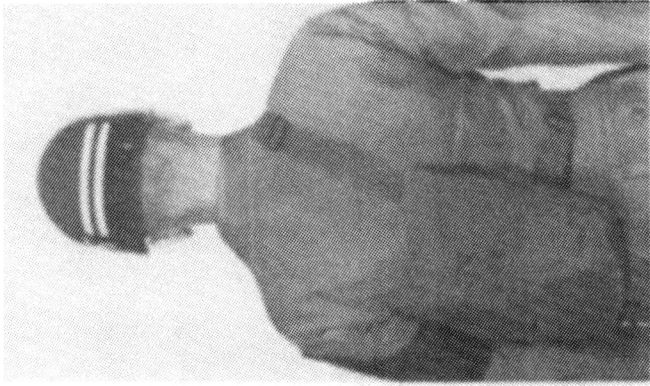

BACK CARRY

LEG CARRY

SIDE CARRY

FRONT CARRY

Figure 81a. Mask carrying positions.

ST 19-180; 189

CHEST CARRY

Figure 81b. Mask carrying positions (Cont'd).

so that in most cases a good fit can be obtained by slight adjustment of the head harness straps. If a mask is too small, the pupils of the eyes will be below the center of the lenses. If the mask is too large, the edges of the facepiece will interfere with ears and throat of the wearer, and the pupils of the eyes will be above the center of the lenses.

(2) Detailed fitting procedure. Have the individual loosen all of the head harness straps so that they are all even. Then have the individual place the mask on his face with his chin resting snugly in the chin pocket. To don the mask, center the head harness pad fairly well down on the back of the head and hold it there with one hand. With the other hand tighten each forehead strap just enough to remove any slack. The strap is best adjusted by a rapid pull or jerk to the rear. Tighten each chin strap until the straps are evenly and moderately tightened. To adjust the temple straps remove the hand from the head pad and adjust the straps to a moderate tightness. These straps should clear the ears. All the straps should be fairly even. After the mask is on, grasp the neck strap and place it around the back of the neck, smoothing it to avoid twisting. Fasten the neck strap on the stud. Adjust the neck strap so that it fits snugly. (See Figures 82, 83, 84, and 85.)

ST 19-180; 190

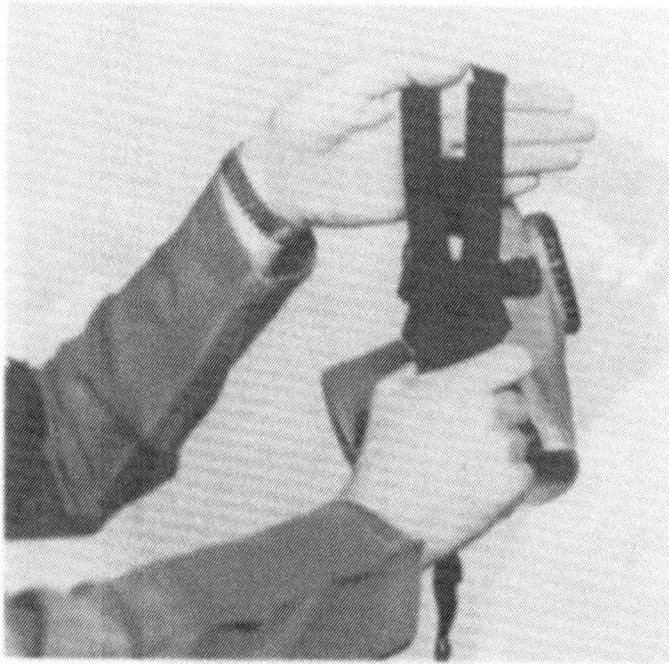

Figure 82. Loosening head harness straps.

Figure 83. Donning mask.

ST 19-180; 191

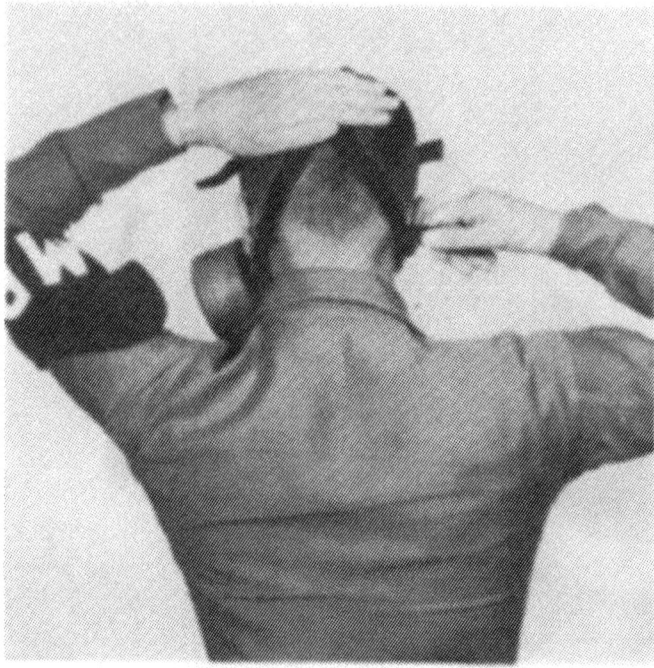

Figure 84. Adjusting chin straps.

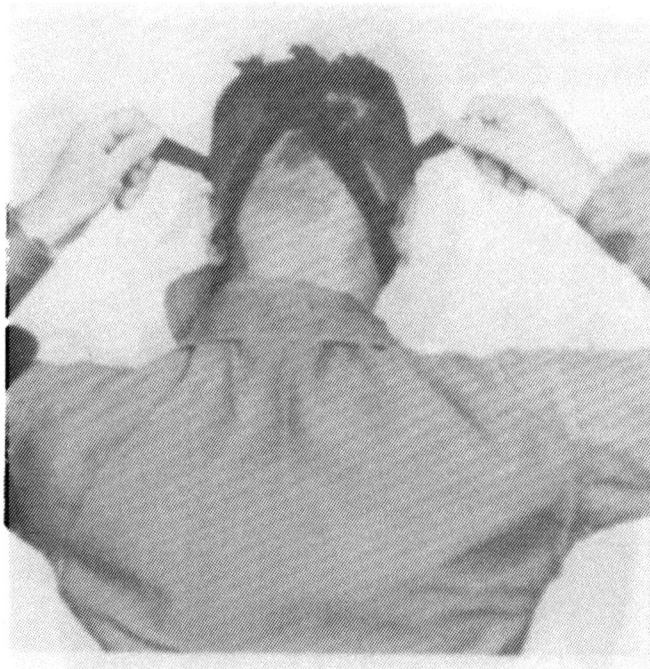

Figure 85. Adjusting temple straps.

ST 19-180; 192

(3) <u>Checking the fit.</u> Inspect the lenses to determine that they are centered over the pupils of the eyes. Check the mask to see that it does not fit so tightly that pressure is exerted on flesh around the eyes, causing them to be partially closed. Check to see that the mask does not press painfully on the nose or cut into flesh at the throat of the wearer. Check edge of the mask for overlap at the ears or for overlap at the chin to the extent that it cuts into the throat. Proper fit is attained when the mask comes well up on the forehead and the edge of the facepiece is within one inch of the ears. If slight gaps or channels are present, carefully adjust the head harness.

(4) <u>Checking for leakage.</u> The best way to check for leakage is to wear the mask in a gas chamber. Before testing the facepiece for leaks, assure that the cannister is screwed tightly to the facepiece. With the palm of the hand over the inlet of the canister, have the wearer inhale normally and hold his breath for 10 seconds. When the facepiece tends to collapse, it is an indication of an effective air seal. (See Figure 86.)

Figure 86. Checking for leakage.

f. <u>Inspections of the mask.</u> Masks must be inspected when issued and periodically afterwards to detect deterioration. Such inspections must be conducted by a police supervisor or someone designated by him. The procedure is as follows:

(1) Remove the facepiece and canister from the carrier, then examine the carrier. There must be no tears or rips. Straps on the carrier must be in good condition.

(2) Examine the canister. Look for holes and large dents in the canister body. Any rust or corrosion may indicate that the canister has been wet. Moisture cakes and damages chemicals, lowering the efficiency of the canister and causing the wearer of the mask difficulty in breathing.

(3) Examine the facepiece carefully, including the head harness, eyepieces, and outlet valve. Head harnesses may lose their elasticity through improper storage, or rubber threads in the elastic straps may break if the head harness is worn too tightly. Eyepieces may be badly scratched, or cracks may have developed near the eyepieces. Outlet valves may stick after disinfection or cold weather. They can usually be cleaned by wiping with a dry cloth.

(4) Put the mask on the face and check it by shutting off the air at the canister. The facepiece should collapse when the wearer inhales and should remain collapsed for at least 10 seconds.

g. Cleaning. Under normal circumstances, each mask will be disinfected, before issue to an individual, when shifted from one individual to another, or once every six months when the mask has been worn by a single individual only. The mask may be disinfected by using a disinfectant solution or by washing it in hot soapy water. THE CANISTER MUST BE REMOVED BEFORE WASHING THE MASK!

h. Storage. Gas masks should have storage facilities similar to those provided for weapons and ammunition. They may be hung from nails by carrier straps. Ideal conditions require cool dry storage and at least semiannual inspection and disinfection.

i. Mask drill. In an emergency, men must be able to don their masks smoothly and with a minimum of interruption to their regular duties. Careful adjustment is far more important than uniformity of movement in gas drills; however, preliminary training may be given by the numbers. Speed is a secondary factor to be developed after the police officers have mastered the "by-the-numbers" drill. Men are taught to mask rapidly and accurately under all conditions. Gas mask drill, including the adjustment to and removal from carrying positions, adjustment of the mask to the face, removal and return to the carrier, and testing for gas, is shown in Figures 87a, b, c, and d.

TO ADJUST MASK--SIDE CARRY

"GAS"

1. At the word GAS, stop breathing, remove headgear with right hand, and open carrier with left hand.

2. Place headgear as directed. Hold carrier open with left hand; grasp facepiece below eyepieces with right hand, and remove mask. (If canister is on right cheek, grasp both sides of facepiece with right hand.)

3. Grasp facepiece with both hands, sliding thumbs up inside facepiece under lower head harness straps. Place other fingers straight and together outside facepiece, above eyepieces. Spread facepiece as shown and bring it up in front of face; at the same time thrust out chin. (CAUTION: Never try to put facepiece on by grasping head harness.)

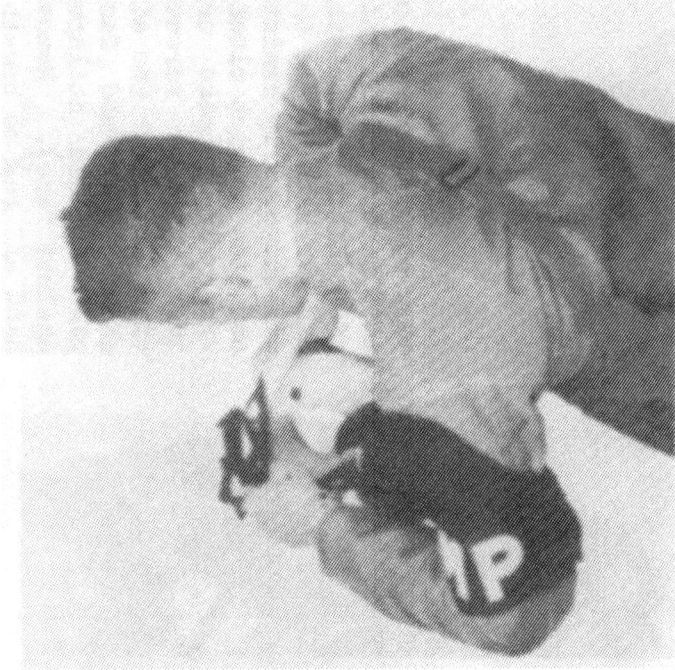

Figure 87a. Masking procedure.

"CHECK"

6. At the word CHECK, close outlet valve by cupping heel of right hand firmly over opening; blow hard to clear facepiece of agent. (Do not inhale.)

7. Test for leakage of mask by placing palm of left hand over air inlet of canister, shutting off air supply. At the same time, grip canister and give a quick clockwise turn to make certain it is screwed tight. Inhale (no air should enter, and facepiece should collapse against face). Remove hand and resume breathing.

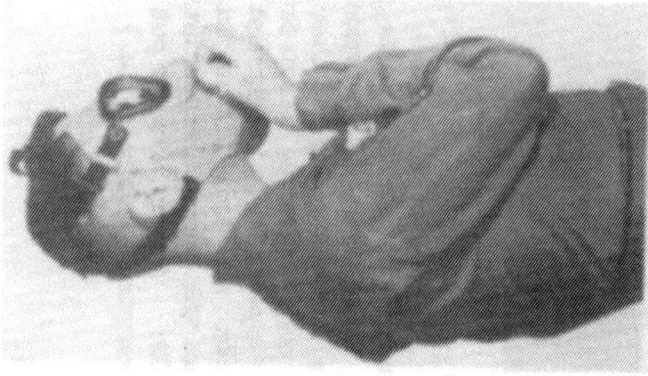

"PLACE"

4. At the word PLACE, seat chin pocket of facepiece firmly on chin. Bring head harness smoothly over head, making certain all head harness straps are straight and head pad is centered.

5. Smooth edges of facepiece on face with upward and backward motion of hands, pressing out all bulges to secure an airtight seal.

Figure 87b. Masking Procedure (cont'd)

TO REMOVE AND REPLACE MASK

"REMOVE, MASK"

1. At the word MASK, remove headgear with left hand and unfasten head harness neck strap with right hand.

2. With right hand, grasp facepiece around outlet valve and remove facepiece with circular motion (downward, outward, and upward).

"COVER"

8. At the word COVER, replace headgear and fasten head harness neck strap.

9. Fasten carrier flap, starting with bottom fastener. Straighten up and place hands down to sides for final position.

Figure 87c. Masking procedure (cont'd).

5. Close carrier flap, starting with bottom fastener.

"REPLACE"

4. At the word REPLACE, insert mask into carrier, twisting mask upward so that facepiece is facing out. (If canister is on right cheek, eyepieces are facing inward.)

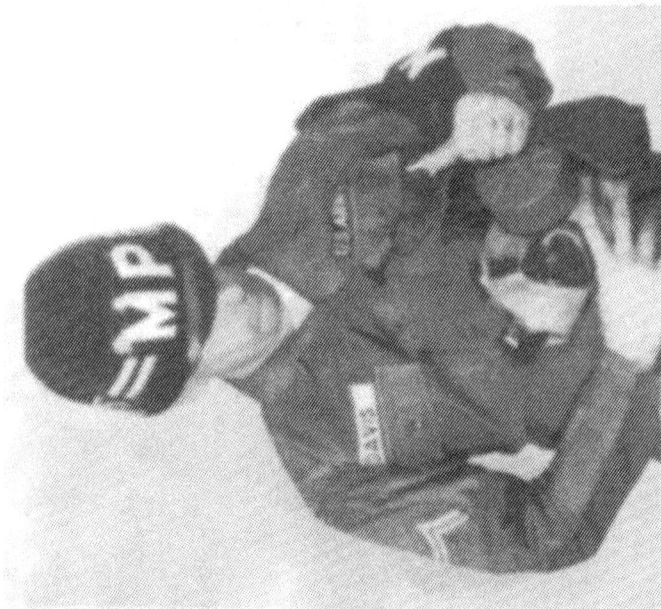

3. Replace headgear. With left hand, fold head harness into facepiece and then open carrier. Holding carrier open with left hand and holding facepiece below eyepieces, start mask toward carrier, chin pocket first, canister away from body, and eyepieces facing downward. (If canister is on right cheek, eyepieces are facing upward and canister is away from body.)

Figure 87d. Unmasking (cont'd).

104. GAS CHAMBER EXERCISES.

a. Purpose. All police officers should be given this exercise annually to establish their proficiency in adjustment of the gas mask. The exercise is conducted in three phases with tear gas (CN). It has five objectives.

(1) To test the efficiency of the mask.

(2) To establish confidence in the mask.

(3) To teach the purpose of gas mask drill.

(4) To teach respect for tear gas.

(5) To test proficiency of the individual in the use of the mask.

b. Gas chamber. Any reasonably airtight room or enclosed space of moderate size will suffice provided it is 100 to 200 meters away from any other activity. A one-room building is satisfactory if it is about seven meters square and fitted with two doors, one at each end. A tent may be used if earth is banked around the outside to prevent the gas from leaking out. Tents should be turned inside out and aired for several days after use before being returned to storage.

c. Requirements for the exercise. An experienced officer should supervise the exercise with medical personnel present or available. Before the exercise the instructor should be certain that each man is familiar with gas mask drill; specific emphasis is placed on adjusting and clearing the facepiece. (The facepiece is cleared by holding the breath, putting the mask on, and then exhaling.) The instructor should inspect the fit of each mask and divide the students into groups according to the capacity of the chamber. The CN capsules are heated by placing a candle on a brick and then placing a tin can punched with holes over the candle. The CN capsules are then placed on top of the tin can. The instructor can tell when a concentration is properly built up by feeling a prickly sensation on his skin.

d. General outline of the exercise. The exercise will be divided into three phases as outlined below. After each phase, the students should be warned not to rub their eyes, since this will cause painful swelling if the eyes have become infected. The men should move upwind, separate, and face into the breeze. Any painful effects will disappear within a few minutes. If the weather is hot, men should be allowed to wash with soap and water as soon as possible to avoid skin irritation.

A CN GRENADE WILL NEVER BE USED TO BUILD UP THE CN CONCENTRATION.

Each phase is explained to the students.

Phase	Position of Mask When Entering Chamber	Action in Chamber	Position of Mask When Leaving Chamber	Purpose
1	On face.	Remain briefly.	On face.	Test efficiency, fit and adjustment of mask; dispel fear of gas.
2	On face.	Remain briefly, test for gas, clear facepiece, and remove mask.	Removed.	Prove presence of gas, practice testing for gas, establish confidence in mask.
3	In carrier.	Put on mask.	On face.	Simulate actual conditions, practice adjusting mask in tear gas.

   e. Phase one. In succession, masked groups are ushered into the chamber and the door closed behind them. Each group stays 1 or 2 minutes to determine proper fit and adjustment of the mask. Meanwhile the officer explains the protection being provided by the mask. On leaving the chamber the men move upwind, keeping the masks on. They are inspected by the officer in charge who checks the fit of each mask before the wearer is ordered to remove the mask. Each man is examined for signs of lacrimation and asked if his mask is comfortable. If a man reports that his eyes were affected by gas while in the chamber, this may indicate a poorly fitting or defective mask. Corrective measures are taken and the student repeats the test until a satisfactory fit is obtained.

   f. Phase two. This phase establishes confidence in the protection provided by the mask. Properly masked, each group enters the chamber in which there is a strong concentration of CN. They test for gas by breaking the mask face seal and allowing a small amount of gas to enter the facepieces. They then clear the facepieces, and take a position across the room from the exit. Each man in turn then unmasks and walks toward the door. A masked officer is stationed there to help him out, first making certain that he has felt an eye effect. To avoid needless loss of the CN concentration, the door is kept open as short a time as possible.

        g. <u>Phase three</u>. Men are carefully instructed in advance about the procedure. With the masks in the carriers, members of the group enter the tear gas filled chamber. Each man goes into the room with his hands at his side. He then puts on the mask and clears his facepiece. The group remains in the chamber for 2 to 3 minutes. Each man of the group then leaves the chamber with the mask on.

CHAPTER 11

THE RIOT BATON

Section I

GENERAL

105. INTRODUCTION.

The riot baton is the most practical weapon for general employment by police in civil disturbances. The riot baton is primarily an
offensive weapon. The intent of its application is to facilitate temporary disablement of an aggressive, riotous, and violent individual. The
riot baton is not a club; it is a weapon which enables the police officer
to deliver specific blows to vulnerable portions of the human body. In
a defensive situation, the riot baton may be used in conjunction with
certain techniques to allow the police officer to counter the attack of
an opponent and subsequently return to the offense. This chapter illustrates the application of the riot baton in both offensive and defensive
techniques. Police officers should be trained to a point where riot baton
techniques are accomplished through reflex action rather than through an
extended thought process.

106. ACCEPTED CHARACTERISTICS OF THE RIOT BATON.

The most practical length of the riot baton is 26 to 36 inches.
It is made from any dense hardwood such as rosewood or walnut which is
not easily shattered or broken. Both ends of the baton are rounded to
preclude unnecessary injury. The suggested diameter of the baton is
1.25 inches. The baton is drilled for the installation of a wrist thong
nine inches from the grip end.

107. POINTS OF IMPACT.

It is important in the application of the riot baton that police officers have a thorough knowledge of the vulnerable points of impact on the human body. Figures 88a and 88b indicate the vulnerable
points of the body which lend themselves to the application of riot
baton techniques. The police officer should attempt to avoid those
blows which produce permanent injury or fatality. Blows to the head
should also be avoided.

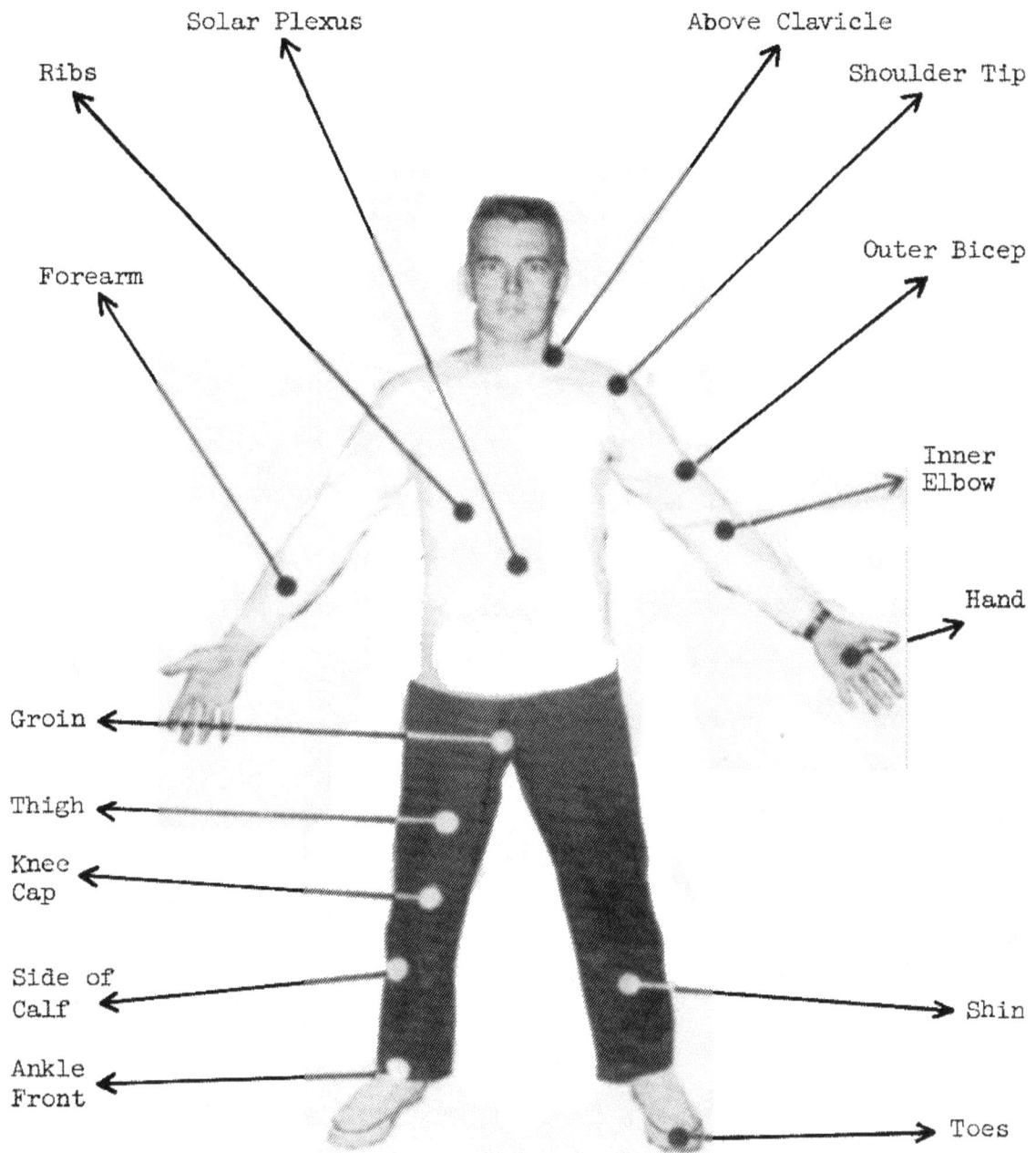

Solar Plexus

Above Clavicle

Ribs

Shoulder Tip

Forearm

Outer Bicep

Inner Elbow

Hand

Groin

Thigh

Knee Cap

Side of Calf

Shin

Ankle Front

Toes

Figure 88a. Points of impact.

ST 19-180; 203

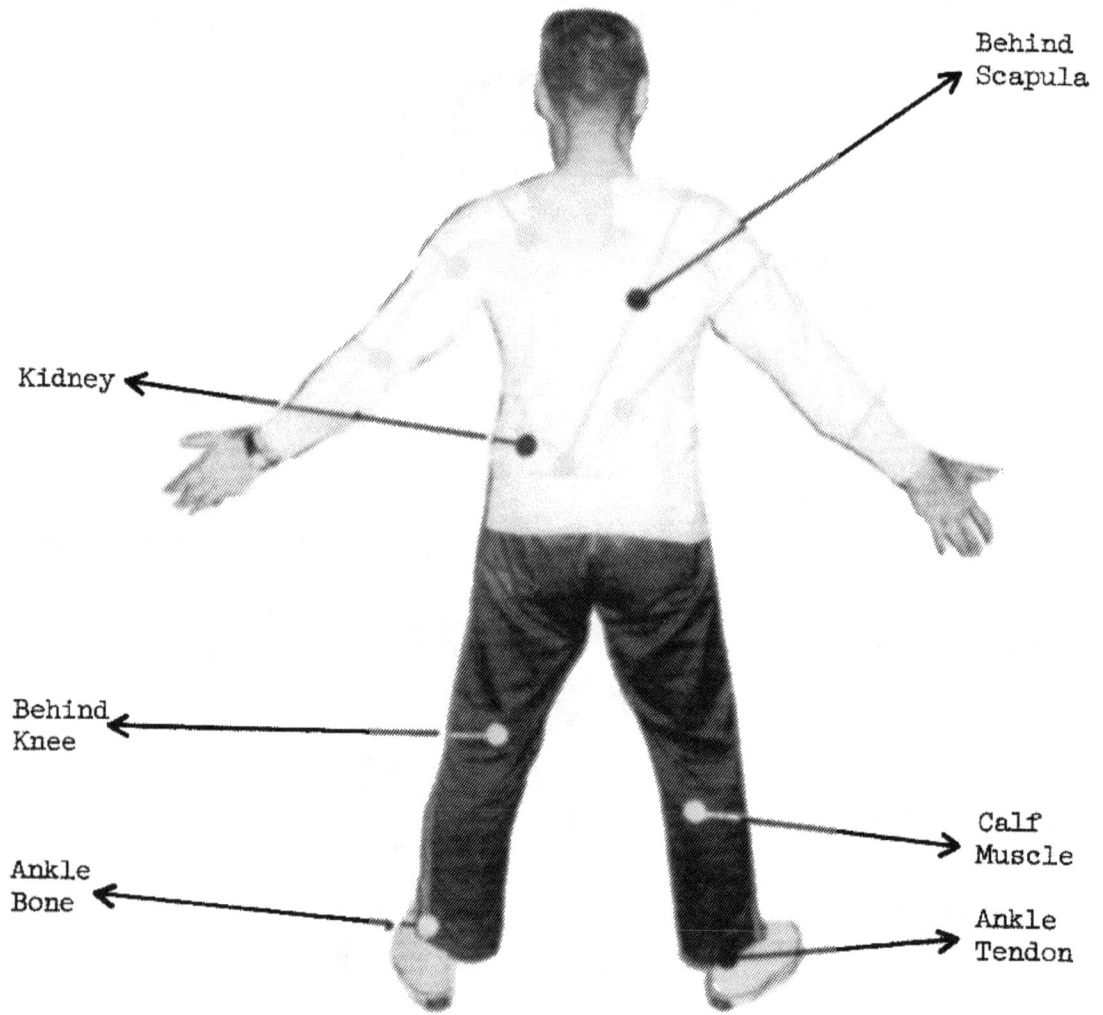

Figure 88b. Points of impact.

ST 19-180; 204

Section II

MANUAL OF THE RIOT BATON

108. BATON GRIP TECHNIQUES.

Three steps are necessary to obtain a secure grip of the riot baton. The thong of the baton is first placed around the thumb. The baton is then held in a position allowing the thong to hang over the back of the hand. The hand is then rolled into the handle of the baton allowing the thong to be pressed into the palm of the hand. This technique of gripping the riot baton provides the individual with a secure grasp and facilitates immediate release of the weapon by merely relaxing his hand. (See Figure 89.)

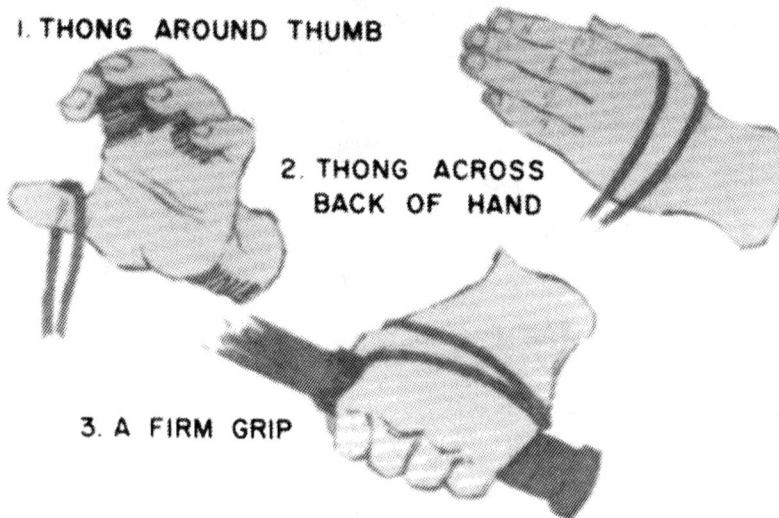

Figure 89. Baton grip.

109. PARADE REST.

Parade rest is the relaxed ready position. The feet are shoulder-width apart. The left palm is facing out. The right palm is facing in toward the body. The hands are approximately six inches from the end of the baton. (See Figure 90.)

Figure 90. Parade rest.

110. PORT POSITION.

The port position is a ready position. It is particularly
well suited for individual combat or defensive tactics. The right hand
and forearm are parallel to the ground. The left hand is level with the
left shoulder. The striking end of the baton bisects the angle between
the neck and the left shoulder. The baton is a distance of approximately
eight inches from the body. The feet are shoulder-width apart. (See
Figure 91.)

111. ON GUARD POSITION.

The on guard position is an offensive ready position. It is
well suited for employment during the advance of riot control formations.
It should not be maintained for unnecessary, prolonged periods of time
since it is tiring to the body. To assume the position the left foot
is placed in advance of the right. The feet are spread apart and the

Figure 91. Port position.

knees slightly bent. (See Figures 92a & b.) The right hand and butt end of the baton are placed snugly against the hip. The body is bent slightly forward at the waist. The left arm is bent sufficiently to provide for a thrust. The baton is pointed at throat level.

112. SHORT THRUST.

The short thrust is accomplished from the on guard position. The body is thrust forward rapidly by advancing the left foot. The left arm is snapped straight, driving the striking end of the baton into one selected vulnerable area of the opponent's body. NEVER DIRECT THE THRUST DIRECTLY AGAINST THE CENTRAL THROAT AREA, SINCE IT CAN CAUSE PERMANENT INJURY OR DEATH! The position of on guard is assumed after delivering the short thrust. (See Figure 93.)

Figure 92b. On guard (side view).

Figure 92a. On guard (front view).

Figure 93.   Short thrust.

113.   LONG THRUST.

    The long thrust is accomplished from the on guard position.
The body is advanced rapidly forward by advancing the right foot.   The
baton is held in the right hand.   The baton is snapped forward driving
the striking end of the weapon into a vulnerable point of the opponent's
body.   NEVER DIRECT THE THRUST DIRECTLY AGAINST THE CENTRAL THROAT AREA,
SINCE IT CAN CAUSE PERMANENT INJURY OR DEATH!   The position of on guard
is assumed after delivering the long thrust.   (See Figure 94.)

114.   BUTT STROKE.

    a.   Position for butt stroke.   The butt stroke position is as-
sumed from the on guard position.   The right hand is elevated until the
baton is almost parallel to the ground.   (See Figure 95.)

    b.   Execution of the butt stroke.   The butt stroke is executed
by advancing the body rapidly with the right foot.   The right arm is
snapped straight and the butt end of the baton is driven to the left,
striking the opponent's jaw.   The left hand is kept even with the left
shoulder.   THE BUTT STROKE MAY BE FATAL TO THE OPPONENT IF EITHER THE
SIDE OF THE NECK OR THE HEAD ARE STRUCK.   (See Figure 96.)

Figure 94. Long thrust.

Figure 95. Butt stroke (preparatory position).

ST 19-180; 210

Figure 96.   Executing the butt stroke.

115.   THE BATON SMASH.

The baton smash may be accomplished either from the on guard or port position.

a. <u>Preparatory position</u>. From the on guard position, the baton is moved to a position horizontal to the ground and approximately chest high. (See Figure 97.)

b. <u>Executing the smash</u>. The smash is executed by advancing the right foot rapidly. Both arms are snapped straight, smashing the length of the baton across the opponent's chest. After delivering the smash, the position of on guard is assumed. (See Figure 98.)

Figure 97. Position for the baton smash.

Figure 98. Execution of the smash.

ST 19-180; 212

116. DEFENSE AGAINST BLOW TO LEFT SIDE OF HEAD.

The defense against an armed opponent's blow to the left side
of the head is accomplished in a manner to facilitate the return to the
offense.

a. Blocking blow. From either the on guard position or the
port position, smartly snap the left hand to the left side of the body
and the right hand up and to the left. The baton is then in a semi-
vertical position which blocks the opponent's blow. (See Figure 99.)

Figure 99. Blocking blow, left side.

b. After blocking, position for counterattack. Immediately
after blocking the opponent's blow, snap both arms up and level with the
baton. The left hand near the left shoulder and the right hand to the
front of the left shoulder. The grip end of the baton is pointing towards the opponent. The position now assumed is the position for the
execution of the baton jab or smash. (See Figure 100.)

Figure 100. Position for the counterattack.

   c. Executing the baton jab or smash. The body is driven forward. The right hand is snapped straight, driving the grip end of the
baton into the opponent's upper body, but avoiding the head. After delivering the jab or smash, the position of on guard is assumed. (See
Figure 101.)

   117. DEFENSE AGAINST BACKHAND BLOW.

   The backhand blow delivered by an opponent can be blocked from
either the position of on guard, or the port position.

   a. Blocking the backhand blow. From the on guard position,
snap both arms straight, out and to the right front of the body. The
left hand is elevated over the right hand so that the grip end of the
baton is pointing down. This position will block the opponent's blow.
(See Figure 102.)

Figure 101. Execution of the jab.

Figure 102. Blocking the backhand blow.

ST 19-180; 215

b. After blocking, position for counterattack. Immediately after blocking the opponent's blow, snap the right hand up near the right shoulder. The left hand is moved down and to the front of the chest. The striking end of the baton should be pointing slightly to the left front and toward the opponent. The position now assumed is the position for the execution of the butt stroke. (See Figure 103.)

Figure 103. Position for counterattack.

c. Executing the butt stroke. The body is rapidly advanced forward by the right foot. The right hand is driven forward and to the left. The left hand is maintained in place as the baton is driven against the side of the opponent's jaw. THIS ATTACK CAN PRODUCE A FATAL INJURY IF ANY OTHER AREA OF THE HEAD IS STRUCK. (See Figure 104.)

118. DEFENSE AGAINST THE LONG THRUST.

The long thrust can be defended against from either the on guard position or the port position.

a. Blocking the thrust. The left hand is moved across the body toward the left. The right hand is moved smartly down and toward the left. The opponent's weapon is engaged and deflected to the left and away from the body. (See Figure 105.)

Figure 104. Executing the butt stroke.

Figure 105. Blocking the Thrust.

ST 19-180; 217

b. Preparation for the counterblow. As soon as the opponent's weapon has been defected, allow the left hand to slide down to the right hand. The riot baton and body are now positioned for delivering a counter blow against a vulnerable point of the opponent. (See Figure 106.)

Figure 106. Preparation for counterblow.

119. DEFENSE AGAINST OVERHAND STAB.

This defensive tactic can best be accomplished from the on guard position.

a. Blocking the stab. As the opponent stabs downward, the baton is moved smartly across the body. The left hand is allowed to move down the baton until it is positioned slightly above the right. The baton is snapped against the wrist of the opponent. (See Figure 107.)

b. Preparation for the counterblow. The body is moved rapidly forward and the baton is directed against a vulnerable point of the opponent's body. (See Figure 108.)

ST 19-180; 218

Figure 107. Defense against overhead stab. Figure 108. Preparation for the counterblow.

120. DEFENSE AGAINST THE UPWARD THRUST.

The upward thrust may be blocked effectively from either the on guard position or the port position.

a. Blocking the upward thrust. The riot baton is brought quickly to a position parallel to the ground and approximately six inches from the lower chest. Both arms are snapped straight down driving the length of the baton downward striking the opponent's wrist. (See Figure 109.)

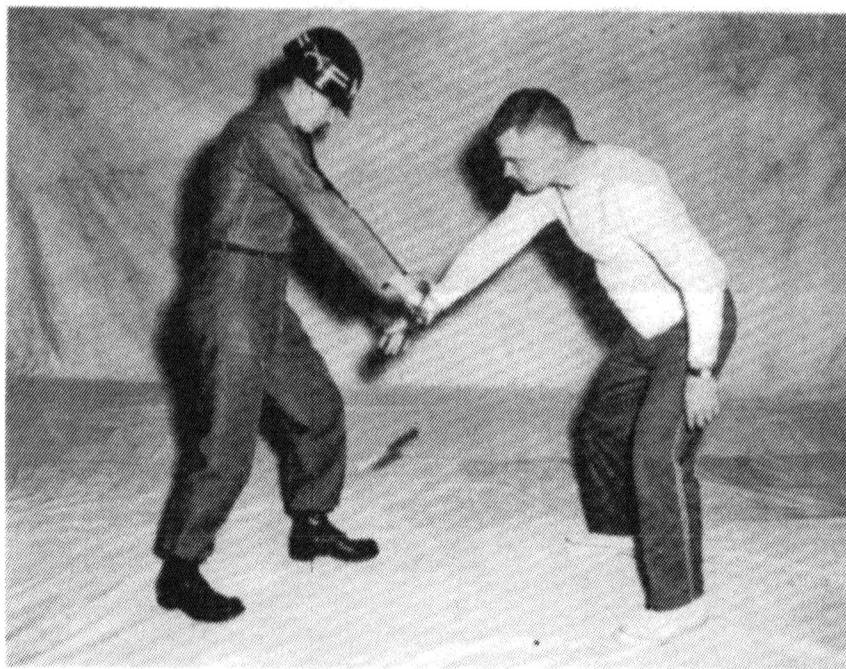

Figure 109. Blocking the upward thrust.

b. Preparation for the counterblow. As the opponent drops his weapon, both hands are snapped up and close to the shoulders. The baton is held across the chest. The counterblow is launched by moving forward with the right foot. The baton smash is executed. (See Figure 110.)

Figure 110. Preparation for the counterblow.

121. DEFENSE AGAINST THE UNARMED MAN.

The riot baton is extremely effective when used against an aggressive violent individual. These defensive tactics are best administered from the port position.

a. Defense against left-handed blow. The body is moved slightly to the rear by withdrawing the left foot. The baton is moved smartly from the port position and a counterblow delivered against the opponent's shoulder or collar bone. (See Figure 111.)

b. Defense against right-handed blow. The body is moved slightly to the rear by withdrawing the left foot. The baton is carried smartly downward across the body striking the forearm of the opponent. (See Figure 112.)

Figure 111. Defense against left-handed blow.

Figure 112. Defense against right-handed blow.

c. Defense against the kick. The kick can be blocked from either the on guard or port position. The baton is directed against the instep of the foot. (See Figure 113.)

Figure 113. Defense against the kick.

d. To break the grasp of an opponent. If the police officer is grabbed by an opponent, the baton can be effectively employed as a defensive weapon.

(1) The baton can be jabbed into the groin of the opponent (See Figure 114.)

(2) The baton may be jabbed into the stomach of the opponent. (See Figure 115.)

e. Preventing the opponent from rearming. Once an opponent has been disarmed, he must not be allowed to regain his weapon. Any blow delivered to a vulnerable point of the body is effective. (See Figure 116.)

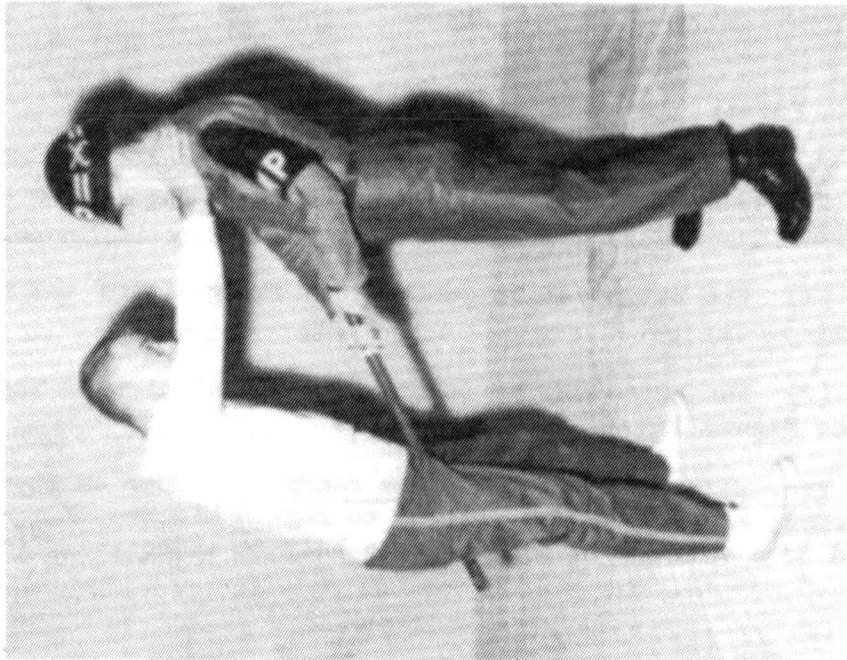

Figure 115. Breaking the grasp of an Opponent.

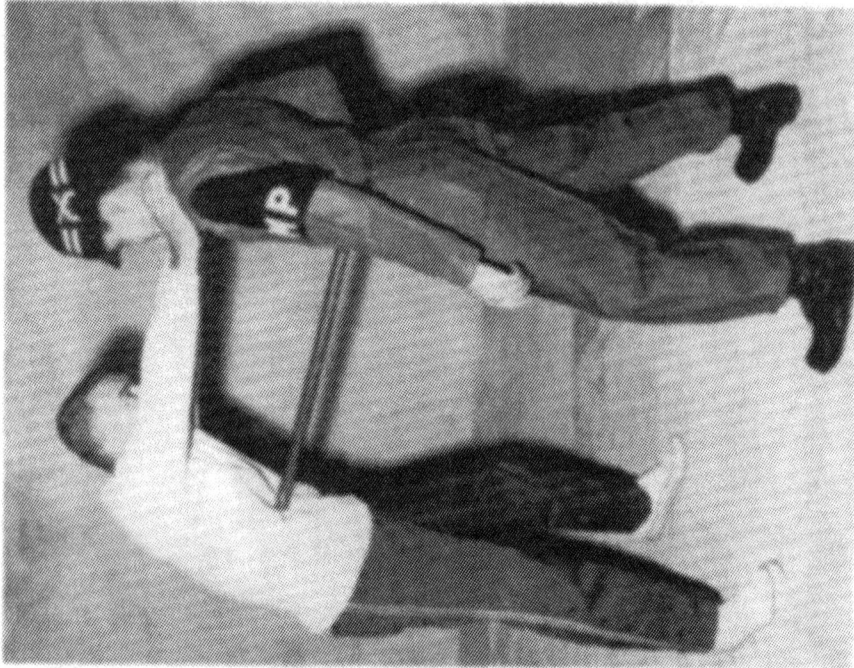

Figure 114. Breaking the grasp of an opponent.

Figure 116.   Preventing the opponent from rearming.

Section III

FATAL BLOWS

122.   GENERAL.

The riot baton can be used as a weapon that will produce death
or serious injury.   It is important for police officers to know those blows
which can be fatal.   Figure 117 illustrates those areas of the body which
when struck by blows with a baton can result in death.

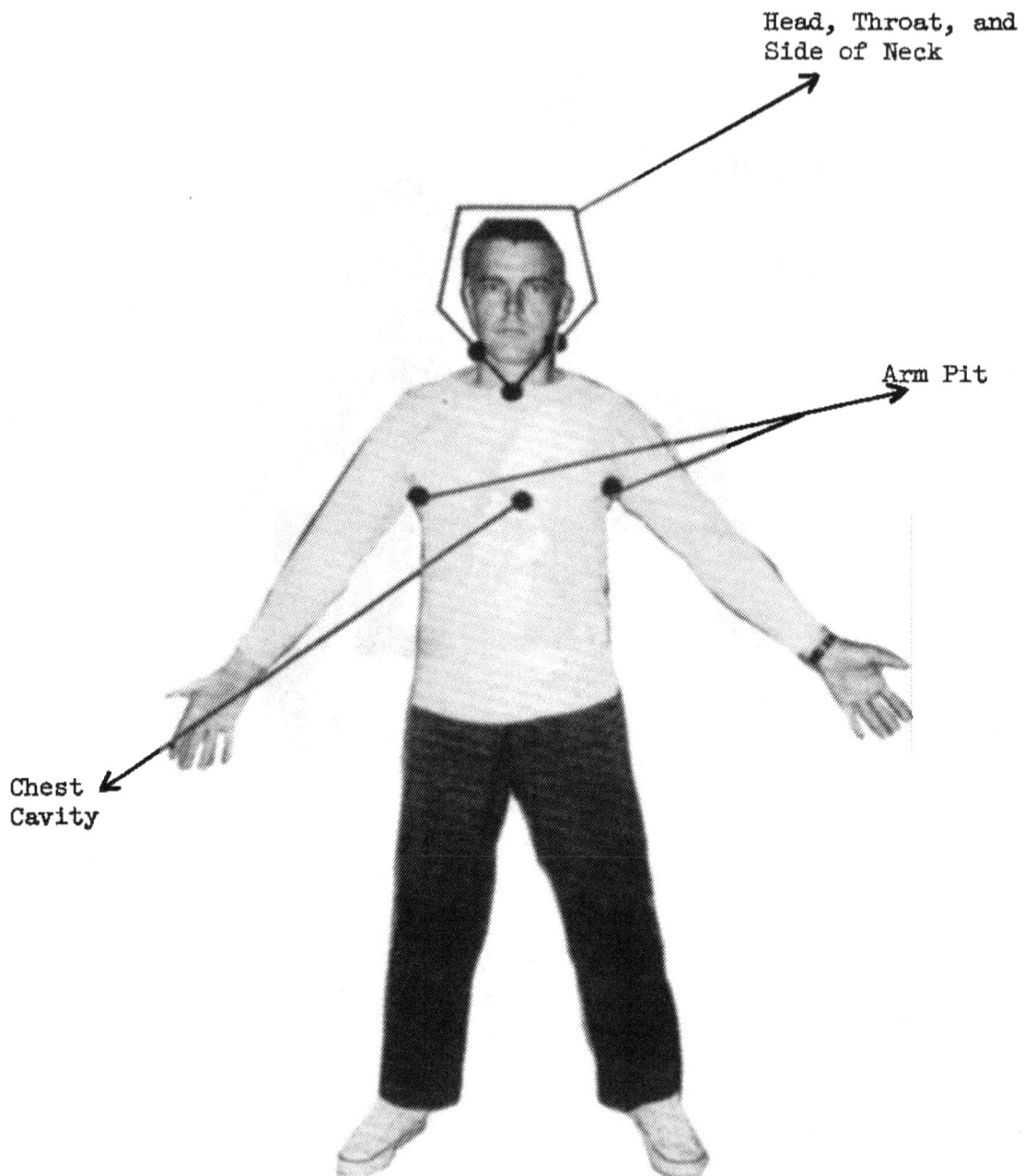

Figure 117.   Possible fatal points of impact.

ST 19-180; 226

123. THE ADMINISTRATION OF A FATAL BLOW THROUGH THE APPLICATION OF THE BATON JAB.

a. Position for execution. The jab may be delivered after completion of the baton butt stroke or from the on guard position. The left hand is raised to the left near the shoulder. The right hand is moved upward and to the left. The relative positions of the hands remain unchanged in the grip of the baton. The grip end of the baton is pointing toward the opponent. (See Figure 118.)

Figure 118. Position for baton jab.

b. Execution of the baton jab, fatal blow. The body is advanced rapidly by moving forward with the right foot. The left arm is snapped forward and the right arm straightened. The grip end of the baton is driven into a fatal point of impact. The baton jab is an offensive maneuver that can be used effectively employing nonfatal points of impact. (See Figure 119.)

Figure 119. Executing the jab (fatal blow).

124. THE ADMINISTRATION OF FATAL BLOWS THROUGH THE APPLICATION OF THE BATON SMASH.

Fatal blows can be delivered to the central portion of the throat area or to the nose of the opponent's body. (See Figures 120 and 121.)

125. ILLUSTRATION OF MINOR DIFFERENCE BETWEEN MODERATE INJURY AND FATALITY.

Figure 122 illustrates a blow delivered to the upper shoulder region of the opponent. Although this blow would probably break the collar bone, it is not considered fatal. Figure 123 illustrates almost the same blow, except that its force is directed against the side of the neck and can cause death.

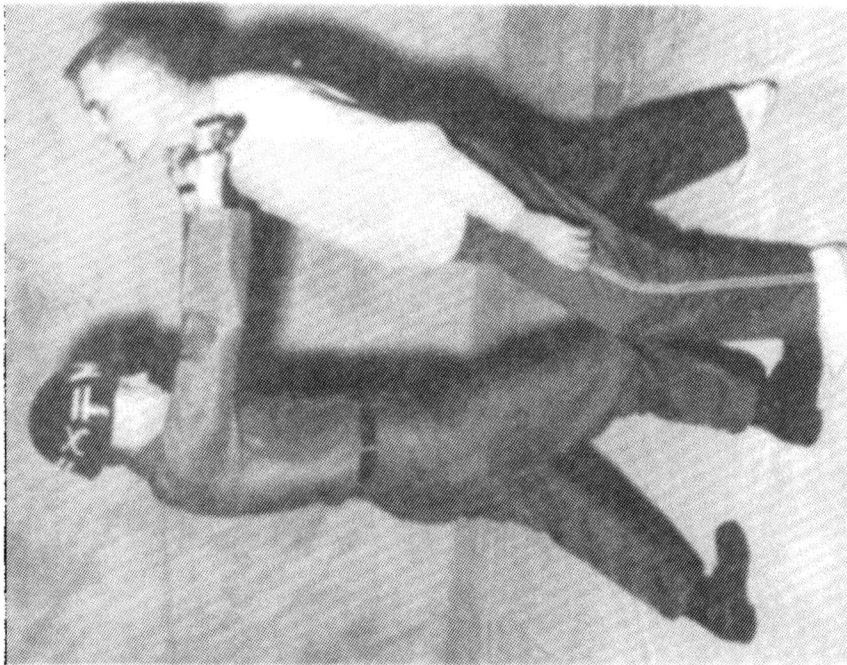

Figure 120. Executing the smash (fatal blow)   Figure 121. Executing the smash (fatal blow).

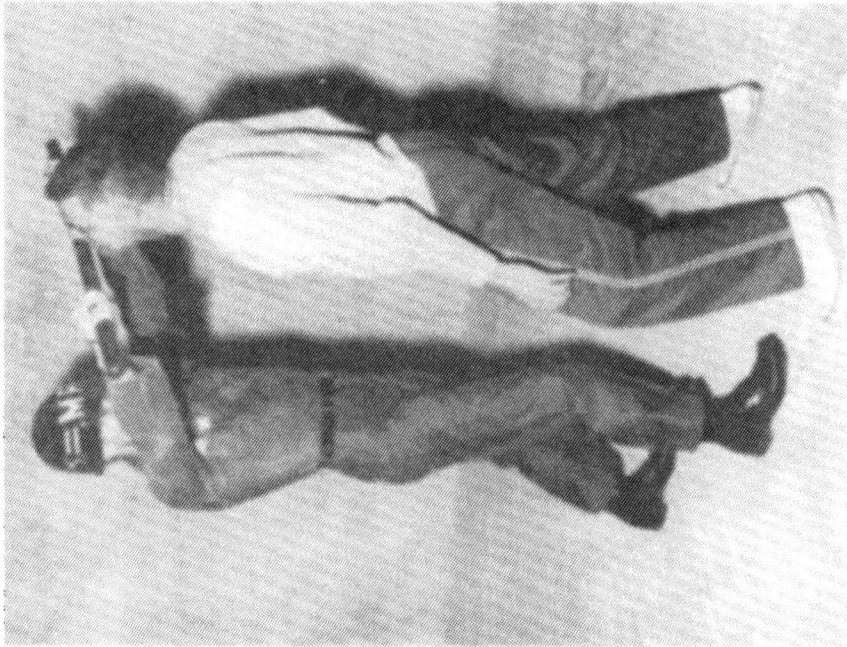

Figure 123. Executing blow to neck (fatal).

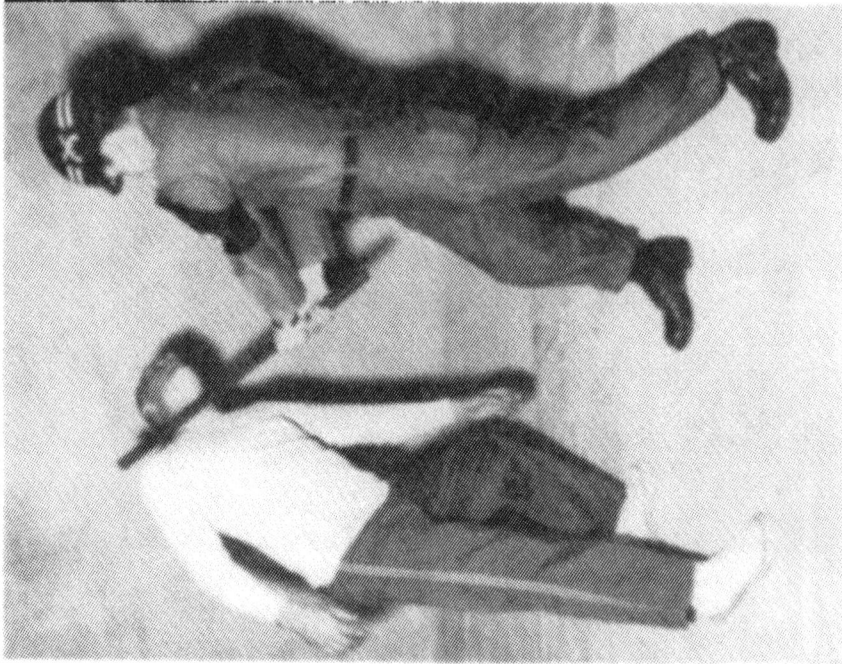

Figure 122. Executing blow to collar bone.

ST 19-180; 230

Section IV

OTHER APPLIED TECHNIQUES

126. GENERAL.

The riot baton is effective in the application of control techniques against hostile personnel. Those considered of particular interest to police officers are discussed in this section.

127. THE CROSS ARM STRANGLE.

a. Step one. Place the right hand, grasping the baton, across the opponent's left shoulder. The hand should rest against the left side of his neck. (See Figure 124.)

Figure 124. Step one, cross arm strangle.

ST 19-180; 231

b. Step two. Rotate the right hand toward the right so that the palm is pointed upward with the striking end of the baton resting against the opponent's throat. Simultaneously, reach the left hand across the right forearm and the opponent's right shoulder. Grip the striking end of the baton with the left hand tight against the right side of the opponent's neck. (See Figure 125.)

Figure 125. Step two, cross arm strangle.

c. Step three. To apply pressure rendering the opponent helpless, spread the elbows apart, pulling him off-balance at the same time. IF MAINTAINED FOR AN EXTENDED PERIOD, THIS HOLD IS FATALITY PRODUCING. (See Figure 126.)

Figure 126. Step three, cross arm strangle.

128. FIGURE FOUR STRANGLE.

a. Step one. Place the right hand grasping the baton across the opponent's right shoulder. (See Figure 127.)

b. Step two. Rotate the right hand toward the left so that the palm is facing down. The baton should be across the opponent's throat in a horizontal position. (See Figure 128.)

c. Step three. Reach across the opponent's left shoulder with the left hand. The left arm is moved under the striking end of the baton, far enough forward so that the baton is able to fall into the bend of the left arm. Lift the left forearm, placing the left hand at the back of the opponent's head. To apply pressure, push forward with the left hand, simultaneously pulling to the rear with the right hand. IF PRESSURE IS MAINTAINED FOR AN EXTENDED PERIOD OF TIME, THIS HOLD IS CONSIDERED CASUALTY-PRODUCING. (See Figure 129.)

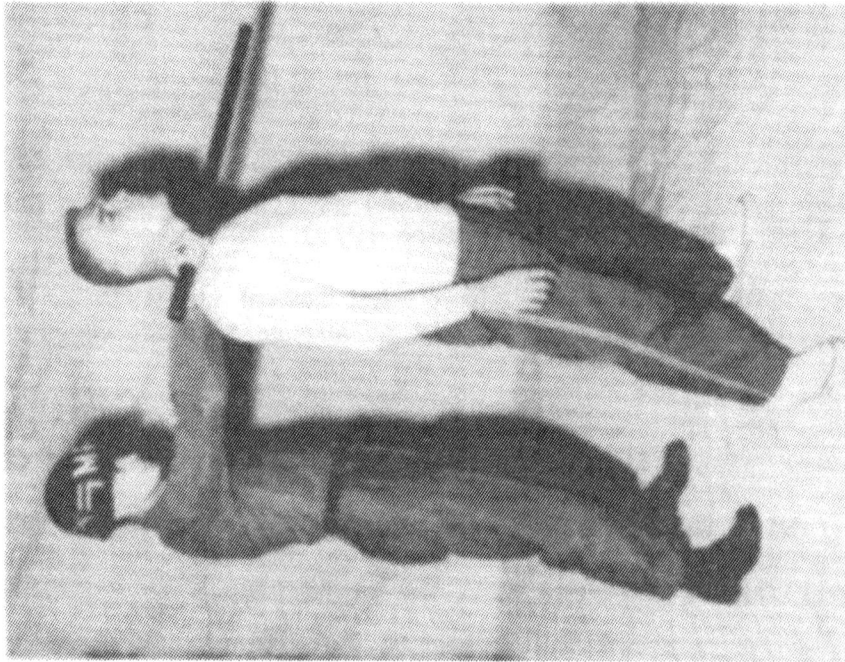

Figure 128. Step two, figure four strangle.

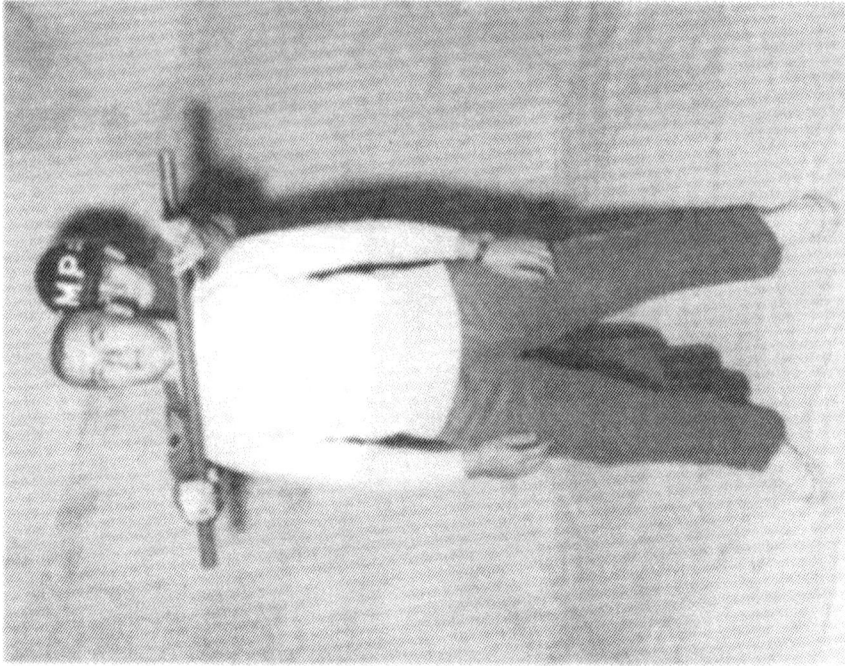

Figure 127. Step one, figure four strangle.

Figure 129. Step three, figure four strangle.

129. BATON COME-A-LONG.

a. Step one. Grasp the center of the baton with the right hand. Rotate the baton to a position that is on line with the right arm and pointed toward the opponent. (See Figure 130.)

b. Step two. Thrust the baton between the opponent's legs with the right arm. Rotate the right hand to a position in which the palm is turned upward. Pull back and up, placing the baton across the upper thighs of the opponent. (See Figure 131.)

c. Step three. With the left hand, reach up and grasp the opponent's collar near the back of his neck. To move the opponent, the right hand is maintained as straight as possible and upward pressure is exerted from the shoulder. Simultaneously, pressure is applied forward with the left hand. The opponent is kept up and off-balance, to his front. (See Figure 132.)

Figure 131. Step two, baton come-a-along.

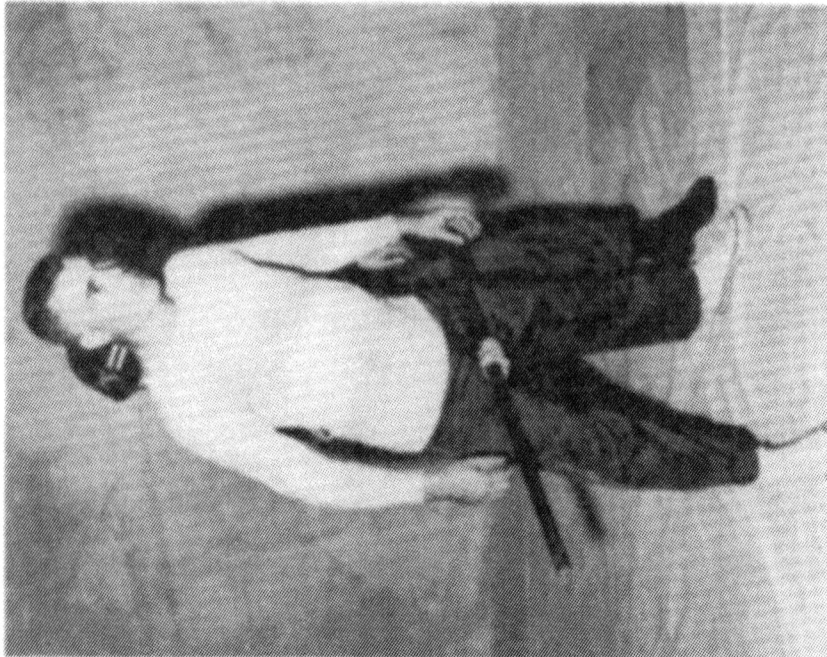

Figure 130. Step one, baton come-a-long.

Figure 132. Step three, baton come-a-long.

130. HAMMERLOCK COME-A-LONG.

a. <u>Step one</u>. With the baton held in the right hand, step forward with the left foot, placing the striking end of the baton between the opponent's left arm and body. As the baton passes to the rear of the opponent's body, push upward and to the rear. (See Figure 133.)

b. <u>Step two</u>. Reach across the opponent's left shoulder with the left hand and grasp the striking end of the baton. (See Figure 134.)

c. <u>Step three</u>. Pivoting on the ball of the left foot, move to the opponent's left rear. Simultaneously exert downward pressure on the striking end of the baton with the left hand in the direction of the opponent's left front. Exert upward pressure on the grip end of the baton with the right hand. Bend the opponent well forward at the waist. (See Figure 135.)

d. Step four. Holding the baton firmly with the right hand, release the left hand and reach across the striking end of the baton and grasp the right side of his face. (See Figure 136.)

e. Step five. With the left hand, force the opponent's face to the left, straightening him up. To apply pressure, press downward with the left upper arm across the striking end of the baton and pull upward with the right hand on the grip of the baton. (See Figure 137.)

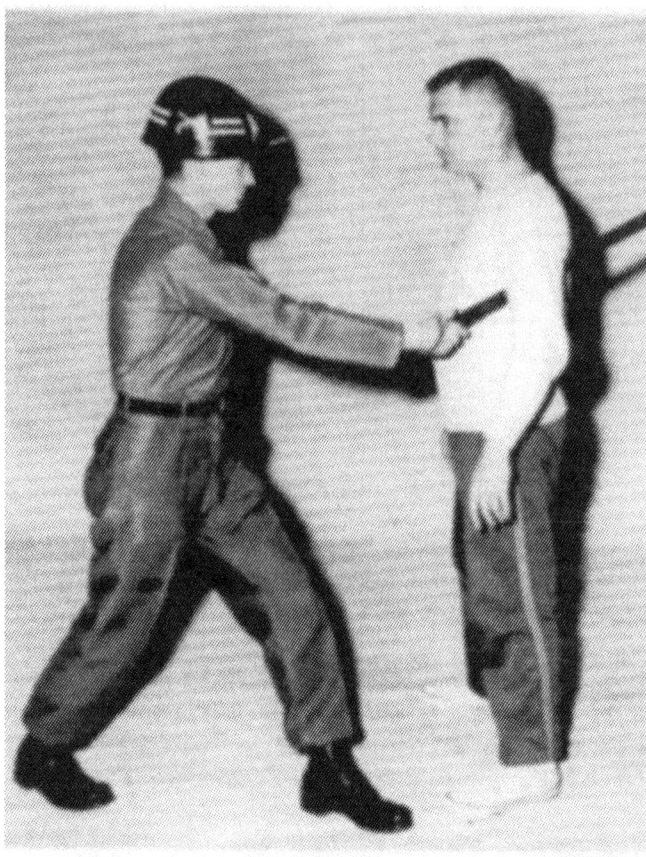

Figure 133. Step one, hammerlock.

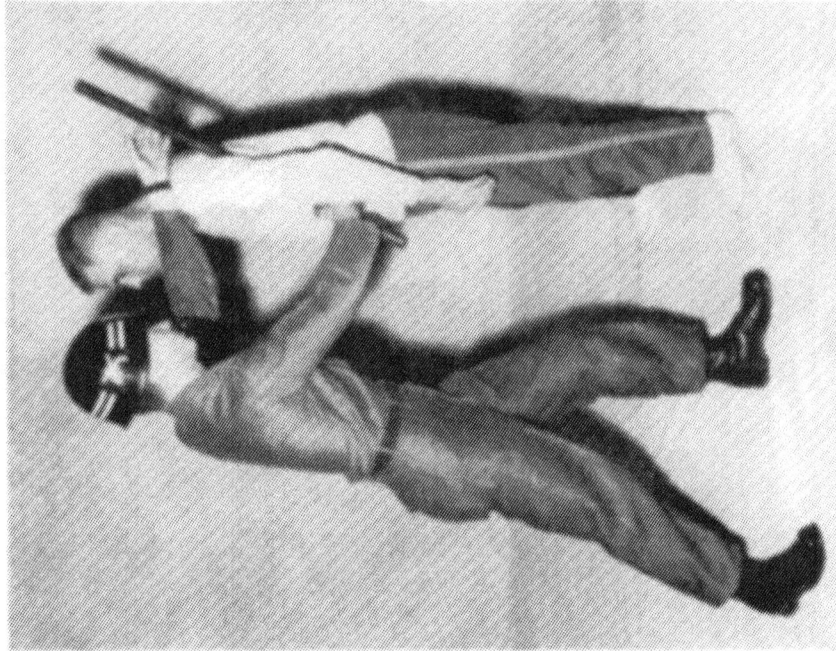

Figure 135. Step three, hammerlock.

Figure 134. Step two, hammerlock.

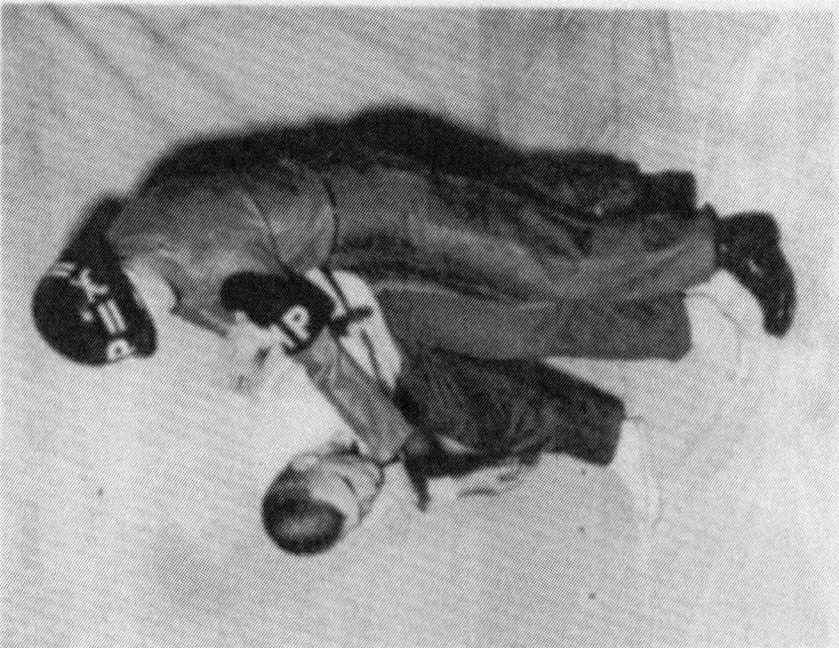

Figure 137. Step five, hammerlock.

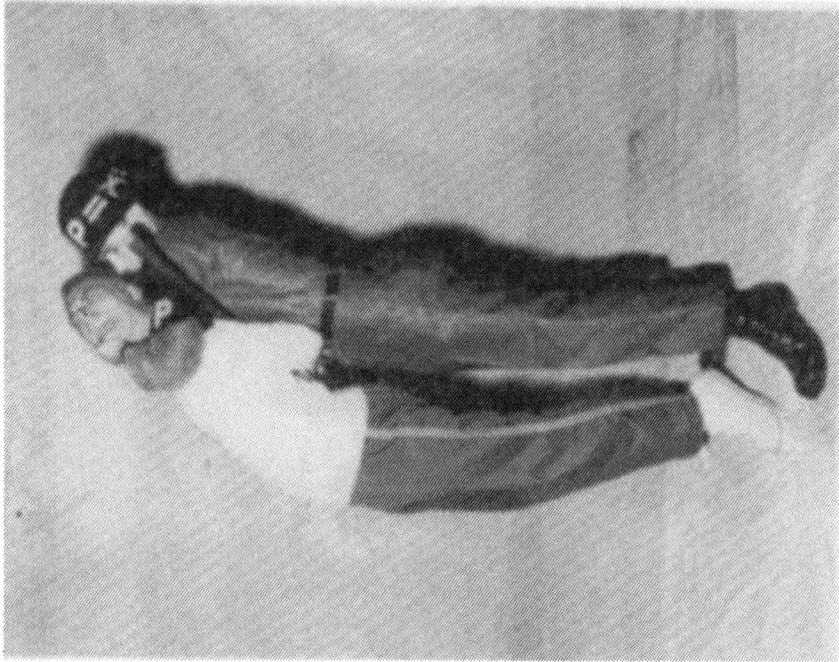

Figure 136. Step four, hammerlock.

ST 19-180; 240

131. TECHNIQUES WITH 30 INCH RIOT BATON.

Figures 138 through 148 indicate various techniques of employing the riot baton with a single hand. These techniques are applied in the same manner as the two-handed techniques discussed in this chapter.

a. The short thrust is delivered with the 30 inch or one-handed baton by thrusting the baton forward parallel to the ground without shifting the feet from the modified boxer's stance. The tip of the baton should strike the opponent at one of the vulnerable points of the body. (See Figure 138.)

b. The butt stroke with a one-handed baton is delivered by advancing the right foot and body weight while striking the opponent with the end of the baton that is exposed below the grip. (See Figure 139.)

c. With the 30 inch or one-handed baton, the defense against the overhand stab is most effective when executed exactly as described for the two-handed baton in paragraph 119a. (See Figure 140.)

ST 19-180; 241

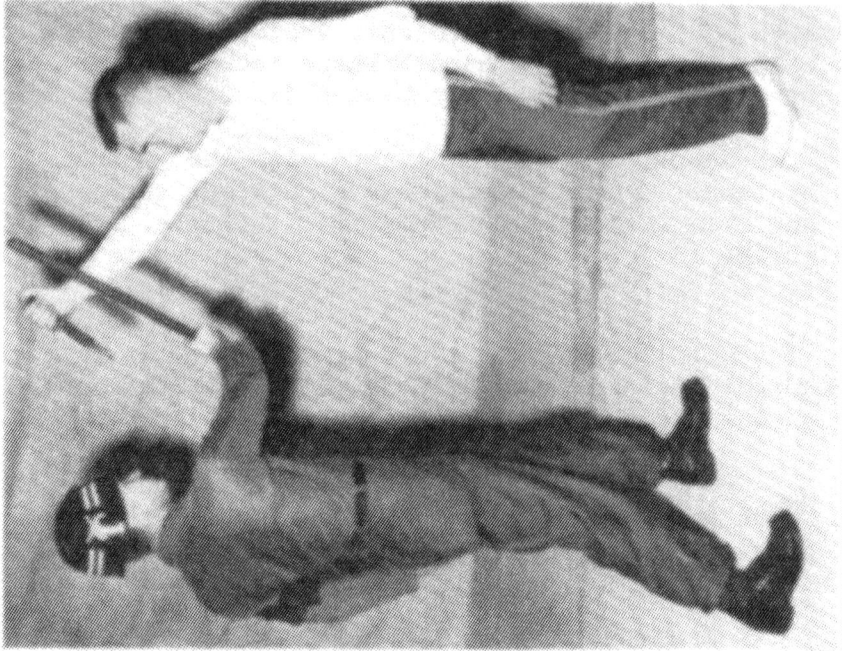

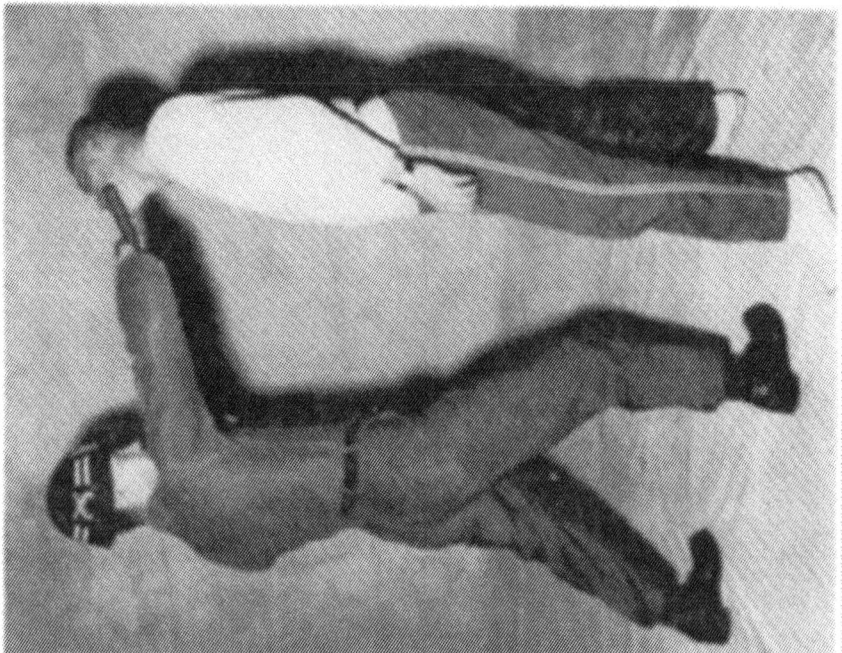

ST 19-180; 242

d. The upward knife thrust is blocked with a one-handed riot baton by delivering a sharp blow to the inside of the wrist of the opponent. (See Figure 141.)

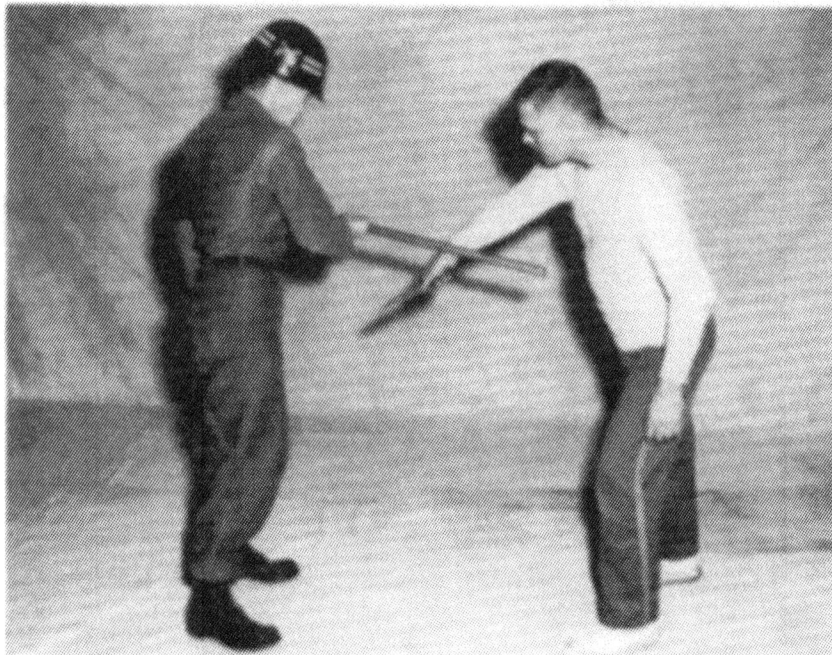

Figure 141. Defense against upward thrust
(one hand).

e. To defend against a kick with the one-handed baton, a sharp blow is delivered to the ankle of the opponent after the opponent's leg leaves the ground to deliver the kick. The defensive blow is delivered to the inside of the ankle if the defender is right-handed and the opponent kicks with his right foot. The defender may strike the outside of the ankle if the opponent kicks with his left foot. (See Figure 142.)

f. If the opponent grabs the baton and attempts to wrench it from the policeman, the policeman grasps the baton with the left hand below the right hand. By shifting the body weight to the left foot and turning the right side toward the opponent, the policeman can then deliver a kick with the right foot to the knee of the opponent. A hard kick with the right foot to the opponent's knee will either disable him temporarily or break his leg. (See Figure 143.)

g. An opponent who is aggressively attempting to grab the policeman can be temporarily disabled by stepping back and delivering a one-handed blow to the back of the hand or to the wrist. (See Figures 144 and 145.)

Figure 142.   Defense against kick (one hand).

Figure 143.   Breaking opponent's grip of baton.

ST 19-180; 244

Figure 144.   Forehand blow to hand.

Figure 145.   Back hand blow to hand.

h. A sharp forehand blow to the forearm of the opponent will either break the forearm or restrict movement temporarily. (See Figure 146.)

Figure 146. Forehand blow to forearm.

i. The one-handed riot baton may be used to down an opponent from the rear. The policeman reaches over the shoulder of the opponent with the left hand and grabs the clothing. With a pull backward with the left hand and by delivering a sharp blow with the riot baton to the back of the knee, the opponent can be downed easily. (See Figure 147.)

j. An effective come-a-long with the riot baton can be improvised by having the opponent cross his hands behind his back and slipping each hand through the leather thong on the riot baton. By twisting the baton until all of the slack is gone, the come-a-long can be tightened or loosened according to the degree of pressure required to secure the prisoner. The left hand grasps the left shoulder or the clothing over the shoulder of the opponent and the opponent is pulled backward slightly so that he cannot pull away from the baton end, which is pressed against the small of the back. (See Figure 148a and b.)

Figure 147. Downing Opponent.

Figure 148a. Come-a-long.

ST 19-180; 247

Figure 148b. Come-a-long.

CHAPTER 12

PHOTOGRAPHY

132. GENERAL.

Special consideration should be given to the selection of the
photographic equipment that can be effectively employed in the support
of riot control operations. A camera must be capable of performing well
under adverse conditions such as flooding by water hoses or exposure to
rain. It should be sturdily constructed to withstand the shock when hit
by sticks or other damaging objects. It should be easily operated when
the cameraman is forced to wear either gloves or a gas mask. The camera
selected should be easily transported by a single man. It is also advantageous to have a camera capable of using interchangeable lenses.
These general considerations are considered applicable to both movie
and still-type cameras.

133. MOTION PICTURE CAMERAS.

Motion picture cameras are highly recommended for use in riot
control operations because of their versatility. Motion picture cameras
are categorized according to their characteristics.

a. The turret type camera. The turret motion picture camera
normally has two or three lenses mounted on an exterior turret. The
lenses are changed by selection and rotation of the turret. The view-
finder must be changed with the lens to correspond with the view as seen
through the lens.

b. Single lens type camera. The single lens camera contains
a single lens which is mounted in the camera body. Normally, this lens
can be removed manually and other lenses substituted as required. If
one lens is substituted for another, it is necessary to change view-
finders. (See Figure 149.)

c. Magazine loading cameras. The magazine loading camera
utilizes a pre-loaded film magazine which is inserted into the camera
body. Reloading of the magazine camera is rapid and easily accomplished
Cameras of this type are usually capable of exposing fifty feet of film
(15.24 meters) before a change in magazines is required.

d. Roll film cameras. The roll film motion picture camera
normally uses a one-hundred foot roll (30.48 meters) of 16mm film. Loading procedures require threading of the film into the camera mechanism
prior to operation. Although loading is usually easily accomplished, it
is time consuming.

Figure 149. Single lens roll film movie camera.

e. Recommended equipment. For riot control operations a type camera is recommended that has the capabilities of the turret lens arrangement and magazine loading. Through the use of this equipment the photographer is able to more easily remain abreast of the situation without being hindered by accessory lenses or untimely reloading requirements. However, other cameras can also be employed successfully.

f. Accessory items. Certain accessory items are frequently used in conjunction with motion picture cameras. A tripod is an important adjunct to the utilization of the telephoto lens. Battery operated electric motors can be used to drive the camera mechanism. For roll type cameras of certain types, specially constructed magazines capable of carrying 500 to 1,000 feet are available.

134. STILL PICTURE CAMERAS.

Still picture cameras have the same general employment as do motion picture cameras in riot control operations. They are divided into categories by type and size.

a. Press camera. The press camera is designed for rugged service and is capable of high shutter speeds, useful in riot photography. This type of camera normally uses either 2.25 by 3.25 inch or 4 by 5 inch cut film. The press type camera employs a ground glass focusing panel and characteristically accepts various lenses. It is an excellent all-purpose camera which can be used in the additional roles of a copy camera, portrait camera, and for general purpose police activities. (See Figure 150.)

b. Miniature cameras. The most widely accepted miniature camera in general use is the 35mm. For police photography, it should have rapidly interchangeable lenses, high shutter speeds, and fast lenses. A photoflash attachment is recommended and should be film that normally provides 20-36 exposures per roll. (See Figure 151.)

c. Sub-miniature cameras. Sub-miniature cameras are those that utilize film smaller than 35mm. They normally utilize 16mm film and are capable of taking from 50 to 60 exposures per roll. Professional models of the sub-miniature cameras possess shutter speeds as high as 1/1000 second and may be used without accessories to photograph items such as documents as close as ten inches to the camera. Due to the capability of these cameras to be installed in unusual objects such as cigarette lighters or umbrella handles, they are well suited for use in covert police photography. Since exposure techniques are not critical, the sub-miniature camera is able to produce excellent results.

Figure 150. Typical press type still camera with accessories.

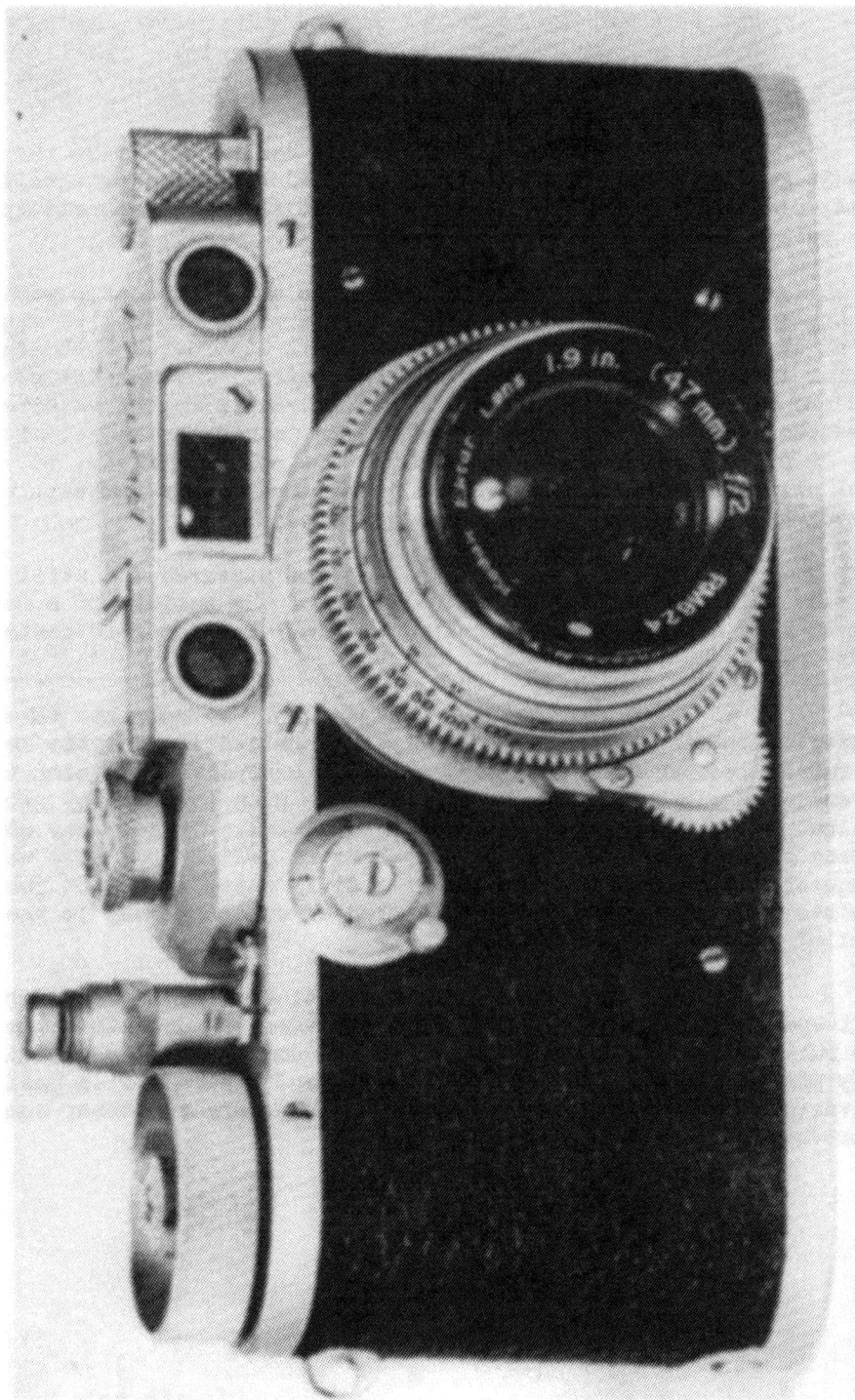

Figure 151. Typical 35mm miniature camera.

135. USES OF PHOTOGRAPHY.

The application of photography can be effective throughout the stages of riot control. It may be used in gathering intelligence data, planning, critiques, training, identification of participants, and public relations.

a. Planning. Vital, sensitive areas such as power stations, banks, and water works may require predetermined protective measures which can be rapidly applied during a civil disorder. Photography can assist in the determination of these measures. Through the use of aerial and ground photography, access and egress routes may be selected. The locations for barricades or police strong points can be selected by analysis of photographs. Photographs allow the police official to view the actual area of a projected operation in advance of his arrival. Aerial photographs lend themselves to use as maps.

b. During riot control. Motion pictures and still photographs provide police with an invaluable record of the actions of a mob. They can be used effectively to identify criminal acts, participants, and mob tactics.

c. Post riot control utilization. Photographs taken during a civil disorder are useful in analyzing mob tactics for the development of future countermeasures. They are also useful in analyzing the effectiveness of police tactics and equipment. Riot photography provides excellent training material for police personnel. It also may be used to defend police commanders against charges of police brutality which are frequently made in the aftermath of a civil disorder. Riot photography assists in the modification or redesign of equipment and in the development of protective devices.

d. Photography in public relations. Photographs provide the police agency with an effective communication medium with which to reach the public. For example, photographs can portray police training, identify police with the public's interests, and record police participation in various public activities such as youth groups and other community improvement projects.

CHAPTER 13

PHYSICAL SECURITY OF VITAL INSTALLATIONS

136. INTRODUCTION.

During a period of civil disorder, careful consideration must be given to the protection of vital community installations. The destruction of public facilities by a mob can create long-lasting adverse effects on the economic and physical well-being of the population and seriously hamper the continuing operation of the community government. The loss of water supplies and power can seriously endanger the health of the community; the appropriation of weapons stored in an armory can increase violence; the destruction of important government buildings can seriously disrupt the procedures of government; mob control of banks, post offices, or hospitals may lead to the collapse of the society; and mob control of communication media can readily gain psychological advantage for further spread of the disorder. Through the application of physical security principles, vital installations can be protected effectively during civil disorders. The use of trained security forces, augmented by protective devices will enable a vital installation to survive the attack of a mob long enough to allow the police commander to employ necessary measures of force. It is important that the security of vital installations be carefully considered in the overall execution of the riot control mission.

137. OBJECTIVES.

Physical security encompasses those actions taken to protect property and personnel from unnecessary damage or destruction. This chapter is intended to present the principles of physical security and concepts in the use of protective measures.

138. RECOGNITION OF SECURITY HAZARDS.

Hazards to property or people are acts or conditions which can result in the compromise of information, loss of life, injury, damage, or the loss or destruction of property. These acts or conditions may be constantly present, or recurring at infrequent intervals. The very possibility that they sometimes do exist is sufficient to be considered risks to security. The degree of risk involved is dependent upon two factors: (1) the probability of adverse effects occurring as the direct result of the hazard, and (2) the degree to which the facility will be affected if the hazard becomes a reality.

139. NATURAL HAZARDS.

Natural hazards occur as the result of a natural phenomenon, although in some instances they can be induced through human action.

Normally, preventive action against damage inflicted by natural hazards is not considered within the scope of physical security; however, in the discussion of civil disorders, it is interesting to note that although riots do not often occur under adverse natural conditions, they may occur in the aftermath. Police officials should be aware of the ramifications that natural hazards can have in a vital installation when evaluating existing security measures.

a. Earthquakes and storms. The violent actions of storms or earthquakes can cause severe damage within a community. The passive defense measures that may be taken are not a part of physical security. In the aftermath of an earthquake or storm, a vital installation can become the target for portions of the population who have been seriously affected The loss of protective lighting, perimeter barriers, alarm systems, patrol vehicles, and communications, create serious breaches in the security status of an installation. Complete and detailed plans should be formulated in advance to assure that the installation will not remain vulnerable for an extended period of time following the occurrence of a natural disaster. The possibility for occurrence of a serious hazard through storm or earthquake may be indicated by the results of historical studies which consider the geographical location of the installation.

b. Extremes in temperature. Extremes in temperature are classified as natural hazards to security. Extremes of heat or cold can have adverse effects on the human body. Individuals become reluctant to take aggressive action, perform patrol duties, or otherwise expose themselves to such weather extremes. Vehicles, communications, and alarm devices may not function properly. Special advance precautions must be taken to insure that acceptable standards of security are maintained.

c. Floods. In some geographical areas floods are a recurring problem. Planning for these conditions should include emergency security measures that replace or supplement measures normally in effect.

d. Reduced visibility. Any natural phenomena which reduce and restrict visibility are considered natural hazards. Such conditions may arise as the result of darkness, snow, rain, fog, or sandstorm. Individuals attempting to penetrate a vital installation will be afforded an increased degree of concealment under any of these conditions. Planning for adequate security should include provision for these occurrences.

e. Fires. The possibility of fire as the result of a natural phenomenon is ever-present. Security personnel must be alert for the early detection of fire to allow for immediate effective action. Fires exceeding the control capabilities of the fire protection unit seriously jeopardize the security of the installation. Fires create excellent diversionary opportunities for pilferers, saboteurs, espionage agents, and professional agitators to attempt to breach security measures.

140. HUMAN HAZARDS.

Human security hazards usually are the result of a state of mind, attitude, weakness, or character trait on the part of one or more individuals. They may be intentional or unintentional, covert or overt. They involve acts of commission or omission on the part of human beings, and therefore cannot be predicted accurately. Security planning should be based on the concept that such hazards exist at each facility. Each facility must then be analyzed to determine what the hazards are and how they may be minimized.

141. PHYSICAL PROTECTION.

To improve the physical security of a vital installation, various safeguards may be employed. Those considered most important are discussed below:

a. Security areas. It is common for activities within a facility to be assigned different degrees of security importance.

(1) Restricted areas. Restricted areas are considered to be those areas which must be subjected to special restrictions and controls for reasons of security. The reasons for security may include the safeguarding of property and material. Access to restricted areas is characteristically rigidly controlled.

(2) Limited areas. A limited area is a restricted area which contains a security interest or other matter, in which uncontrolled movement will permit access to such security interest or matter, but within which access may be prevented by escort and other internal restrictions and controls.

(3) Exclusion areas. Exclusion areas are defined as restricted areas which contain an item of security interest which is of such a nature that access to the area constitutes access to the item. They may also be defined as areas containing items of security interest which are of such vital importance that the proximity resulting from access to the area is equivalent to access to the item.

b. Perimeter barriers. A perimeter barrier defines the physical limits of a protected area. It is designed to impede or restrict access to the protected area by unauthorized personnel; however, it does not preclude entry by a determined intruder. Perimeter barriers perform the following functions:

(1) They create a physical and psychological deterrent to innocent entry and to persons attempting or contemplating unauthorized entry into the area.

(2) They delay intrusion into an area and aid in the detection and apprehension of intruders by security personnel.

(3) They facilitate more effective utilization of security guard forces.

(4) They channel the flow of personnel and vehicles through designated controlled access points. Perimeter barriers may be natural or man-made. Certain topographical terrain features such as mountains, cliffs, canyons, rivers, marshes, and deserts are considered natural barriers. Most natural barriers require additional man-made safeguards to realize their maximum potential deterrent to unauthorized entry. The most common structural barrier in use today is the wire fence, normally found in the form of chain link, barbed wire, or concertina. Clear zones should be maintained on either side of a perimeter barrier. When it is not possible to establish clear zones due to property lines or natural features, the height of the fence should be increased accordingly.

c. Protective lighting. The ability to see is important to security personnel. Protective lighting is designed to provide uninterrupted visibility during the hours of darkness. Light has some intrinsic value as a deterrent but its primary purpose is to provide illumination. The proper use of light permits observation from a distance thereby reducing the requirement for security guard personnel. Protective lighting is an aid in preventing covert interferences but is of little value in overt situations when blackout conditions are necessary.

(1) Continuous lighting. Continuous lighting consists of a series of fixed lights arranged to provide overlapping cones of light to a given area during the hours of darkness. Two primary methods of employing continuous lighting include glare projection and controlled lighting.

(a) Glare projection. Glare projection is lighting in which the surrounding territory is illuminated. It permits the security guard to see an outside area but restricts the ability of an individual in the outside area from viewing the guard.

(b) Controlled lighting. Controlled lighting permits the adjustment of light to fit the particular instance. It normally consists of lighting a specific object, passage, or barrier to the requirements of the specific situation.

(2) Standby lighting. Standby lighting is similar to continuous lighting except that it is usually activated through an intrusion detection device or other automatic means. It may also be operated manually as required by the security force. Standby lighting is used under abnormal conditions.

(3) Movable lighting. Movable lighting normally consists of movable searchlights. It is primarily used to supplement the main lighting systems discussed above.

(4) Emergency lighting. Emergency lighting may duplicate any of the other types of systems discussed. Its use is limited to emergencies in which the primary lighting system becomes inoperative. A power source must be assured.

(5) General considerations. The applications of protective lighting vary as required by specific situations and types of installations. It may be necessary to use a combination of several types of lighting systems in a facility. It is important that police officials be familiar with the differences in lighting systems and be able to select the best system for the facility concerned.

(6) Power. The primary source of power at a vital installation may be the local community power utility. It is suggested that an alternate power source be available for use in situations where power interruptions are frequent or during emergency conditions. Both multiple and series circuits can be utilized to advantage in protective lighting systems. Circuits should be arranged to insure that failure of one lamp will not darken an extended area in which protective light coverage is required. Periodic inspections should be conducted of all electrical circuits to detect, repair, or replace worn parts, tighten connections, and check the condition of insulation. Lights should be scheduled for replacement when 80 per cent of their rated life has been attained. Light poles of protective lighting systems should be positioned a minimum of ten feet inside the fence line. Feeder electrical lines should be installed underground to reduce the possibility of sabotage or vandalism.

d. Identification and control. The purpose of identification and control is to assure that only authorized personnel are allowed access to a secured area. The identification and control system must be simple, readily understood, and easily operated. One method for identifying personnel is personal recognition. Usually, one person should be responsible for the proper identification of approximately thirty people. A personal recognition system is not feasible for utilization in large facilities. In these facilities, an artificial system of identification should be developed and applied. The most practical method of identification of personnel at large installations is the use of a special pass or badge. For efficient use, passes or badges must be of tamper-resistant construction. Normally, metal-rimmed or plastic envelope devices are not considered tamper-resistant. Laminated or embossed devices are considered tamper resistant when several other features are incorporated. Other features might include a clear and intricate background design which is difficult to reproduce, a clear and recent photograph, the signature of the validating official, and a secret characteristic known only to facility officials.

e. Alarm systems devices. An alarm system is the manual or automatic medium through which warnings of potential or imminent dangers are transmitted.

(1) Alarm communication systems accomplish the purposes outlined below.

(a) They can reduce security personnel requirements through substituting mobile security guards for fixed posts and foot patrols where practical.

(b) They can be used to replace other protective methods which cannot be used for various reasons.

(c) They provide additional protection to vital areas.

(2) Under some conditions, a practical and economical alarm system can consist of improvised alarm devices such as tin cans containing stones and positioned on wire fences. When the fence is breached, the noise created by the rattling tin cans immediately alerts guards to an unauthorized entry. Trip flares can also be employed effectively under certain circumstances.

f. Protective communications. A security force should not depend solely on the regular communications system of a vital installation. The force should also have a communication capability which is adaptable to use with an emergency power supply. Protective communications systems will normally vary according to analysis of several different factors. Normally, more than one of the following methods of communication should be included.

(1) Capability for local exchange and community telephone service.

(2) A capability for either point-to-point or mobile communication.

(3) Telephone and teletype capability for either commercial service or private line operation.

(4) Public address units.

(5) The use of visual signals.

(6) The application of certain audible signal devices such as whistles, bells, and sirens.

g. Security guard forces.

(1) General. The use of security guard forces in the protective plan of a vital installation considers the employment of men or animals as barriers between the potential intruder and the material being protected. The security guard force provides for rapid response to alarms or situations threatening security, apprehension of individual violators, and identification of individuals entering, departing, or working in a secured area.

(2) Personnel requirements. The number of personnel required for the security of a vital installation can be determined only after careful analysis is made of the facility. It can be assumed that increased manpower will be required in the event of a civil disorder that has the potential of affecting the installation.

(3) The use of dogs. Consideration should be given to the use of dogs in the operations of the security force. Sentry dogs are valuable assets to the security force since their extreme sensitivity to odor and sound alerts handlers to intruders at ranges of 150 to 200 yards during hours of darkness and under adverse weather conditions. While the dogs may be used at any hour of the day, nighttime is the dog's natural hunting time and he will usually be more inquisitive and alert when working at night than during the day. Sentry dogs should be trained to disarm violators on command, to climb ladders and other obstacles, and perform other aggressive feats to protect his handler. Dogs, unlike human beings, are considered to be incorruptible and completely loyal. The addition of dogs to a security force will provide the security guards with a distinct psychological advantage. Dogs will generally offset any numerical advantage enjoyed by intruders and will enable the security guard to apprehend violators who might have otherwise escaped detection.

APPENDIX I

INCIDENTS

The following extracts are news items extracted from the New York Times during the year 1961. They provide a brief survey of the magnitude of civil disturbances and riots which occurred throughout the world during that year. In some instances the basic causation factors are obvious, while in others they are not. These incidents were caused by either dissatisfaction within the population or by pressure or influence from an opposing ideology of domestic or foreign origin.

551 HURT IN OSAKA RIOT; POLICE BREAK UP MELEE

OSAKA, JAPAN, Friday, Aug. 4 (AP)--Club-swinging policemen charged through Osaka's slums at dawn today, breaking up a third consecutive all-night riot. Officials expect another battle tonight.

The police listed 551 persons injured, including 389 policemen and eight Japanese newsmen and cameramen, since the fighting broke out in the poverty-stricken Nishinari district Tuesday night. The demonstrators were angry at the way the police had handled an auto accident that caused the death of an aged male pedestrian.

Six thousand policemen have been alerted. Officials estimate that at one point last night, 5,000 steel-helmeted policemen fought 3,000 rioters. The police have arrested 97 persons.

18 HURT IN HARLEM AS CALYPSO PARADE TURNS INTO A RIOT

A calypso parade that moved rhythmically up Seventh Avenue in Harlem, New York City, suddenly turned into a bottle-throwing brawl yesterday afternoon. Eighteen persons were hurt in the riot, including ten policemen. Six of the injured were among eleven persons arrested.

Bottles crashed onto sidewalks between 141st and 142d Streets during the ten-minute riot. Mounted policemen charged angry mobs, merchants locked their stores and scores of people who had been watching the parade ran for cover.

The trouble started at 4:30 P. M. as the end of the fourteenth annual West Indies Day parade was approaching 141st Street, three blocks south of the dispersal point.

Spectators Move Out

The last float held a calypso band in full swing, and surrounding it were dozens of young girls and boys in scant costumes who shuffled along the sidewalk, arm in arm, to the captivating drum beat.

When a few male spectators went out to join the dancers, the police yelled, "Get back, get back along the sidewalk!" One man shoved a patrol man who tried to pull him back, and then both lost their balance. Other patrolmen joined in, and the man was soon handcuffed. However, he broke away, and the first of dozens of bottles came smashing onto Seventh Avenue.

Angry crowds moved in on policemen wrestling with the handcuffed man. One of the first bottles thrown from the five story tenements along the avenue hit the neck of one mounted patrolman, who was felled to the ground. The air previously filled with calypso music and steel drums, now was filled with sirens of patrol cars, the swearing of policemen and the crashing of bottles.

Mounted policemen hunched low over their horses as they galloped up and down the avenue trying to force the people onto the sidewalks. Women carrying babies shouted incoherently and ran.

Nearly 300 patrolmen were trying to disperse 2,000 persons at the height of the riot.

"It was a most unfortunate incident," said the Rev. O. D. Dempsey, vice marshal of the parade. "This was due to the heat, and also one fellow was mocking another fellow. Something like this can happen in a minute in Harlem. There is so much unrest, so many problems."

VIOLENCE IN INDIA MARS UNITY GOAL

NEW DELHI, INDIA, June 24-----A wave of violence in the State of Assam appears to have gravely marred the quest of Prime Minister Jawaharlal Nehru for Indian unity.

Recent outbreaks in the State had underscored--and, according to some observers, encouraged--linguistic rivalries in several parts of India. They also have added to discord between Hindus and Moslems.

The center of recent unrest is Cachar District, in southern Assam. At least nineteen deaths and hundreds of cases of arson, looting and other property damage have been reported there in the last five weeks.

Yesterday the district, just east of East Pakistan, was declared a disturbed area. This means that a curfew and other stern police measures will be enforced while political and religious leaders attempt to restore harmony.

Disturbances Spreading

Reports are still incomplete on the havoc caused by attacks last Monday by a mob of about 10,000 persons in Hailakandi, a subdivision of Cachar. A report said last night that disturbances in the rural areas of Cachar District were gradually spreading.

The Cachar outbreaks have emphasized the rivalries that have plagued Assam for years. At least forty persons were killed and about 52,000 left homeless in rioting last summer in Brahmaputra Valley in central Assam.

The state is a polyglot of peoples. About 6,000,000 inhabitants, according to latest estimates, claim Assamese as their mother tongue. But the state also has about 4,000,000 persons who speak Bengali, 1,000,000 who speak tribal languages and 500,000 others.

Those who speak Assamese look askance at the long-standing Bengali influence in business and public life. They want Assamese to be the sole official language.

Tribesmen Favor English

The Bengalis of Assam, spearheaded by those in Cachar, want their language to be official. The tribal people who dwell in the hills of southern Assam are fearful of both Bengali and Assamese domination and want English to be retained until it can be replaced by Hindi, India's national tongue.

There have been several moves for separation of certain areas from Assam. Early this month Home Minister Lal Bahadue Shastri of the Central Government proposed a formula under which English would be retained for the present. Bengali agitation was called off.

Last Monday's outbreak was said to have been instigated by anti-Bengalis. Reports from Hindu organizations put the responsibility primarily on Moslems. They say that up to 1,000,000 Moslems have immigrated illegally into Assam in the last ten years from East Pakistan.

Official figures indicate that the immigration total is substantially below 1,000,000, but still enough to worry the Assam government. Chief Minister B. P. Chaliha of Assam, a Hindu, has talked of erecting a barbed-wire fence along the largely unpatrolled East Pakistan frontier.

Moslems Accused

Some Bengali Hindus have accused Moslems in the Assam government of encouraging the immigration to increase their support. The Bengalis say that in order to curry favor most Moslems in the state give Assamese as their mother tongue, whether they speak it or not.

Reports reaching New Delhi often appear incomplete and sometimes contradictory. The situation is considered critical, especially in view of Hindu-Moslem rioting early this year in central India and the effect the Assam situation might have on agitation for the creation of a Sikh-dominated state in Punjab.

PARIS ALGERIANS RIOT FOR 4 HOURS; PROTEST CURFEW

PARIS, Oct. 17--Thousands of Algerian Moslems clashed violently with the French police and security forces here tonight. At least two Moslems were officially reported killed and scores of persons were believed to have been injured.

Besides the dead, a Prefecture of Police communique issued at midnight listed "several" Moslems injured and about ten policemen hurt.

It was the most serious outbreak of violence between the Paris police and the Algerian Moslem community here since the Algerian rebellion began almost seven years ago.

Meanwhile, a mob of about 1,000 Europeans killed four more Moslems as communal strife continued in the western Algerian city of Oran.

20,000 Reported Involved

Estimates of the number of Moslems involved in the clashes in Paris, which took place in the center of the city and in its immediate suburbs, ran as high as 20,000. The number of Algerians who live and work in the Paris region is about 200,000.

The rioting, which began about 7:30 P. M. ended about four hours later. It was reported that 7,500 Moslems had been arrested during the fighting.

The violence started as a protest against police curbs imposed twelve days ago on Moslems in the greater metropolitan area. Moslems were warned to stay off the streets between 8:30 at night and 5:30 in the morning and Moslem cafes were ordered closed at 7 in the evening.

ST 19-180; 265

The order for tonight's demonstration, which quickly got out of hand, was believed to have been given by the clandestine Algerian rebel leadership in France. It was said that similar demonstrations could be expected on other nights this week.

Police Try to Block Way

About 6 P. M. groups of several hundred Moslems started marching toward the gates of Paris from the industrial suburbs of Nanterre, to the west; Aubervilliers, to the north, and Choisy-le-Rio, to the south.

At the same time, Moslems began marching out of their two main quarters in Paris itself--the Goutte d'Or behind the Place Pigalle in Montmartre and the Left Bank Latin Quarter near the Halle aux Vins and the Jardin des Plantes.

At least 7,000 police and special Republican Security companies struggled to block the marchers coming into the city and to break up the Moslems surging into the center of town. Some of the police wore bullet-proof vests and all were armed and carried truncheons. The main areas of the fighting in the city were in Saint-Germain-des-Pres, the Opera, the Madeleine, the Place de la Concorde, the Champs Elysees and around the Place de l'Etoile. At the edges of the city the most serious clashes occurred at the Rond Point de la Defense just beyond Neuilly.

With each succeeding charge by the police the fighting became more intense. One report said that the security forces had come under fire from a submachine gun, in which one policeman was wounded.

Some of the Moslem groups chanted "Algerie Algerienne" (Algerian Algeria) as they marched toward the lines of police. This has been the Algerian nationalist slogan designed to match the French Right-wing cry of "Algerie Francaise."

In the region of the Opera and near the Rond Point de la Defense to the west of the city, the Moslems smashed store windows, slashed tires and turned over cars.

Many to be Expelled

The Prefecture of Police communique said that a "great part" of Moslems arrested would be sent back to Algeria this week as well as those Algerian shopkeepers in Paris who followed a strike called for tomorrow in Algeria and France by the Algerian rebel leadership.

There was immediate concern expressed in responsible circles here that the outbreak of Moslem violence would be met by an outburst of terrorism directed against the Algerians by members of the French Right-wing extremist Secret Armed Organization.

ST 19-180; 266

This, it was said, could lead to a situation in Paris similar to that in Oran, where bloody strife between the Europeans and Moslems has become almost a daily occurrence.

On a minor scale such a scene took place tonight near the Rond Point de la Defense when French motorists jumped out of their cars and, seizing whatever was handy as a weapon, attacked the Moslem demonstrators. No serious injuries were reported in this clash, however.

The communal fighting in Oran has taken thirteen lives--twelve Moslem and one European--since last Thursday and at least forty-five persons have been injured as a result of the outbreaks.

Tonight local authorities there clamped down with stringent measures to try to halt the growing violence.

Today's violence followed the funeral of a European settler who was stabbed to death last Saturday as he leaned over to help a child injured during that day's fighting.

Young Europeans entered the center of the city bent on revenge. They hurled over stalls in a Moslem open-air market, sacked Moslem stores in the vicinity, attacked Moslem merchants and strollers and set fire to cars driven by Moslems.

Meanwhile it was disclosed today that President de Gaulle received three Algerian rebel leaders secretly in the Elysee Palace June 10, 1960, to discuss peace two weeks before official negotiations began.

This was revealed by Louis Joxe, French Minister for Algerian Affairs, in a statement before the Senate. He broke official silence on the oft-rumored meeting because all of the principals who might have been compromised by the disclosure have since been killed.

The rebel agents, Si Salah, Si Mohammed and Si Lakdar--were active guerrilla leaders in Algeria itself and were operating independently and in defiance of the rebel Provisional Government installed in Tunis, according to M. Joxe's account.

Their offer to rally up to 10,000 rebel fighters to General de Gaulle's offer of the "peace of the brave" and self-determination for Algeria was frustrated eventually by the treachery of one of the agents, Si Mohammed. He turned on his associates, executed some implicated in the negotiations and arrested others.

He and the one remaining principal were killed subsequently by French forces, M. Joxe said.

SCHOOL TORN BY RIOT IS SHUT BY BALAGUER

CUIDAD TRUJILLO, Dominican Republic, Oct. 17 (SP)--The University of Santo Domingo, scene of student rioting, was ordered closed today for the remainder of the year.

A decree by President Joaquin Balaguer said the shutdown was necessary while Congress considered a bill that would modify the autonomy under which the university has operated.

About 500 angry students--of a total enrollment of 4,500--continued demonstrations today against a recently appointed rector, Jose Manuel Machado. They considered him "too pro-Trujillo."

They tore down pictures of the late dictator, Generalissimo Rafael Leonidas Trujillo Molina, shattered windows and shouted that they would continue demonstrating until the rector was removed.

Two busloads of police swarmed over the campus but there was no evidence they were using force against the rampaging students.

The police seemed to congregate around a large statue of the Generalissimo in front of the administration building. The rioters, who oppose the whole Trujillo family, members of which remain influential in the Government, had said the statue would be their next target.

7 BOLIVIANS KILLED AS POLICE HALT RIOT

LA PAZ, Bolivia, Oct. 24--At least seven persons were killed and about fifty were injured as a result of riots and other violence in La Paz last night.

Despite the technical state of seige now in effect, a demonstration was called by university students and drivers of buses and taxis to protest against a Government measure increasing prices for gasoline.

The demonstrators clashed with the police in the northern part of the capital. Tear gas was used at the beginning, but the demonstrators were able to make an attempt to burn some police stations. The police and the militia then opened fire against the crowds and restored calm.

The Government appeared today to be in full control of the situation and conditions here seemed almost normal. However, the recent unrest and violence are interpreted as part of an effort by opponents of President Victor Paz Estens-soro and his National Revolutionary Movement to oust the Government. The militia has been placed on an emergency status, and armed soldiers, policemen and members of the militia are patrolling the capitol.

Members of the political opposition are being imprisoned in increasing numbers.

TURKEY ARRESTS 80 IN PLOT ON REGIME

ISTANBUL, Turkey, May 9--The Government announced tonight that it had smashed a plot against Gen. Cemal Goursel's regime by supporters of deposed Premier Adnan Menderes. About eighty persons were reported to have been arrested.

Officials said the plotters had planned an armed revolt and had been so "infamous as to request assistance from a power with a foreign ideology.' The foreign power was not identified.

Sources close to the military junta that ousted the Menderes regime last year said the arrests had been carried out in Istanbul, Ankara and another unspecified area. Those rounded up were not identified.

The first arrests were announced in Istanbul, where about forty persons were detained.

Official quarters did not make clear the nature of the armed action that was intended against the Government, but unofficial reports said plotters had planned to strike May 27, the first anniversary of the military coup d-etat that overthrew the Menderes regime.

A terse Government communique said those arrested would be tried soon.

The communique called them sympathizers of Mr. Menderes' disbanded Democrat party. Mr. Menderes and other ousted leaders are on trial for crimes against the state.

FRONTIER REPORTED CLOSED

DAMASCUS, United Arab Republic, May 9 (AP)--Official sources here said Turkey closed her frontier with Syria today following anti-Government riots in three southern Turkish districts bordering on the Syrian area of The United Arab Republic.

Dispatches from the Syrian border said 100 Turks had been killed or injured in demonstrations in the districts of Urfa, Eintab and Kalaf.

There was no indication of how many of the 100 casualties were dead.

Reports from Aleppo, Syria, said the demonstrators had protested against rising taxes and the increase of Turkish Army salaries by the regime of Gen. Cemal Gursel.

THREE ALGERIANS SLAIN BY FRENCH DURING RALLY

ALGIERS, May 9 (AP)--Three nationalist demonstrators were slain and about ten wounded by French riot forces in a small town in eastern Algeria today.

Algerians in Djidjelli marched through the town waving the green and white rebel flag and chanting nationalist slogans. They clashed with the French forces, who opened fire.

Earlier, troops and riot police broke up a similar demonstration at Marengo, about fifty miles from Algiers. No deaths were reported.

While the new upsurge of nationalist rioting occurred in the two small towns, a plastic bomb, apparently set by Right-wing Europeans, exploded in front of the home of Louis Cardona, director of the newspaper journal D'Alger. He was about five yards away and was shaken up.

BOLIVIANS IN NEW RIOT;
ONE KILLED IN PROTEST OF RISE IN PRICE OF GASOLINE

LA PAZ, Bolivia, Oct. 25--One person was killed and ten were injured in new riots in La Paz last night. Demonstrators protesting a Government decision to increase the price of gasoline clashed with the police and militia.

The situation appeared quieter today, however, as the Government provided emergency transportation in the bus drivers' strike over the Government decision to increase the price of gasoline but not to raise transportation rates. The Interior Minister, Eduardo Rivas Ugalde, announced that the Government had imprisoned 200 persons on charges arising from Monday's rioting.

10,000 IN RANGOON RIOT AGAINST U. S.

RANGOON, Burma, Feb. 21--Burmese soldiers used gunfire today to break up the biggest anti-United States demonstration ever seen in this neutral nation.

Steel-helmeted soldiers opened up with automatic weapons on a crowd estimated at 10,000 persons moving on the United States Embassy. The demonstrators were protesting the reported supplying of United States marked arms to Chinese Nationalist guerrillas operating in the Burmese jungle along the Thailand border.

United States officials are investigating to determine how any such weapons got to the guerrillas, former soldiers of Generalissimo Chiang Kai-shek. The guerrillas stayed behind when Chinese Nationalist forces escaped to Taiwan after the Chinese Communists conquered mainland China in 1949.

The police threw up barricades twenty-five yards from the embassy and used tear gas and fire hoses to fight off most of the rioters. Some demonstrators, however, stormed the barricades and battled the police with sticks and stones.

Soldiers then rushed to the embassy. A Government order banning gatherings of ten or more persons was read, but the demonstrators, believing the troops would not shoot, shouted anti-United States slogans and moved forward.

The troops knelt and opened fire. Most of the shots were aimed in the air. The demonstrators fled.

About 2,000, however, went on a rampage through the streets of the city--stopping automobiles and smashing shop windows.

Demonstrators threw tomatoes at the embassy last week in a small-scale demonstration against the arms shipments.

Charge Denied by Taiwan

The Ministry of Information denied in Taipei, Taiwan, Monday that Nationalist China had sent United States--supplied arms to the anti-Communist guerrillas operating in Burma.

The statement included an assertion that United States weapons were used only for defense of Taiwan and islands off the Chinese Mainland held by the Nationalists.

EMBASSIES ATTACKED IN CAIRO

CAIRO, Feb. 15--Rioters sacked and set fire to the Belgian Embassy here today. A mob also stoned the British and United States Embassies and attacked the offices of United Nations and the United States Embassy library as protests against the death of Patrice Lumumba.

Piles of Belgian secret documents were burned, but security officials managed to salvage some of them. The Belgian coat of arms over the front door of the Embassy was pulled down.

Meanwhile, a reliable source indicated that the United Arab Republic had decided to extend substantial financial and military aid to the Government of Antoine Gizenga, which the Government recognized yesterday as the "legitimate national government of the Congo."

The news of Mr. Lumumba's death was broken to his three children by the headmistress of the school where they were staying.

106 ARRESTED IN PARIS

PARIS, Feb. 15 (AP)--The Paris police arrested 106 persons in clashes with mobs in front of the Belgian Embassy today. Several persons were injured. Six Negro students were injured in fights with police in Lyon.

A fresh wave of violent protests over the death of Patrice Lumumba occurred today.

U. N. FLAG DESTROYED IN ACCRA

ACCRA, Ghana, Feb. 15(Reuters)--Ghana was reported today to have demanded the arrest of anti-Lumumba forces in the Congo as demonstrators tore up a United Nations flag outside the United Nations regional offices here.

About 3,000 persons took part in the demonstration outside United Nations Headquarters.

ACCRA EMBASSY BESIEGED

ACCRA, Feb. 15 (UPI)--Hundreds of demonstrators protesting the death of Patrice Lumumba ripped the United States Seal from the American Embassy today and three rifle shots shattered an embassy lamp.

BELGIAN CONSULATE ATTACKED

AMSTERDAM, The Netherlands, Feb. 15 (AP)--Communist youths charged the Belgian Consulate behind a shield of sixteen girls today, but the police stopped them. Two policemen were injured.

ST 19-180; 272

YUGOSLAVS OFFER APOLOGY

BELGRADE, Yugoslavia, Feb. 15--The Yugoslav Government apologized to the Belgian Ambassador, Marcel Goosse, today for yesterday's attack on his Embassy by demonstrators protesting the death of Patrice Lumumba.

Heavy police guards were still mounted around Western embassies today, but there was no sign of further violence.

NEW PROTEST STAGED

BELGRADE, Feb. 15 (Reuters)--Students held a new protest meeting on the death of Patrice Lumumba today. They then marched to the Belgian Embassy.